Origins of Christ's New Covenant

Origins of Christ's New Covenant

Somewhere Beyond Belief
Volume I

Alfred D. Holcombe, B.S.L., LL.B

and

Suzanne M. Holcombe

Copyright © 2002 by Alfred D. and Suzanne M. Holcombe.

Library of Congress Number:		2002092222
ISBN:	Hardcover	1-4010-5909-0
	Softcover	1-4010-5908-2

All Rights Reserved by Authors

No part of this book may be reproduced or transmitted in any form or by any means without the permission in writing from the authors

This book was printed in the United States of America.

To order additional copies of this book, contact:
Xlibris Corporation
1-888-795-4274
www.Xlibris.com
      Orders@Xlibris.com
      15359

Acknowledgement

We hereby thankfully acknowledge all those who, in past ages, have labored under duress and oppression to gain spiritual knowledge and understanding and heroically struggled to pass it down to others. We prayerfully hope that this book will, in its own way, afford another reliable stepping stone on the foundations laid by those who came before us.

With blessings in Christ,
Al and Suzanne

http://www.somewherebeyondbelief.com

CONTENTS

PART ONE

CHAPTER ONE
CONSIDERING SCIENTIFIC AND SPIRITUAL REASONING **21**
- SCIENTIFIC REASONING 22
- SPIRITUAL REASONING 29

CHAPTER TWO
TRANSPOSITION OF SPIRIT ENERGY INTO PHYSICAL BODIES **36**
- BINARY SOULS 37
- SPIRIT INFUSION INTO PHYSICAL BODIES 43
- WITH OR WITHOUT A BINARY MATE 51
- DIAGRAM ONE: TRANSPOSITION OF SPIRIT ENERGY INTO PHYSICAL BODIES 54
- DIAGRAM TWO: INDIVIDUAL SOULS: DIVISION OF THE BINARY SOUL 56
- DIAGRAM THREE: STAR OF ISRAEL: AT-ONE-MENT OF MALE AND FEMALE ENERGIES 58
- DIAGRAM FOUR: STAR OF ISRAEL: AT-ONE-MENT WITH ALL SPIRIT FORCES .. 60

CHAPTER THREE
EXILED IN LOWER STATES OF CONSCIOUSNESS **61**
- MICHAEL: THE ARCHANGELIC IMAGE OF JESUS THE CHRIST 61

THE FIRST AND LAST ADAM 72
THE FIRST AND LAST EVE 74
EVOLUTION AND CREATION 83
EVE BITES THE APPLE 87

CHAPTER FOUR
ISRAEL'S DIVINE GENEALOGICAL TREE AND THE DIVINE LINEAGE 90
THE ENMITY BETWEEN TWO SEEDS 90
   Cain Versus Abel: 94
   Lamech Versus Enoch: 96
MELCHIZEDEK ESTABLISHES ISRAEL 99
   Abraham and His Sons: Ishmael Versus Isaac 103
   Isaac and His Sons: Esau Versus Jacob 105
   Jacob and His Twelve Sons: Reuben Versus Judah ... 107
   Judah and His Sons: Zerah Versus Pharez 112
TABLE 1: THE SEVEN GENERATIONS OF ENOCH AND CAIN 118
TABLE 2: THE DIVINE LINEAGE 119

PART TWO

CHAPTER ONE
PROPHET ISAIAH 127

CHAPTER TWO
PROPHET JEREMIAH 152

CHAPTER THREE
PROPHET EZEKIEL 181

CHAPTER FOUR
PROPHET DANIEL 213

CHAPTER FIVE
OTHER LATTER DAY PROPHETS OF THE HEBRAIC AGE 232
- PROPHET HOSEA 232
- PROPHET AMOS 235
- PROPHET MICAH 238
- PROPHET ZEPHANIAH 250
- PROPHET HAGGAI 252
- PROPHET ZECHARIAH 256
- PROPHET MALACHI 266

CHAPTER SIX
THE NEW COVENANT: PAVING THE WAY TO HIGHER DIMENSIONS 279
- THE OLD COVENANT 280
- THE NEW COVENANT 281
- TERMS OF THE NEW COVENANT 285
- THE PURGING FIRE OF THE HOLY GHOST 288
- THE MYSTICAL CHURCH BODY OF CHRIST 290
- THE 144,000 FORERUNNERS 300

PART THREE

CHAPTER ONE
THE SONS OF JACOB RETURN 307
- TWELVE GREAT ARCHANGELS: FRUIT YIELDING TREES 307
- TWELVE SONS: TWELVE APOSTLES ... 310
- THE DIVINE GENEALOGICAL TREE 318

CHAPTER TWO
JOSEPH
A SOUL INCARNATION OF JESUS OF NAZARETH 321
- THE BRIGHT MORNING STAR 321
- JACOB'S PREDICTION 323
- JOSEPH'S BLESSING 324
- TWO PROPHETIC DREAMS 327
- MANNA FROM HEAVEN 332

CHAPTER THREE
REUBEN
A SOUL INCARNATION OF APOSTLE PETER? 337
- JESUS SELECTS HIS APOSTLES 337
- JACOB'S FIRST SON: REUBEN 339
- JESUS' FIRST APOSTLE: PETER 344
- PETER'S SPIRITUAL AWAKENING 349

CHAPTER FOUR
BENJAMIN
A SOUL INCARNATION OF APOSTLE PAUL 351
- JACOB'S TWELFTH SON: BENJAMIN 352
- SAUL SON OF KISH: A SOUL INCARNATION OF BENJAMIN 354
- KING SAUL'S FALL 358
- PAUL AS SAUL OF TARSUS 362
- BLINDED BY THE LIGHT 366
- BORN OUT OF TIME 369

CHAPTER FIVE
DAN
A SOUL INCARNATION OF JUDAS ISCARIOT 374
- CAIN 374
- DAN 377
- DAN'S BLESSING 379
- SATAN AND HIS SONS 381
- A KING OF TYRUS: PROBABLE SOUL INCARNATION OF DAN 382
- A PHAROAH: A SON OF SATAN 384
- KING NEBUCHADNEZZAR: A SON OF SATAN .. 385
- JUDAS ISCARIOT 387
- A SON FORFEITS HIS HEAVENLY CROWN 389

CHAPTER SIX
EPHRAIM AND MANASSEH
APOSTLES JOHN AND JAMES 394
EPHRAIM 395
APOSTLE JOHN: A SON OF ZEBEDEE 397
MANASSEH 404
APOSTLE JAMES: A SON OF ZEBEDEE 407

CONCLUSION 411

Preface

We are summarily warned by Beloved John in The Book of The Revelation that the name of anyone who adds to the prophesies written in the Bible, or who takes away from the words of that sacred book of prophecy, shall be removed from the Book of Life.[1] Apostle Peter added that no prophecy of the scripture is of any private interpretation because it came not in ancient times by the will of man but through holy men who spoke as they were moved by the Holy Ghost. The writings in this book, *Origins of Christ's New Covenant,* do not violate the sanctity of those hallowed precautions. There is no attempt here to rewrite the Bible nor to alter its words; albeit numerous versions have been written and handed down through many centuries during which the scriptures have undergone a considerable number of translations. The ancient writings sequentially written in the King James Version of the Bible remain in this book unaltered from their known original form. In fact, biblical passages are herein quoted word for word to illustrate the origins of Jesus Christ's New Covenant as the Bible describes its development in its spiritual sense: as opposed to its letter understanding. Apostle Paul defined a clear distinction between two characteristic understandings of scriptural writings.[2] He

---

[1] Rev. 22:18-19.
[2] 1 Cor. 2:9-15; 2 Cor. 3:3-6.

went so far as to say that when the Bible is read according to its letter meanings, its spiritual message is lost. This work relies upon the hypothesis that biblical interpretation is commensurate with the level of spiritual knowledge and understanding attained in past and current life experiences.

The Bible is a body of spiritual knowledge built up through many centuries of man's learning experiences, and — like a diamond with many facets — it can be interpreted on multi-dimensional spiritual levels. Important scriptural threads, often symbolic and allegorical in nature, have remained coded, in order that the answers to the deeper spiritual mysteries would remain secreted away from those of a negative spiritual nature who would misuse them. Many of these bits and pieces of spiritual enlightenment are pavement blocks on the Way made passable into heaven, from which pathway those of a negative nature are barred because of what the disobedient angels did on earth in the beginning. It is in these sealed verses that many spiritual mysteries remain secreted, waiting to be revealed to those who appropriately seek understanding of them, intending to do only good with that which is revealed to them. A spiritual seeker who reads the Bible according to its letter meaning is inclined to fall short of understanding its deeper meanings, being not sufficiently spiritually quickened to be able to tune in to vibrational frequencies of the Spirit which inspired the original writers. When this is understood, one begins to realize that the Bible is a divinely-inspired work, filled with valuable knowledge locked in symbols for safekeeping. Because of this built-in protection, various biblical editors and translators, who did not possess a sufficient understanding of its symbols, were rendered unable to manipulate scriptures to suit their own biased purposes. This is one notable reason why Jesus spoke in parables. It was one form of protection against authorities who at that time opposed His teachings, which militated against the Law of Moses. Those who had by that time attained to a sufficiently high level of consciousness were able to understand the spiritual meanings He fashioned in His discourses. This was exemplified in His message about Eliljah, who, Jesus taught, had reincarnated as John the Baptist — the Master explained that those who had *"ears to hear"* would understand it to be the truth, in the spiritual sense.[3]

This work is dedicated to the proposition that the New Covenant brought in by Jesus Christ, as foretold by Prophet Jeremiah,[4] is the way the *"strong spiritual meat"* contained in the scriptures can be received and understood through the Spirit of the Holy Ghost. Jesus promised GOD would send the Spirit of Truth and other Comforter in His name to those who were His, after He was transformed, translated into heaven and empowered by GOD the FATHER.[5] Knowledge acquired by those who have attained to higher states of consciousness is presently being divulged to many on earth in accordance with Daniel's prophecy that when the time came for Michael to stand up — the time of redemption — knowledge would be increased.[6] We have now arrived at that prophesied time; which, as will be discussed, coincides with the three and half thousand year period after Moses

---

[3] Mt. 11:10-15.
[4] Jer. 31:31-34.
[5] Jn. 14:15-17,26; 15:26; 16:7,12-15.
[6] Dan. 12:1-4.

brought in GOD's basic Law;[7] known as the Mosaic Law. The cream of spiritual understanding is currently being raised to the top of the consciousness of each soul who has become one of Christ's; activated by the Christ consciousness, in accordance with the promised terms of His New Covenant.

The New Covenant is central to the writings in this book. As explained herein, the roots of the New Covenant were planted in Judaism, and from those roots grew up a Divine Genealogical Tree of Life on earth. These writings accordingly expound on developments from the time of the descent of angels into the earth plane and describe man's struggle through the ages to acquire spiritual knowledge and understanding of his earthbound condition in flesh. Also included are reincarnative scriptural threads found intricately woven through the spiritual fabric of the Bible.

The concept of the lower-self (soul energy) and higher self (angelic energy) is elaborated upon because of its crucial importance in reaching an understanding of man's earthly relationship to his heavenly estate in higher dimensions of consciousness. Also discussed, is the importance of spiritual patterns expressed in family lineages as seen in the Divine Genealogical Tree emphasizing the all-important Divine Lineage and its inseparable relationship to the Bible's illuminating three-to-four generation rule. Mankind's spiritual evolution is also examined as seen in the children of Israel who incarnated on earth in the beginning as part of the Adamic generation and subsequently reincarnated in successive embodied

---

[7] Prophetically known as "*a time, times and half a time*" (Dan. 12:7).

experiences, as they have flowed through the generations in different cultures and races. They have currently reincarnated to fulfill an important role as will be explained.

Largely esoteric, the Bible preserves the *"strong meat"* of spiritual truth, which the Hebrews writer described as being understood only by those who have their senses exercised to discern both good and evil; in contrast to the shallower understanding of those he referred-to as *"babes unskillful in the word of righteousness."*[8] For these above reasons, the reader is asked to carefully contemplate the spiritual meaning of the biblical verses relied upon in this work, while considering the correlated footnotes which provide biblical authority.

---

[8] Heb. 5:12-14.

PART ONE

—CHAPTER ONE—
CONSIDERING SCIENTIFIC AND SPIRITUAL REASONING

Whenever we take the time to reflect upon what manner of individuals we are, and how we came to manifest as intelligent life on this far-flung planet, we are inclined to puzzle at the fact of our isolation away off here in space, sole intelligent inhabitants of the earth insofar as is yet generally known — indeed, the thought occurs, why did we come into existence at all? Birthed as fractious helpless infants, demandingly dependent upon parents and others for our very existence, we blithely wend our way through life, all the while subtly aware that some curious unfathomable fate stealthily and irrepressibly stalks us, each day pervasively impressing upon us a non-discerned bit of age until we at some point rather precipitously revert into an inevitable decline to unceremoniously die. Opinions of what happens next fill a broad spectrum of man's ideas according to his level of spiritual knowledge and understanding.

Distinguished author H. L. Mencken wrote that he was utterly convinced that upon drawing his last breath he would simply cease to exist, and fade back into the same state of non-existence from which he had come at birth. However, it appears he was uncertain about that conclusion because he expressed his wish that in the event he might have diagnosed his situation incorrectly that he be permitted to stand before the heavenly gate to express his heartfelt regrets, and say he was sorry.

Arabian prophet Omar Khayam took a different view of the matter. After reflecting on man's situation, he dolefully noted that, to his knowledge, nobody had ever satisfactorily demonstrated their return into their flesh body after once having died, so he accepted his own eventual and inevitable death as final. He further declared that life on earth has at least some contemporary certainty attached to it, whereas whatever might possibly follow was, to him at least, remote and speculative. And so he wrote that a man is wise to take the cash and let the credit go — enjoy life here on earth because it is a sure thing, and not be concerned about what may or may not come afterward.

SCIENTIFIC REASONING

Many ideas have occurred to man whenever he has contemplated the origins of his existence. When the scientific age dawned, a man named Charles Darwin emerged from his studies to present to the world a seemingly strange and novel idea. It had nothing to do with man's spiritual origins, but rather was concerned with the way organisms had physically developed and adapted on the earth. Our species, he theorized, had grown up from some now uncertain transient primitive existence having roots that extend far back mainly out of sight into the dim past. He presented compelling substantiating evidence to back his contention that man had evolved from some remote animal ancestry not in our time able to be accurately traced. His hypothesis was presented in such a reasonable way, and supported by fossils and other credible forms of material evidence, that it immediately attracted the foremost minds of his time from among those who sought some definitive and reasonable explanation for man's having been brought into being.

The theory did not include any explanation about possible creative spirit forces by which man might have been developed. For example, invisible forces existent at higher levels than man's knowledge and understanding which could have guided, directed and moved physical beings in what might have been an intended and contemplated evolutionary progression. Had man's spiritual aspect played a role in his having developed as an intelligent animal distinctly set apart from and above the other species found living on this planet? Could the Apostle Paul's writing long after the fact of man's appearance on the earth, teaching that the worlds were framed by the Word of GOD so that things which are seen were not made of things which do appear?[9] — explain man's earthly appearance as a flesh being brought into material existence by ethereal forces ordinarily invisible to him?

The Darwinian Theory militated against those who held strong fundamental religious beliefs, who sensed that all of Creation had been the work of One Divine Creator, Who, for reasons known to HIM, brought mankind into existence at a much later time

---

[9] Heb. 11:3.

than the earth — and even pre-human creatures — were created. But religious scholars were at that time limited in their understanding of how spirit manifests in flesh in the third dimension, and so blindly opposed Darwin's theory of evolution.

Scientific inquirers, many of whom had little interest in abstract spiritual matters they considered irrelevant in the scheme of things, quickly hearkened to Darwin's clarion call, envisioning unique new fruits of truth and knowledge yet to be unveiled on his evolutionary vine. They eagerly took up the trail, and with painstaking care traced evidential leads back to some infinitesimal ambiguous cells that had somehow sparked into life countless millennia ago. Through many years, these patient investigators meticulously set in place pieces of what they believed to be man's mysterious physical origins. They carefully reconstructed vestigial linkages until they theorized an evolutionary system explaining man's flesh beginnings. The tracing of man's development on earth, to them, stood as much as proved beyond any rational doubt. Yet, despite all its findings, science still has not been able to explain what forces guided man's existence, the creation of the solar system, and the unfathomable universe which encompasses everything physical.

By the reckoning of science, man has simply evolved in some abstract way, advancing from forbears who were simple creatures in the evolutionary chain into ever more complex beings, while following the lead of much simpler creatures who struggled though the ages, striving to merely survive environmental conditions. Could these primitive creatures have been part of some spiritual design intended to eventually produce material man? According to the theory of evolution, as science has presented it, man has been programmed to walk the earth for a reasonable but indeterminate length of time until death. By that reasoning, man, who possesses a better developed brain, is otherwise set equal to other animal life forms possessing inferior reasoning capabilities. But if that be the case, what reasonable purpose can there be for such a creative development as man?

Such an elementary sequential process suggests that each person lives but a brief existence on the earth, a sense of consciousness entering into him at the time of birth as if from out of nowhere. He is seemingly predestined to expire as the result of death of the flesh body to return — where? — why? To a state of non-existence? as apparently H. L. Mencken and Omar Khayam believed. Such a process would insure man's mortality beyond the faintest shadow of a doubt: he would have come from nowhere, predestined to return nowhere, for no particular reason. If that be the case, would it not represent a waste of time and effort on the part of whatever forces took the time and trouble to create such a temporal transient being as man? — not to mention the vast universe in which he has manifested, and of which he is obviously an integral part. The question arises: why and how would a living being as complex as man evolve through many centuries, systematically striving to elevate himself under earth's conditions, if that be the case? Of what conceivable use is his further self-development if his ultimate destination is a place in the ground with a stone marker set over his grave? Stated another way, of what value is his flesh body to him or anyone if it has no other predestined fate or prospects than to rot in the ground? Thus. if there is no potentially eternal aspect in man, then what is the purpose for his elaborate physical design and existence? Does he possess his personal identity, uniquely and peculiarly his own, and a brain comfortably afloat in cerebrospinal fluid enabling him to articulate thoughts, and even to imagine abstract concepts in quite baffling ways — without any sensible reason or purpose?

If man's advancement to his current level of knowledge, understanding and mental competence has come about as the chance result of some ineffable conglomeration of purposeless forces — or forces not directed toward any potential benefit to mankind — then his outlook is indeed bleak, for it is apparent that further development of his flesh body is valueless if his fate has already been sealed, predestined to end in death. If it be true that there is no way for man to seek his own immortality, then he is doomed. If there are no higher-vibrational eternal dimensions of existence to which mankind may in some reasonable way aspire, and if he is unable to colonize other planets in the time remaining before earth meets the fate of all objects in orbit around other objects, then his fate is indeed sealed. But in that event, what happens to him? We might well ask: What is this thing all about, anyway?

On its face, the evolutionary theory as it now stands appears to correctly and accurately portray how man's physical aspect, his flesh body, apparently came into existence: but having said that, what force brought it into existence? Obviously there is more to a man than his physical self. As science itself instructs, every effect has a cause. What is the cause of mankind's complex existence? Science has little more than begun to understand it: what has been learned to date leaves us far short of knowing why man has become what and who he is.

Man is set above the animals around him in ways suggesting that there must be reasons for the considerable differences in their construction. A major advantage accruing to man is his innate reasoning and imaginative capacity, characteristics so contrastingly clear-cut that in some extreme comparative examples one human individual may so far exceed another as to make for an inexplicable enigma. Consider that such a radical imbalance offends the notion that fairness of creation would seem to equitably require a closer measure of equality among individuals than is seen manifested. This is particularly true if one presumes the creation of mankind was heavenly engineered by a higher intelligence — for example, a Creator existent in some much higher dimension than earthly man — GOD.

If the evolutionary theory is a true account of man's physical development — if his origins are as simplistic as evolutionists believe them to be — then we need only understand his appearance on the earth as a mammal existent at a higher level of mentality than the other animals around him. If this be the case, then we are compelled to accept the deflating presumption that homo sapiens is at best the un-exalted result of an evolutionary process aimed at some vague and indefinable goal in which man is only an insignificant byproduct cast off from the development of mammals as the result of undesigned randomness. The obvious benefit of the doctrine of survival of the fittest, as understood today, is to provide the concept of a three-dimensional earth arena in which a fitful struggle continually takes place among the creatures that inhabit it: a war in which mankind is better able to survive than his competitors solely by reason of his fortuitous superior physical-mental development. Such an idea is an empty shell.

What science has learned suggests an inglorious past and future for mankind, portraying him as the more or less chance product — even byproduct — of an apparently aimless evolutionary process, proceeding haphazardly according to certain physical patterns and forces man calls nature. That being the case, he responds to no particular force or energy, yet has progressed without any apparent fixed or certain ideals or goals. Such a process would derogate the ordinary rules of development, under which any unguided, undirected, purposeless and apparently useless pattern inevitably turns out to be moot, redundant and self-terminating. If GOD brought all earthly wonders into existence in accordance with Darwin's theory — which in part theorizes that selectivity ensures survival and adaptation — then there is no need to look beyond man's mental and physical being to understand his existence, and we may as well all become hedonistic atheists, and devote ourselves entirely to selfish enjoyment during our comparatively brief time on earth.

Science has learned that the human body functions by electro-biochemical energies and the illuminated Dr. Albert Einstein concluded as the result of his studies that there is no waste of energy in the entire universe, as far as he could ascertain. That noted, should we not realistically consider that some energy, as yet not scientifically discerned, existent at an extremely high frequency level, might somehow be the source from which a crucially important part of man's body materialized? This prospective contemplation presents itself as the conjectural line of demarcation separating scientific reasoning from spiritual reasoning.

SPIRITUAL REASONING

> *For the letter killeth but the spirit giveth life. (2 Cor. 3.6)*

> *Howbeit when the Spirit of truth, is come, he will guide you into all truth.... (Jn. 16:13)*

The Hebrew Bible, commonly known as the Old Testament, based on the Law of Moses, was originally written in Hebrew and Greek. The thirty-nine volumes of the Old Testament were written one by one on scrolls made of skin as the Jews composed them, and consisted of from twelve to twenty scrolls of different sizes. The first five books of the Old Testament came to be known as the Pentateuch, and succeeding books were added to those foundational writings. Only after the invention of printing were they united into one book.

A brief summation of Old Testament history records that in 621 B.C. the Book of Deuteronomy was discovered by a priest who took it to his king, who forthwith effectuated its mandates.[10] The Book became the law of the land, albeit its origins were obscure, and turned out to be the fusion of two great forces in Jewish religious life: the priestly and the prophetic. The priests leaned toward sacrifices, rituals and prophesies, whereas the prophets were drawn toward expressing the Lord's requirement of moral uprightness and the inner life, as well as foretelling what was to come. In Deuteronomy the two interests were combined, and the priestly aspect became the symbol of the spiritual religion, while worship became less personal and more national in its scope. Its writings became the foundation of the Old Testament in the days of prophets on the order of Zephaniah, Nahum, Jeremiah, and Habakkuk, who wrote between the Scythian invasion of 627 and the destruction of Jerusalem by the Babylonians in 586. The Sadducees accepted only the Law as scripture; and the Pharisees went so far in their attachment to the Law that they remained fanatically devoted to it; which made them all the more difficult to convince when Jesus of Nazareth brought in His New Covenant. When the Master spoke of clean and unclean food, he in effect swept away the basic Levitical legislation — the priestly contribution to the Law.[11]

> The line of demarcation between the Old Testament and the New was drawn by the Lord the Son of GOD when He announced the terms of His New Covenant through Prophet Jeremiah, as is later discussed. It once and for all entirely removed the concept of a group or national way to salvation — a predominant Jewish belief — and replaced it with the fundamental principle that GOD would write His Law into the inward parts and hearts of each individual, so no one

---

[10] 2 Ki. Chh. 22-23.

[11] Mk. 7:18-19.

needed to teach others to know the Lord, because each would know Him from the least to the most. That was effectuated when Jesus Christ brought in His New Covenant, although it is yet to be generally accepted.

Briefly recapitulated, biblical writings evolved through various translations, and eventually different versions of biblical writings followed. The great one of the Middle Ages was the Vulgate, a Latin translation by St. Jerome about the end of the fourth century, based on earlier Latin translations. Other translations followed, such as the Wyclif version translated into German in 1382 to 1388; the later Catholic translation of the Old Testament made by Gregory Martin in 1578 to 1582; and Luther's new translation into German, which was completed in 1534. Coverdale's English Bible followed Luther's arrangement of the Old Testament, and William Tyndale brought in his New Testament translation in English in 1525.

The order in which the respective books encapsulating the Bible are preserved is important, because it reflects a flowing pattern of growth, consisting first of the fall of angels, then of evolution/creation, the fall of man, the law of GOD and the redemption of man. Without relying on any scientific discoveries or measurements, the Holy Bible explains in an allegorical and abstract way understandable to even unlearned men, rudimentary details of the origins of the universe, as well as the engineering of the earth in a manner enabling it to eventually accommodate human life. Science, on the other hand, is based on data and theories, which nonetheless have enabled man to understand, at least basically, how creation evolved, after having come into existence. The Bible supplies no scientific data to prove its teachings about subjects which have transcended man's ability to conceive of his unimaginably complex origins and existence, which matters still confound him because of his limited ability to see clearly into dimensions remote from him in his current condition. Because of this dichotomous situation, man has been — and still is — reliant upon much more knowledgeable heavenly sources to fill in missing blanks. The Book of Hebrews explains that faith is the substance of things hoped for, the evidence of things not seen: that it is through faith that we understand that the worlds were framed by the Word of GOD, so that things which are seen were not made of things which do appear.[12]

> *For now we see through a glass darkly, but then face to face: now I know in part; but then shall I know even as I am known. (1 Cor. 13:12)*

Man is unable in this earth plane of existence to observe with his natural eyes that which is native to sublime higher dimensions of existence. To do so he must enter into much higher states of consciousness than are natural to him in his human condition. He needs to develop what has become known to some as his "*third eye*", his spiritual sensory organ able to perceive that which remains invisible to the naked eye. As Apostle Paul taught, those who try to understand spiritual matters by their letter meaning — that

---

[12] Heb. 11:1,3. Cf. Heb. 11:27 - Moses endured when he forsook Egypt leading the children of Israel in their Exodus because he was able to see the Lord who was invisible to those He led (Heb. 11:27).

which is exclusively available through the intellect — will in effect "*die*" in a spiritual sense.[13] This, it is contended, is because a living spirit is able to receive its Spirit sustenance from the living GOD, who reveals spiritual truths by HIS spirit. The carnally-oriented natural man, Paul taught, receives not the things of the spirit of GOD for they are foolishness to him, because of his inability to discern between natural earthly and heavenly spiritual matters. It was when the exalted prophets of Israel, on the order of Isaiah, Jeremiah, and Ezekiel, were able to be quickened by GOD's Holy Spirit, that they were enabled to receive HIS unblemished Word.

The eminent Dr. David L. Cooper[14] explained that certain biblical writings exemplify this above-described principle: that when a man has the Spirit of GOD in him he has access to GOD's truth, but when he does not have it, he cannot be assured he will correctly interpret HIS Word:

> "The prophets were not always inspired. This fact becomes evident when one reads their messages and statements which they sometimes made concerning the coming of the Word of the Lord to them on given occasions. At times the people went to them and sought information. These men of GOD would then go to HIM in prayer, and HE would respond. Whenever HIS spirit was in them, they spoke infallibly. Under

---

[13] 1 Cor. 2:9-15.

[14] Messiah: His First Coming Scheduled, (abridged edition), Cooper, David L., Th.M., PhD., Litt.D., 1941, Biblical Research Society, LA, CA pp. 65-66.

those conditions they were not prone to error.

On other occasions, when the Spirit was not inspiring them, nor was the hand of the Lord upon them, they could and did draw wrong conclusions. As an illustration, consider the case of Nathan. According to 2 Sam. 7, David informed the prophet concerning his desire to erect a temple for the Glory of GOD. Immediately he approved the royal purpose and assured the king that GOD would be with him. When he gave this bit of encouragement, he was speaking as a man to his friend. He saw no reason why such a an excellent idea would be in error.

But that night the Word of the Lord came to him,[15] reproving him for what he had said to the king and commanding him to countermand his advice given in the energy of the flesh. The reason assigned by the Lord for preventing David from building the temple was that he was a man of war and blood. When the Spirit of the Lord was upon Nathan, he of course spoke infallibly. On other occasions, when the Spirit was not in him, he could, as in this situation, make a mistake."

No question about it, compelling scientific evidence supports the evolutionary theory of man's development on the earth, and that scholars in the fields of neuroscience and quantum physics have taken im-

---

[15] Job 33:15-18.

portant steps forward in attaining knowledge and understanding of energies that relate to the human mind, emotions and the physical body. But science has yet to find a way to discern, much less measure, subtle energies which lie beyond reach of man's natural mind. When he attempts to resolve higher dimensional enigmas solely by way of his lower-consciousness scientific reasoning, he finds himself lacking in his ability to conceive of the missing pieces which fit into, and fill out, a more complete picture of the heavenly mystery puzzle. This higher dimensional source of knowledge, from which may be elicited scientifically unmeasurable truths, can only be effectively sought through divine inspiration and faith; fundamental reasons for which restriction are explained in detail in this work. It is therefore contended that those who arbitrarily opt to constrain their seeking of spiritual truths within the parameters of scientific reasoning, restrict themselves to only a comparatively minimal portion of the knowledge available to man when he attains to higher levels of consciousness: — the Christ Consciousness being the uppermost.

—CHAPTER TWO—

TRANSPOSITION OF SPIRIT ENERGY INTO PHYSICAL BODIES

That human beings are spirit descendants, products of a divine heritage, was confirmed by Asaph, Chief Musician to King David, when he remarked, *"Ye are Gods, and all of you are children of the Most High."*[16] Ages later, Jesus of Nazareth attested to the spirit divinity alive within each individual's physical temple when He declared, *"Is it not written in your law, I SAID, YE ARE GODS?"*[17] With faith many accept this as truth; yet details of how spirit manifests in the third dimension still remain elusive to human understanding. There is a great deal that needs to be learned of this complex and intriguing subject, for which reason the following two chapters are designed to explicate in a basic simplified esoteric, physiological and biblical manner how the Spirit of GOD interfaces with the flesh body.

---

[16] Ps. 82:6.
[17] Jn. 10:34.

BINARY SOULS

> *So **God created man in his own image**, in the image of God created he him: **male and female created he them**. (Gen. 1:27)*

The Bible reveals that GOD the FATHER of all creation remains ineffable and undefinable by man's intellectual faculties, and until enlightened by the Christ and the Holy Spirit, he is unable to even know HIS name.[18] Yet, despite all of man's unanswered questions, the Bible also discloses that GOD is the spirit image of Adam and Eve. Therefore GOD the FATHER, though HE is implied to be masculine throughout scriptures, is the totality of both male and female energies. This continuity of male eminence is repeated throughout biblical scriptures, causing many to mistakenly believe that this divinely-inspired book is predominantly male-oriented. From an esoteric perspective, however, biblical references which appear to allude solely to male singularity often take into account his female expression, as exemplified in the Book of The Revelation. That man and woman are inseparably paired, as was foreordained from the beginning, is enigmatically disclosed in John's vision of the heavenly city. Especially noteworthy are specific biblical passages which denote only males as inhabiting the New Jerusalem — no scriptural references to women residing in this paradisiacal structure are recorded. Except that it be understood that male and female soul energies are considered as One, we may be hard pressed to understand a woman's position in the newly-restructured heavenly city — the New Jerusalem:

---

[18] Rev. 3:12.

> .... *at the gates twelve angels, and names written thereon, which are the names of the* **twelve tribes*** *of the children of Israel:.... and the wall of the city had twelve foundations and in them the names of the* **twelve Apostles** *of the lamb . . . And he measured the wall thereof, an hundred and forty and four cubits according to the* **measure of a man that is of the angel**. *(Rev. 21:12-17)*

**Jacob's 12 male sons*

This state of oneness existent between a particular man and woman may be somewhat perplexing and difficult to understand because of their obvious physical separation in the flesh, but here we refer to a combination of male and female spirit energies conceived together as one unit in higher realms of existence before the advent of Adam on earth.

In accordance with the Divine Will, the Eternal Son, in harmony with GOD's Holy Spirit, co-created a particular hierarchy of angelic beings in the similitude of His FATHER's Spirit. They can best be defined as single units of male and female energy which divided into binary souls when they descended into the dense, lower realms of earthly existence.[19] In other words, these angelic beings systematically decelerated in energy and through a process of polarity, took expression as individual souls able to manifest in two individual flesh bodies, as did Adam and Eve. Though they became separated in lower dimensions at the beginning, binary souls remained attached at the soul level with each other, their angelic higher self and

---

[19] Each individual is an expression of GOD attached in union to an angelic form standing ever at HIS throne (Mt. 18:10 cf. Mt. 18:4-5; Lk. 20:36; Mk. 12:25).

with GOD through seven spirit vortices[20] commonly known as chakras, which compose the ethereal template of the physical body. These vortices then interfaced — as they still do — with seven major nerve ganglia, and were expressed throughout the physical body by the Nervous System's electro-chemical circuits and bodily fluids; in particular the blood.

An understanding of the sacred attributes of the male and female genders is gained from the Book of Genesis, which reaches back to primordial time when God created the Adamic race. Before Eve was created, Adam possessed both male and female energies and was considered androgynous because these compatible energies were as One.[21] When Adam desired a helpmeet, woman was drawn into existence and consequently he was transformed from his androgynous state into male and female.[22] Because he had been created in GOD's image, his female counterpart created from his metaphorical rib represented an expression of the divine female image of GOD the FATHER on earth:

---

[20] The seven vortices, chakras, are analogous to Revelation's Seven Churches. The Seven Spirits of GOD are the celestial Archangelic messengers who stand guard over them (Rev. 1:20). They are the same seven spirits who are sent forth into all the earth (Rev. 5:6). The Book of Proverbs teaches that wisdom (feminine in nature) was the contributive force which "*hewn out the seven pillars*" — seven chakras of man's spiritual edifice — his soul (Prov. 9:1-2).

[21] That man and women were One since the beginning is reflected in Adam and Eve as explained in the Chapter: "Exiled in Lower States of Consciousness." Refer to Gen. 2:23-24; Eph. 5:28-33; Mk. 10:5-9; Mal. 2:14-15; Mt. 19:4-7).

[22] Gen. 2:21-25.

> *So ought men to love their wives as their own bodies. **He that loveth his wife loveth himself** . . . For this cause shall a man leave his father and mother, and shall be joined unto his wife and they two shall be one flesh. **This is a great mystery:** but I speak concerning Christ and the church. Nevertheless, let every one of you in particular so love his wife even as himself; and the wife see that she reverence her husband. (Eph. 5:28-33)*

When this transformation took place, energies of the binary souls became physically mirrored in a man who possessed, to a lesser extent, female hormones and a woman who possessed, to a lesser extent, male hormones. Unlike his female counterpart who possessed two "x" sex chromosomes, the male possessed "xy" sex chromosomes. Significantly, it is the male's "xy" sex imprint which determines the gender of the offspring and also his sperm population which statistically determines how males and females are produced in almost equal numbers. Scientific discoveries in the field of genetics support ancient biblical writings which have long taught that before the separation of the genders took place, man who was created in GOD's image, possessed the full masculine and feminine blueprints, as reflected in his "xy" sex chromosomes. This data provides compelling evidence that Eve, who was created from Adam's rib lacking the "y" chromosome, was attached in spiritual, mental and physical union with him from the beginning:

> *And the rib, which the Lord God had taken from man, made he a woman, and brought her unto the man. And Adam said, this is now bone of my*

> *bones and flesh of my flesh: **she shall be called woman because she was taken out of man**. Therefore shall a man leave his father and mother and shall cleave to his wife; and **they shall be one flesh**. (Gen. 2:23-24)*

Because the Eternal Son, Co-creator of all,[23] inherited His FATHER's male and female attributes, it is reasonable to conclude that these creative powers — in attunement with GOD — lie at the roots of creation. The Book of Proverbs allegorically provides a symbolic understanding of these operative forces by subtly disclosing that wisdom was a contributive feminine attribute used by the Lord in the creation of universes, and that this life force had been with Him before the beginning:

> *Say unto wisdom, Thou art my sister, and call understanding thy kinswoman: ... (Prov. 7:4)*

> *Happy is the man that findeth wisdom and the man that getteth understanding ... she is a tree of life for them that lay hold upon her. (Prov. 3:13-18)*

> *The Lord possessed me (wisdom) in the beginning of his way, before his words of old. I was set up from everlasting, from the beginning or ever the earth was. When there were no depths, I was brought forth; when there were no fountains abounding with water. Before the mountains were settled, before the hills was I brought forth: While as yet he had not made the earth, nor the fields, nor the highest part of the dust of the world. When he prepared the heavens, I was there: when he set a compass upon the face of the depth: When he es-*

---

[23] Ps. 33:6; Eph. 3:9-10.

> *tablished the clouds above: when he strengthened the fountains of the deep: When he gave to the sea his decree, that the waters should not pass his commandment: when he appointed the foundations of the earth: Then I was by him, as one brought up with him: and I was daily his delight, rejoicing always before him: Rejoicing in the habitable part of his earth; and my delights were with the sons of men. Now therefore hearken unto me, O ye children: for blessed are they that keep my ways. (Prov. 8:22-32)*

From scriptures it appears that the female attribute is the feminine force of the Holy Spirit that nourishes and gives life.[24] However, the source of her physical origins remains with the man from whose metaphorical rib she was extracted. Accordingly, man remains the mental attribute, the "*head*" of this mystical union as explained in Ephesians' illuminating verses. The head is symbolic of the mental aspect: the intelligent, reasoning and logical mind of the male attribute. Because husband and wife are an integral part of the mystical body of Christ — the Co-creator and Maker — His Spirit can draw their soul forces together as One into a single cohesive binary unit.

> *Wives submit yourselves unto your own husbands as unto the Lord.* **For the husband is the head of the wife even as Christ is the head of the church:** *and he is the savior of the body. Therefore as the*

---

[24] This is exemplified in the Book of Proverbs which teaches that Wisdom (feminine in nature) was the contributive force which carved out the seven pillars — seven chakras of man's spiritual edifice — his soul (Prov. 9:1-2).

> church is subject unto Christ, so let the wives be to their own husbands in every thing. Husbands, love your wives, even as Christ also loved the church and gave himself for it: That he might sanctify and cleanse it with the washing of water by the word. That he might present it to himself a glorious church, not having spot or wrinkle or any such thing; but that **it should be holy and without blemish.** (Eph. 5:22-27)

Masculine and feminine energies which polarize the seven sacred ethereal whirlpools — chakras — of our binary souls are much more dynamic than we have yet to fully realize. In higher levels of consciousness, we are endowed with cultivating and creative abilities which far surpass our finite human intellect:

> Verily, verily I (Jesus) say unto you. He that believeth on me, the works that I do shall he do also and greater works than these shall he do, because I go to my Father. (Jn. 14:12)

SPIRIT INFUSION INTO PHYSICAL BODIES

Because man's angelic higher self was initially created in the image of GOD, and subsequently patterned by numerous astral and experiential conditions, it is imprinted with a unique spiritprint which only a particular male and female can share. Based on this ethereal print, binary souls were held together by an astral pulse and gravitational pull when they incarnated as complementary physical mates in the first generation of the Adamic lineages. The process of spirit infusion into flesh was explained by Apostle Paul who taught that we are composed of two bodies: the terrestrial and the celestial. As will be explained, the celestial body is composed of two types of energies: the angelic higher self and the binary soul; the latter composed of two individual souls.

1. Man's Angelic Higher Self:

> *For when they shall rise from the dead, they neither marry, nor are given in marriage but are as the angels which are in heaven. (Mk. 12:25)*

Multifarious angelic hierarchies carry out GOD's work in complex ways throughout our boundless cosmic universe. Yet man's celestial reflection, as seen in his angelic higher self, is distinguished from other angels composing different hierarchies because of its unique spiritprint. Unlike other angels, this angelic being intentionally subjects itself to the human condition which potentially enables it to be positioned higher in the celestial echelons when its individual soul portion effectively overcomes cycles of life and death in earth's sphere of existence. Scriptures teach that Jesus who had assumed the human condition when he was "*made a little lower*" than the angels, had reached a state of at-One-ment with GOD and was exalted to sit at HIS right side. The Lord, the Son, declared that a comparative state of at-One-ness could be achieved by man if he would but believe and abide in Him:

> *That they all may be one; as thou, Father art in me, and I in thee, that they also may be one in us; that the world may believe that thou hast sent me.*

And the glory which thou gavest me I have given them; that they may be one, even as we are one. I in them and thou in me, that they may be made perfect in one; and that the world may know that thou hast sent me, and hast loved them, as thou hast loved me. (Jn. 17: 21-23)

Man's angelic higher self cannot wholly express itself in the earth plane because the physical body cannot effectively accommodate its highly-charged spirit energy. Therefore, in order for it to express itself in a dimension incompatible with its energy composition, it must interface with three mediums, the binary soul and its two individual souls (male and female). Accordingly, the more spiritually quickened an individual soul becomes, the more it is able to accommodate receptions from its angelic self, which stands ever at the Throne of GOD. When this occurs, there is less resistance in the seven spirit fields of the soul and consequently it becomes less accountable to karmic, third dimensional laws. Paradoxically, the same seven major vortices also bind the individual soul to the 3rd dimension in accordance with karmic laws. In other words, man's soul is the medium through which the angelic higher self can manifest; yet the soul is also the medium which keeps him earthbound in accordance with his earthly desires and works. As the individual soul gradually overcomes forces which lower its frequencies in the seven vortices, the polarity between karmic laws and the physical world weakens. Thus the liberated soul gradually begins its protracted ascension into higher realms of existence — higher levels of consciousness — where it will eventually majestically merge in full union with its angelic higher self and with GOD.

2. The Individual Soul:

Upon its entry into materiality, the angelic spirit was transformed into a binary soul which took expression in two individual souls. The individual soul is that part of our spirit anatomy which is influenced and patterned by life's experiences. It contains energy which has become enmeshed in earth's dense plane, and as previously noted, is subject to 3rd dimensional laws. It is this portion of the etheric anatomy which expresses itself repeatedly through reincarnation until such time as it overcomes desires and conditions that bind it to the world. These energies are continually recycled until the soul has reached an acceptable state of perfection. Only when the individual soul gradually overcomes negative vibrational forces which confine it to the earth plane, can it fully unite with its binary soul and merge at-One with its angelic higher self and GOD. Once attuned, the transformed soul becomes part of a complete portion (microcosm) which fits within the greater complete portion, our universal GOD (macrocosm).

Christ, man's Maker, is empowered to unite the individual soul with its binary soul and its angelic higher self. When He returns to take dominion at His second coming, the twelve heavenly gates[25] which have been closed since the removal of the Tree of Life from the earth plane, will reopen and translation into higher realms will take place for those who have sufficiently perfected themselves. Thus, man is under compulsion to overcome conditions that weigh heavily on his soul in order to become raptured into an energy wave so intense that translation into higher

---

[25] Rev. 21:12.

realms can take place.[26] On the other hand, individual souls who have accumulated low-frequency vibrations in their seven spiritual vortices through negativity, by misuse of their free will, will not be able to accommodate the quickening force able to induce this spiritual metamorphosis. Scriptures caution that they will consequently need to undergo further life cycles of development and purification until they are able to attain to an acceptable elevated state of consciousness.[27] This process is exemplified in the following biblical verse, which instructs that souls will no longer need to "*go out*" from higher dimensions once they have overcome laws that bind them to earth's sphere of existence:

> *Him that overcometh will I make a pillar in the temple of my God, and **he shall go no more out**. ... (Rev. 3:12)*

Jesus instructed that only those who are as pure as children will behold GOD's face. This becomes feasible when an individual soul has sufficiently overcome the forces of this world and merged at-one with its angelic higher self which stands ever at the throne of GOD. Once this is understood, it becomes clear that in order for this merger to take place, a quickening process is required in order to reunite the two ethereal bodies. The quickening process which allows for the unification of the soul with its glorious angelic body can be accomplished when one becomes as simple, meek and humble as a child,

---

[26] 1 Cor. 15:50-52; 1 Thess. 4:15-17; 2 Cor. 5:10.

[27] Rev. 20:5 explains that insufficiently quickened souls will have another 1,000 years following the first universal resurrection to purge themselves from obstacles that have found expression in their seven spirit vortices.

while attuning to GOD through Christ's intercession.[28] As Jesus explained to His disciples, the greatest in heaven is one who is as humble as a child, and it is that individual's angelic spirit self who beholds the face of GOD. This concept is expressed in the following biblical verse which implies that an innocent child's soul is capable of attuning to its angelic self which stands ever at the Throne of GOD:

> . . . *verily I say unto you, except you be converted, and become as little children, ye shall not enter into the Kingdom of Heaven. Whosoever therefore shall humble himself as this little child, the* **same** *is greatest in the Kingdom of Heaven . . . Take heed that ye despise not one of these little ones for I say unto you that in heaven* **their** *angels do always behold the face of my father in heaven. (Mt. 18:3-10)*

The Master further expounded upon the higher and lower self concept during a discussion with Nicodemus, a ruler of the Pharisees, who would come to Him by night to discuss life's deeper mysteries. In one particular discourse, Jesus instructed that He was concurrently in heaven and on earth:

> *And no man hath ascended up to heaven but he that came down from heaven, even the son of man which* **is** *in heaven. (Jn. 3:13)*

The Master simultaneously existed on earth and in heaven because His perfected soul was able to communicate with its angelic higher self which remains ever before the Throne of GOD in heaven. Not only was Jesus empowered to become the world's Savior but He had during His earthly sojourns attained to a

---
[28] Heb. 7:25.

state of complete humility and perfection as that of a child, and was able to behold the face of GOD:

> *Not that any man hath seen the Father save he which is of God, he hath seen the Father. (Jn. 6:46)*

> *. . . ye have neither heard his (GOD's) voice at any time, nor seen his shape. (Jn. 5:37)*

3. The Physical Body:

The life of the flesh is in the blood. . . . (Lev. 17:11)

The physical body is the encasement of the individual soul and also to lesser, varying degrees its angelic higher self. As previously noted, the physical body is the product of scaled down angelic energy manifested through natural laws via the soul's seven spiritual vortices, which interface with seven major nerve ganglia, including the seven major ductless glands of the endocrine system, including the blood. We are spiritually, emotionally and physically the sum total of all our life experiences, and accordingly our bodies have become molded by these vibrational energies through the electrical-chemical process of our Nervous System. These energies have found expression in numerous bodily characteristics: body type, skin, eye and hair color and even predisposed conditions such as congenital ailments. Genetics indeed play a crucial role in our physical and mental constitution, as science has learned. However, at the root of genetics lies spirit energy, which science despite all its technological advancement, has yet been unable to effectively discern and measure.

That life is present in the human body only for as long as blood circulates, demonstrates it to be the physical medium by which soul forces are expressed in the body. Without blood to oxygenate neural tissues, the nervous system could not execute its chemical-electrical spark; the heart would stop beating and the body would be rendered lifeless. Paradoxically, blood is also the physical medium which keeps the soul encased in the physical body — the consequence of Eve's infraction [29]— and was the medium Satan manipulated in order to keep souls bound to materiality, as will be explained in the next chapter. From a biological point of view, bone is a living structure with blood flowing through it. It is in a continuous state of growth and remodeling, and significantly it is in its marrow that red and white blood cells are produced. Thus the blood, the life giving force in Adam's metaphorical rib bone taken out of him to create Eve, was suggestive of the physical medium which accommodated the transposition of his binary mate's soul forces on earth. And because Adam was immaculately created in the spirit image of GOD from the beginning, the soul forces composing the genders became the divine imprint of man's Creator on earth.

That GOD admonished man not to eat of any manner of blood[30] may well indicate that lower energies contained in animalistic life forms are disruptive,

---

[29] "*Unto Adam and his wife did the Lord God make coats of skins, and clothed them.*" (Gen. 3:21)

[30] Lev. 17:10-11.

because they are carried into the human blood where spirit energy merges with flesh.[31]

WITH OR WITHOUT A BINARY MATE

Jesus attested to the mystical union of the sexes when He explained to a group of Pharisees that man and woman were created from the beginning as One for the purpose of fulfilling GOD's grand design. His explanation reflected the same meaning of Oneness expressed in Genesis 2:23-24 by Adam, when Eve was created to be his wife:

> *. . . he which made them at the beginning made them male and female. For this cause shall a man leave father and mother, and shall cleave to his wife and* **they twain (two) shall be one flesh**. *Wherefore they are no more twain but one flesh.* **What therefore GOD has joined together**, *let no man put asunder. (Mt. 19:4-7)*

It is apparent from scriptures that the Adamic lineages and subsequent generations surrendered to carnal desires, and in doing so strayed from opportunities of being joined in harmonic marital relationships with their respective binary mates. As a result

---

[31] The Eucharist symbolizes the life giving essence of GOD's Holy Spirit restored to mankind by the shed blood of His Son (Lev. 17:11). Fulfilled contritely, it quickens the soul by shedding light on its weaknesses, inducing it to make changes and propelling it into action (good works). Because spirit merges with the mental and physical bodies, its positive effects can potentially purify the blood from negative disturbances (Jn. 6:53-63; 1 Cor. 11:24-32).

of the Adamic transgression, which increasingly led to man's misuse of free will, a lower state of consciousness obscured his spiritual understanding, which to this day constrains him from effectively acquiring heavenly knowledge. Because of a lack of knowledge and understanding, men and women have been retarded in their ability to recognize that a true husband and wife relationship is one that has heavenly origins, and is bonded together by the living GOD.

When an individual has made profound changes, follows GOD's Will and believes in the intercessory power of the Christ, transformation into a new being can take place. Unless these positive changes are first made within, there is always a risk of attracting the negative polarities of an unsuitable partner because of the natural desires of the flesh. Individuals who become involved in any committed relationship with a mate of the opposite sex, without first having been enlightened by the Spirit of Truth and without guidance to the right partner, will often experience lingering cravings at the soul level which cannot be explained or satiated. This instinctual craving often causes discontentment that bears fruit in domestic violence, adultery, sexually-transmitted diseases, emotional abuse, depression, crimes of passion, negative family lineages and a host of other maladies that fit within a karmic framework. It would be wise, therefore, for individuals not to seek union with one of the opposite sex until spiritual transformation has taken place in order to better discern one's spiritually-appropriate mate.

It is by aligning our will with GOD and by attuning ourselves to Christ, who in turn sends the Holy

Ghost[32] that Divine Providence begins to move those who are receptive and like-minded to meet. This may involve unusual forms of guidance which often only spiritually-sensitive souls are able to discern. What the intellect may recognize as only a chance meeting or coincidence may actually be the workings of ethereal forces drawing souls together. That noted, it would be futile for any soul to seek its binary mate unless guided by GOD's Holy Spirit for the reason that one's soul counterpart may not have incarnated in a current life cycle, or may be tied to another karmic relationship. Thus it would behoove a soul to first seek to understand its relationship with GOD in order to fulfill its current life mission on earth, be it with a highly-polarized mate or binary mate or even without a mate. Once a divine rapport has been established with the CREATOR, a soul is better positioned to discern divine guidance in such matters, and avoid frivolous unions that may be guided by carnal attraction or delusions.

> *But seek ye first the kingdom of God, and his righteousness; and all of these things shall be added unto you. (Mt. 6:33)*

As spiritual knowledge and understanding increases, the scales of human ignorance will fall from our blinded eyes and knowledge of our heavenly heritage will become common. Empowered and enlightened with this awareness, mankind will undergo a process of involution and return to his beginnings — his heavenly origins — the resplendent state of his angelic body, and return to a state of At-Onement with GOD.

---

[32] Jn. 16:13.

Diagram 1

The following diagram explicates in an oversimplified form the transposition of spirit energy into physical bodies. Though man (xy) and woman (xx) became divided in their individual physical bodies, they remain attached at the soul level to seven spiritual vortices, holographically representing the seven greater spheres illustrated in this diagram.

TRANSPOSITION OF SPIRIT ENERGY INTO PHYSICAL BODIES

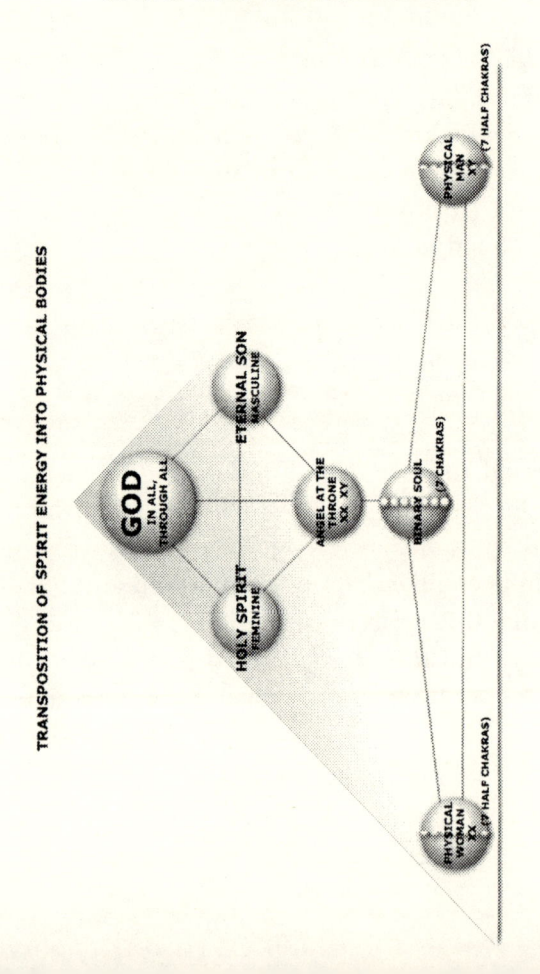

Diagram 2

The seven half-spheres (half-chakras) illustrated in the two triangles, represent the split image — two individual souls — of man and woman's polarities after having been divided. After the separation, they interfaced through a process of expansion and contraction (as in the pulsating effect of a heartbeat), portrayed by the short and long interconnecting lines in the respective triangles. In between expansions and contractions, their energies apparently meet, but the intervals cannot be measured in this dimension because of the speed at which this occurs (beyond the speed of Light). It is the energy contained in this astral pulse that keeps their spheres in rhythm even though they became physically separated. On the physical plane, this energy became synonymous with the bloodline which, in turn, nourishes all neural tissue of the Central Nervous System, including those responsible for the electrical impulses that originate in the sinoatrial node of the heart. This natural pacemaker, in turn, stimulates contraction which moves the blood to all other vital organs of the body. Without blood, there would be no electrical-chemical spark, the heart would stop pumping and the physical body would be rendered lifeless. As will be discussed in the next chapter, the blood is the bridge between spirit forces and the physical body and is the physical medium Satan manipulated to keep the soul earthbound.

> *"And the rib, which the Lord God had taken from man, made he a woman, and brought her unto the man. And Adam said, This is now bone of my bones, and flesh of my flesh, she shall be called woman, because she was taken out of man." (Gen. 2:22-23)*

INDIVIDUAL SOULS: DIVISION OF THE BINARY SOUL

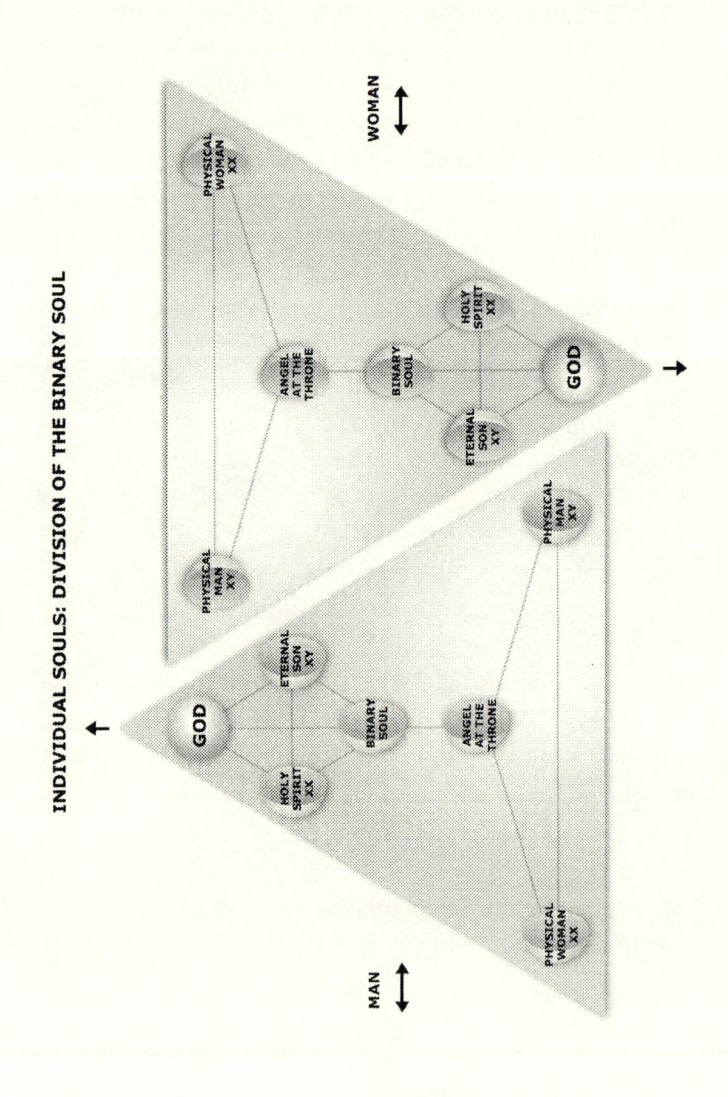

Diagram 3

The Star of Israel, by one understanding, represents the at-One-ment of male and female energies. In this diagram, the individual soul has been quickened by the Christ Spirit Light and consequently has merged with its binary soul, its angelic higher self and with GOD. The seven half-spheres have interlocked in polarity to form seven complete, harmonious spheres. Because the binary soul has merged with its angelic higher self, it no longer undergoes cycles of expansion and contraction, it has involuted and become one sphere (heart center of the star) instead of two. When these souls merged with the Christ Spirit, the GOD-head, illustrated at the extremities of the diagram, formed the polarity required in order for the energies to flow in all directions, thereby eliminating the duality of their feminine and masculine poles.

> *"Wives submit yourself unto your own husbands, as unto the Lord. For the husband is the head of the wife, even as Christ is the head of the church: and he is the saviour of the body. . . . For this cause shall a man leave his father and mother and shall be joined unto his wife, and they two shall be one flesh. This is a great mystery: but I speak concerning Christ and the church." (Eph. 5:22-23)*

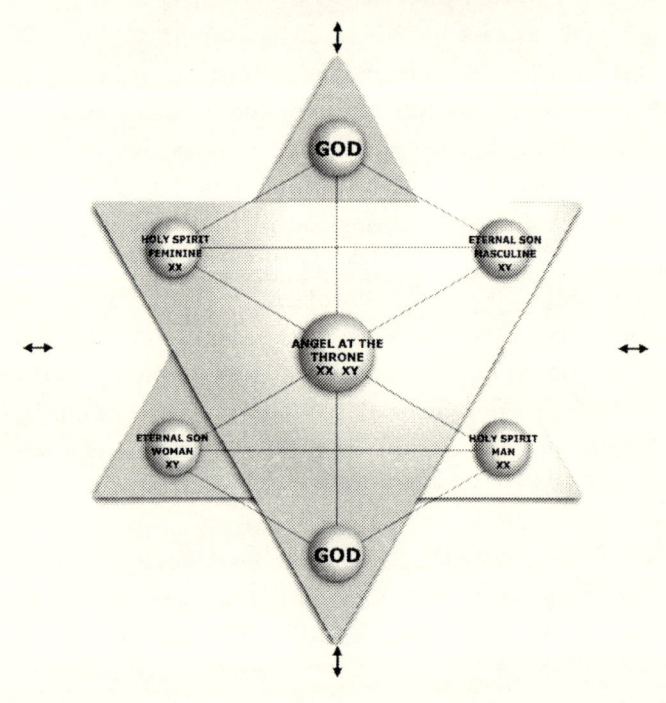

STAR OF ISRAEL: AT-ONE-MENT OF MALE AND FEMALE ENERGIES

STAR OF ISRAEL
AT-ONE-MENT OF MALE AND FEMALE ENERGIES

Diagram 4

The Cross at the center of the diagram is symbolic of Jesus' Crucifixion. Through the Atonement He unified all spirit forces by polarizing from top to bottom, His masculine force and the feminine force of GOD's Holy Spirit. This polarized, from left to right, the energies of the male and female half-chakras which had dualized the astral rhythm through the physical body's sympathetic and parasympathetic neural conduits. Consequently, the elements: earth, wind, fire and water which are linked to man's emotions, human psych and nature, are no longer divided in matter but have returned to a zero-point energy. The twelve intersecting lines of the six-point star symbolize the polarity of the 12 gateways (xx/xy xy/xx) leading into higher levels of the eternal heavenly-New Jerusalem into which a soul, after having reached at-One-ment with GOD, is able to re-enter (Rev. 21:9-23 Cf. Rev. 3:12). The twelve protruding lines radiating into the circle represent spirit influences of the twelve sons of Jacob; the twelve Apostles and the twelve zodiacal signs. Unlike figure 1, in which the physical woman is portrayed as xx, she has now polarized with the masculine energy of the Son, and is therefore labeled as XY. Likewise, the physical man who was labeled as xy, has now polarized with the feminine energy of the Holy Spirit, and is therefore labeled as XX. The woman has become like the man, and the man has become like the woman — they are ONE.

"That they may all be one; as thou Father, art in me, and I in thee, that they also may be one in us; that the world may believe that thou hast sent me." (Jn. 17:21)

STAR OF ISRAEL: AT-ONE-MENT WITH ALL SPIRIT FORCES

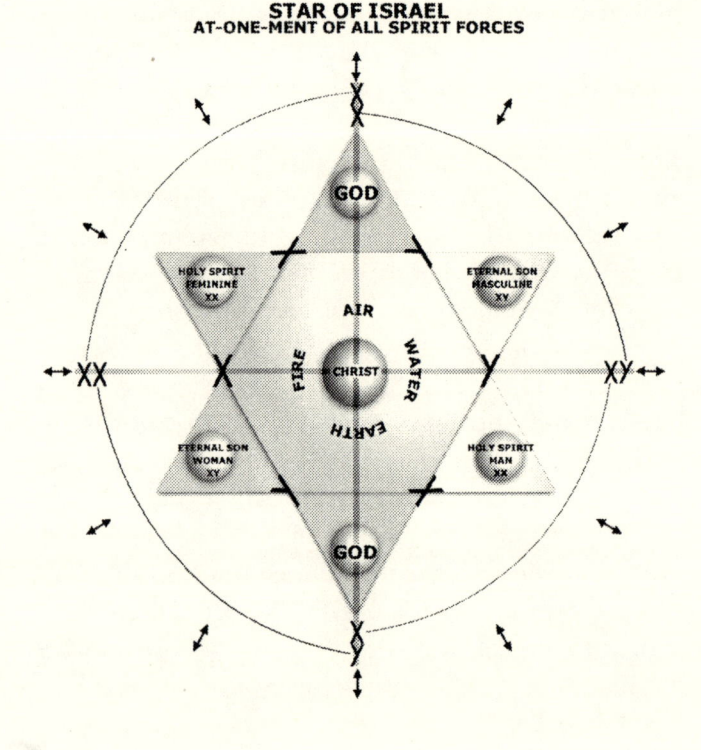

**STAR OF ISRAEL
AT-ONE-MENT OF ALL SPIRIT FORCES**

—CHAPTER THREE—

EXILED IN LOWER STATES OF CONSCIOUSNESS

MICHAEL:
ARCHANGELIC IMAGE OF JESUS CHRIST

GOD's Holy Spirit is energy existent in divers vibrational patterns above all: through all and in all.[33] All things in all dimensions are composed of different energy frequencies vibrating at different wavelengths, the highest and most powerful known as Light energy.[34] From this eternal Light, our UNIVERSAL GOD willed HIS Eternal Son into consciousness [35] and it was through His inherited Holy Spirit, in accordance with His FATHER'S Will, that the earth and all things were in turn created.[36] To interact with the angelic hierarchies He had created, He scaled down a por-

---

[33] Eph. 4:6.

[34] Rev. 21:23-24.

[35] GOD the FATHER is the SUPREME HOLY SPIRIT from which the Son's Spirit was drawn. In 325 A.D., it was decided by a voting process undertaken by Church officials at the Council of Trent that GOD the FATHER and the Son were defined as the same entity. The Bible presents evidence that though the Son is at-One with the FATHER in Spirit (1Jn.5:7), He nonetheless remains an independent Being (1Jn. 4:15-16; Rev. 12:10; Mk. 1:11; Jn. 14:26; Jn. 3:16; 1Jn. 3:23).

[36] Ps. 33:6; 1 Cor. 8:6; Eph. 3:9-10; Heb. 1:1-2; Jn. 1:1-5.

tion of His own Light energy and metamorphosed Himself into the lesser reduced frequency levels of an Archangel, more powerful than all the others He had created. This great Archangel came to be known as Michael which, when translated, means: "*He Who Is Like God.*"[37]

Prophet Daniel predicted that mankind would increase in knowledge during the latter days pending the Lord's return. That knowledge of Michael's identity is now beginning to rise to the surface of man's consciousness, offers us a marker as to where we are presently situated in respect to the apocalyptic timetable.[38] To better understand Beloved Michael's archangelic identity, it is helpful to refer to John's vision in The Revelation. In one of His visions, John allegorically identifies the Son of GOD, "*KING OF KINGS AND LORD OF LORDS*" as One riding on a white horse[39] battling against the forces of darkness during the prophesied period of the tribulation. In this same vision, He brandishes a metaphorical sword — his voice — with which He will smite the nations:

> ***And out of his* mouth goeth a sharp sword*** *that with it he should smite the nations: and* ***he shall rule them with a rod of iron:*** *and he treadeth the winepress of the fierceness and wrath of Almighty God. And he hath on his vesture and on his thigh*

---

* "For as his name is, so is he...." (1 Sam. 25:25). — Given to us by previous generations, the spiritual breakdown of our earth name helps us understand our current state of being because of its inherited ethereal vibrations.

[38] Dan. 12:4-12.

[39] Rev. 6:2; Rev. 19:11-19.

ORIGINS OF CHRIST'S NEW COVENANT

> *a name written, KING OF KINGS, AND LORD OF LORDS. (Rev. 19:15-16)*

* *rider on the white horse*

The rider on the white horse is ordinarily associated with Michael, the highest of all the Archangels empowered to lead GOD's heavenly army. That Michael appears to be the rider is brought to light in the Book of Thessalonians which reveals, that at the time of Armageddon, the Son of GOD will descend from heaven **with the voice of the Archangel** and that this voice has the power to **raise the dead to life**:

> *For the **Lord himself shall descend from heaven** with a shout, **with the voice of the archangel**. . . . and with the trump[10] of God; and **the dead in Christ shall rise first**: Then we which are alive and remain shall be caught up together with them in the clouds to meet the Lord in the air; and so shall we ever be with the Lord. (1 Th.4:16-17)*

The below-noted verses in the Book of John correlate in meaning with the above-noted verses in Thessalonians to substantiate that the voice to raise the dead to life and to execute judgement during the prophesied period of tribulation, will be that of the Son of GOD, having the voice of an Archangel. This correlates the Son of GOD with His scaled-down form as Michael the Archangel. No heavenly being is empowered to undertake such a role, unless He is

---

[40] Thessalonian's Lord, voice of the Archangel and trump are cross-referenced as being the same as revealed in the Book of Psalms which reports, "*God is gone up with a shout, the Lord with the sound of a trumpet.*" (Ps. 47:5)

the archangelic image of the Lord the Son of GOD Himself:

> *Verily, verily, I say unto you,* ***The hour is coming*** *and now is,* ***when the dead shall hear the voice of the Son of God and they that hear shall live****. . . . Marvel not at this: for the hour is coming in the which* ***all that are in the graves shall hear his voice****. (Jn. 5:25-28)*

A continuity of expression found in the verses of the Book of Thessalonians and The Revelation provides us with more information on the identity of He whose voice will be heard. Thessalonians reports that the rider on the white horse is prophesied to appear in the brightness of His coming; while The Revelation indicates that the Lord will return in a countenance that shines as the sun. Considered together, these verses again link Jesus the Lord with the Eternal Son's metamorphosed archangelic image, Beloved Michael.

> *And then shall that Wicked be revealed, whom* ***the Lord shall consume with the spirit of his mouth, and shall destroy with the brightness of his coming****. (2 Thess. 2:8)*

> *And out of his (rider) mouth* ***goeth a sharp sword*** *that with it he should smite the nations . . . (Rev. 19:15) Cf. And he (Lord) had in his hand seven stars: and out of his mouth went* ***a sharp twoedged sword: and his countenance was as the sun shineth in his strength****. (Rev. 1:16)*

> *Repent, or else I will come unto thee quickly, and* **will fight against them with the sword of my mouth**. *(Rev. 2:16)*

The name "Jesus Christ" had not, as of the time of the Hebrew prophets, been revealed. He was, however, metaphorically identified in the Old Testament as bearing different titles. This is seen in Prophet Isaiah who, in describing His different entitlements, significantly records Him to be a Prince:

> *For unto us a child is born, unto us a son is given; and the government shall be upon his shoulder; and his name shall be called Wonderful, Counselor, the mighty God, the everlasting Father,* **the Prince of Peace**. *(Isa. 9:6)*

Prophet Daniel was told by Archangel Gabriel during a vision that a Prince was predestined to fulfill an exalted role during the period of indignation. Significantly, this Prince would hold the title of "*Messiah*" — a title later attributed to Jesus Christ.[41] It was further revealed to Prophet Daniel that Michael shall "*stand up*" during this time of great "*trouble.*"[42] Coinciding with Michael's return to the earth plane, Daniel is instructed that many would "*awake*,"[43] which symbolically refers to the "*dead*" who will hearken to the voice of the Lord, as previously noted in the Books of Thessalonians and John. In accordance with a time prophesied as the "*end*," Daniel learns that Satan is also destined to stand up against the "*Prince of princes*" but will be defeated.[44] The Book of Daniel

---

[41] Dan. 9-25.

[42] Dan. 12:1.

[43] Dan. 12:2.

[44] Dan. 8:19-25.

reveals more clues identifying the Lord on the white horse, foreordained to spearhead the battle against the forces of darkness during Armageddon, to be Michael, the Prince of Peace. In the New Testament, the Lord's heavenly appellation as Prince remained — no other heavenly sons or princes can claim this title of Savior except for the Lord the Son of GOD who manifested as Jesus of Nazareth on earth:

> *Him hath God exalted with his right hand to be a* **Prince and a Savior**. . . . *(Acts. 5:31)*

As previously noted, the Eternal Son created all other sons in accordance with GOD's Master Plan. That Archangel Satan was also created by divine design is disclosed in revealing and somewhat enigmatic terms by the bestowal of his prestigious position as "*Son of the Morning*."[45] Because the Eternal Son of GOD, the "*First Bright Morning Star*,"[46] co-created everything in accordance with His FATHER's Will, Satan therefore remains one of His ethereal offspring, a subordinate prince in the heavenly hierarchy:

> *By **the word of the Lord**[47] were the heavens **made**; and **all the host of them by the breath of his mouth**. (Rev. 33:6)*

---

[45] Is. 14:12-14; Is. 54:16. The dragon, devil, Satan and the Serpent are all the same entity (Rev. 12:9). Lucifer who is also biblically inscribed as having incarnated in the earth plane can be considered the same entity. [The name Lucifer, meaning "Light Giver," was another name given to Satan by St. Jerome and other church fathers. (A Dictionary of Angels; Davidson, Gustav. Free Press. 1967.)]

[46] Rev. 22:16.

[47] Rev. 19:13.

Although Satan was endowed with free will, he eventually proved to be negative when he sought to aggrandize himself above GOD and establish a kingdom of his own on earth.[48] When he defied GOD's harmonious laws in higher levels of existence, chaos ensued and its vitriolic effects subsequently rippled down to lower dimensions of existence. To overcome this fallen prince's adversarial disturbances, the Son of GOD as Michael, set out to cleanse and restructure the heavenly realms, and henceforth entered the earth plane to correct what was taking place under the rule of Satan. That spirit finds expression in materiality is a concept that must first be understood in order to comprehend Michael's personification in the earth plane. His key role in the celestial realms was to restore order from the chaos which had developed under Satanic rebellion. Relatively, as Adam, the first earth manifestation of the Son of GOD,[49] He undertook the same role in this sphere of existence in accordance with third dimensional laws. His spiritual battle continued to take expression against Satan, a heavenly son who became His adversary, in the same plane of existence where the Adamic offence took place.[50] As The Revelation explains, it was during His incarnation as Jesus that He overcame the dragon with the power of His own shed blood and made the way passable above the veil for mankind.[51] In brief,

---

[48] Satan was covering angel over the earth (Ezek. 28:12-19). Cf. Mk. 3:23-26; 11:18.

[49] Lk. 3:38. Cf. Rev. 22:16 which teaches that during John's vision in the Revelation, the Lord discloses that He was: "*the root and the offspring of David, and the bright and morning star*" thereby confirming his earliest earth incarnation as the root parent, the first Adam. Also refer to Jn. 2:13-17.

[50] Rom. 5:19; Mt. 18:18.

[51] Heb. 6:19-20.

Michael as Lord of the Way is an overpowering Spirit force who stands at the door of the highest states of consciousness available to man.[52] As Jesus of Nazareth, He opened and became the "*Way*" leading into heaven when He established a human pattern which man could emulate to attain to truth and life while in the earth plane:

> ***And there was war in heaven: Michael and his angels fought against the dragon and the dragon fought and his angels.*** *And the great dragon was cast out, that old Serpent called the Devil, and Satan, which deceiveth the whole world: he was cast out into the earth and his angels were cast out with him. And I heard a loud voice saying in heaven, Now is come salvation and strength and the kingdom of our God and the power of his Christ:. . . .* ***and they overcame him by the blood of the Lamb.*** *. . . Woe to the inhabiters of the earth and of the sea! For the devil is come down unto you. . . . knoweth that he hath a short time. (Rev. 12:7-12)*

(Michael's identity will be further discussed in detail in other works in this series.)[53]

As allegorically noted in the Book of Genesis, the cleansing process began in higher levels of existence when the First Light was divided from the darkness.[54] The First Light is analogous to the Eternal Son of

---

[52] Dan. 10:21.

[53] Cf. Metatron: From Adam to Enoch to Jesus of Nazareth. Holcombe, Alfred D., B.S.L., LL. B., and Holcombe, S.M. Xlibris 2002.

[54] Gen. 1:3-4. Cf. "*Then spake Jesus....I am the light of the world: he that follows me shall not walk in darkness but shall have the light of Life.*" (Jn. 8:12)

GOD who created other generations of Light in harmony with GOD's Holy Spirit; while darkness is analogous to the fallen son, Satan, who created inharmonious generations of his own deficient, negative spirit. It was through this cosmic division that spirit energies, negative and positive angelic spirit forces, took expression in matter. Thus Satan and his legions were removed from higher realms of Light, and thereafter their vibrational energy took conscious expression on earth where they have continued to spread chaos. Under His leadership, the Son of GOD as Michael, along with a wave of positive angelic spirit forces, assumed 3rd dimensional states of consciousness in order to incarnate in flesh bodies that would enable them to continue the cleansing process of spiritualizing the earth with lineages of GOD's Spirit.[55]

That man's angelic higher self decelerated from higher states of consciousness and became encased in a physical body after the Adamic fall,[56] is encrypted in allegorical terms in Old and New Testament writings. Although some scriptural meanings need to be decoded through the same Holy Spirit which inspired the original authors of the written words, other biblical verses leave no doubt concerning man's celestial nature. One example is found in the Old Testament when Jacob in a dream observed angels

---

[55] Gen. 1:28.

[56] Though there exist different angelic hierarchies, some angels do not assume a human condition. Man's angelic self, created in the first generations of Light, always remains an angel and is that part of his ethereal anatomy which stands ever at the throne of the FATHER. Cf. Mt. 18:10; Lk. 20:36; Gen. 6:3; Mt. 22:30; Mk. 12:25 and Lk. 20:36.

ascending and descending a ladder which extended between heaven and earth.[57] In the same dream, the Lord God explained to Jacob that it was his seed who would inherit the land, and form the spiritually-blessed families of the world. By visualizing Jacob's dream and discerning its symbolic meaning, it becomes apparent that the angels ascending and descending the ladder are indicative of man's angelic nature as well as his ascent and descent into higher and lower realms of existence. Another biblical example attesting to man's angelic nature is found in the New Testament when Jesus explained to a group of chief priests and Pharisees that after death man could assume the condition of an angel.[58] Jesus' words clearly suggest that man must undergo an angelic metamorphosis from his incarnated state in order to be drawn into one of the appropriate mansions in other realms of existence once the physical body expires. His comments confirm that the angels ascending and descending the rungs of Jacob's ladder are analogous to mankind's struggle to climb through higher states of consciousness into the heavenly realms via cycles of life and death. That man must undergo a process of spirit quickening in order to ascend to higher realms of existence[59] suggests that when his angelic energy entered the earth plane, it had to have undergone a deceleration of its light frequencies to assume the human condition. The following biblical verses expound on this principle:

> *For we see Jesus, who **was made a little lower than the angels**. . . . For verily he took not on him the*

---

[57] Gen. 28:12-14.

[58] Mt. 22:30; Mk. 12:25; Lk. 20:36.

[59] Jn. 6:62-63; Eph. 2:1-5, 18-22.

> *nature of angels; but he took on him the seed of Abraham. Wherefore in all things it behooved him to be made like unto his brethren. . . . (Heb. 2:9-16)*

The phrase "*was made a little lower than the angels,*" refers to the process of spirit deceleration from higher to lower states of consciousness. The earth Son of God, Jesus, perceived in terms of angelic spirit energy, subsequently decelerated into a lower form of energy — the soul — in order to effectively interface with a flesh body able to accommodate 3rd dimensional laws. From this perspective, Jesus expressed in flesh was indeed made lower than an angel, because His physical body could not accommodate the full charge of His extremely powerful spirit energy. It should be emphasized, however, that even though He underwent spirit transformation in order to assume the same human condition as His brethren,[60] He unconditionally ranks higher than all other heavenly angelic powers or principalities with the exception of GOD the FATHER Himself. Accordingly, because of His Divine Preeminence as the Eternal Son who inherited His FATHER's spirit without measure,[61] He was predestined to fulfill a unique mission which would, in part, involve the salvation of mankind:

> ***Being made so much better than the angels, as he hath by inheritance obtained a more excellent name than they.*** *For unto which of the angels said he at any time, Thou Art My Son, This Day Have I Begotten Thee? And again, I Will Be To Him a Father, and He Shall Be To Me A Son?. . . . But unto the Son He saith, Thy Throne, O God, Is For Ever and Ever: A Sceptre Of Righteousness Is*

---

[60] Heb. 2:16-18.
[61] Jn. 3:34.

> *the Sceptre Of Thy Kingdom. And Thou Lord, In the Beginning Hast Laid the Foundation Of The Earth: And The Heavens Are The Works Of Thine Hands. (Heb. 1:2-10)*

THE FIRST AND LAST ADAM

Apostle Paul expounded on Jesus' explanation of the angelic metamorphosis when he disclosed that man possesses two bodies: one natural (physical), the other spiritual (soul/angelic spirit energy), *supra*.[62] According to Paul, the flesh body first underwent development in materiality through an evolutionary process before it could accommodate higher states of consciousness, as noted in the following biblical verse:

> *Howbeit, that was not first which is spiritual, but that which is natural; and **afterward** that which is spiritual. (1 Cor. 15:46)*

Significantly, after noting that the flesh part of man was first, after which came the spirit, Paul insightfully linked the first earth manifestation of the Son of GOD to Adam:

> *And so it is written, **the first man Adam was made a living soul; the last Adam was made a quickening spirit** . . . **The first man is of the earth**, earthy; **the second man is the Lord from heaven.** (1 Cor. 15: 45-47)*

---

[62] 1 Cor.15:35-50 - Based on the Pauline writings, man must undergo a purging process to be quickened and transformed into a pure angelic form because nothing that remains corrupted by the earth can take on the heavenly mantle of incorruptibility.

The Son of GOD was made a living, breathing soul when He incarnated in a flesh body as the first Adam. As the second and last Adam, He later became known as Jesus, the Lord incarnate who had overcome third dimensional laws by the quickening of His FATHER's Holy Spirit, and was resurrected to HIS right side.[63] In the Book of The Revelation, the risen Christ disclosed through John the identity of the first and the last Adam. In this particular vision, John identifies the Lord as having a great "*voice*," which again links Him to the voice of the Archangel Michael, *supra*.

> *I (John) was in the Spirit on the Lord's day and heard behind me **a great voice**, as of a trumpet. . . . **I (Christ) am the Alpha and the Omega, the first and the last**. . . . (Rev. 1:10-11)*
>
> *. . . **I am the first and the last**, I am he that liveth, and was dead; and behold, I am alive for evermore. (Rev. 1:17-18)*

That Jesus of Nazareth had incarnated as the root parent, the first Adam, is further disclosed in the following New Testament writings:

> *Now that **he (Jesus) ascended** what is it but that **he also descended first** (as in Adam) in the lower parts of the Earth. **He that descended is the same also that ascended** up far above all heavens. (Eph. 4:9-10)*
>
> *In whom we have redemption through his blood, even the forgiveness of sins: Who is the image of **the invisible god the firstborn of every creature**. (Col. 1:15)*

---

[63] 1 Pet. 3:18 confirms Jesus was quickened by the Spirit of GOD. Cf. Heb. 1:1-3.

> *Nevertheless death reigned from Adam to Moses, even over them that had not sinned after the similitude of Adam's transgression **who is the figure of him that was to come.** (Rom 5:14)*

THE FIRST AND LAST EVE

Because the Son of GOD incarnated as the first and last Adam,[64] created in His FATHER's male and female image, it follows that there existed a first and last Eve. That Adam's complementary binary soul,[65] Eve, eventually appeared as Beloved Mary is subtly revealed in the Bible and in one particularly revealing Marian apparition. Individuals from around the world who have been blessed to behold the Blessed Lady in authentic Marian apparitions, have confirmed that She, in a maternal sense, often addresses mankind as Her children. Yet Eve is the first woman identified in the Book of Genesis as the Mother of all. That being the case, it is evident that Beloved Mary assumed the same parental entitlement because She had previously been a soul incarnation of Eve:

> *And Adam called his wife's name **Eve** because she **was the mother of all living**. (Gen. 3:20)*

One of the most famous Marian apparitions occurred in Lourdes, France, in 1858. During one of eighteen apparitions, the Blessed Lady identified herself to a poor peasant girl, Bernadette Soubirous, using the following words, "*I Am The Immaculate Conception.*" This

---

[64] 1 Cor. 15:45-47.

[65] Refer to Chapter: "Transposition of Spirit Energy In Physical Bodies."

statement was striking because it was ostensibly the first known declaration by Mary that She had not been conceived according to physical laws and implies a deeper meaning than Mary's own virginal birth by Her earth mother. Scriptures confirm that Adam was the first earth Son of GOD created without being subjected to 3rd dimensional laws.[66] From Adam, the first woman was drawn into materiality also without the physical act of copulation, as symbolized in her extraction from his rib. Therefore, Eve, the first Mother of all — Beloved Mary's first soul incarnation — created from Adam's metaphorical rib, could rightfully be considered the first Immaculate Conception. The disclosure of Her identity in Lourdes fits within a divine plan that explicates how woman was brought into material existence through divine laws. For this reason, this particular Marian apparition merits serious and careful consideration.

By connecting scriptural verses found in Genesis and in The Revelation, a continuity of expression reveals an intriguing association between Eve and Mary, despite the fact that these two books were written in different ages by different authors and were thereafter translated and edited numerous times by different authorities. In the below-noted Old and New Testament verses, the first woman biblically known to have experienced the pain associated with childbirth was Eve. The Book of The Revelation teaches that Mary also underwent physical childbirth; while the synoptic gospels inform us that She immaculately conceived Jesus without being subjected to third dimensional laws. Therefore, it appears that Eve, the first Mother of all living, had successfully overcome third dimensional laws, and later as Mary was able to

---

[66] Lk. 3:38.

immaculately conceive Her offspring through the Holy Spirit, which was the means of procreation before the Adamic infraction took place. Stated another way, Mary who had been immaculately conceived from Adam's rib, had in turn, immaculately conceived Her binary male imprint[67] — Jesus — through the Holy Spirit. This supports the biblical tenet that it was the Holy Ghost who spiritually induced Mary's earth pregnancy.[68] The Holy Ghost thus is synonymous with the Divine Spark that set in motion conditions in Her mental, spiritual and endocrine system that brought about in the physical plane the expression of the Son of GOD on earth. The following biblical verses disclose this pattern from beginning to end:

> *Unto the woman (Eve) he said,* ***I will greatly multiply thy sorrow and thy conception;*** *in sorrow shall thou bring forth children and thy desire shall be for thy husband, and* ***he shall*** **rule** ***over thee.*** *(Gen. 3:16)*

> *And she (Mary) being with child cried,* ***travailing in birth and pained to be delivered . . .*** *and she shall bring forth a man child (Jesus) who was to* **rule** *all nations with a rod of iron and her child was caught up unto God and to his throne. (Rev. 12:2-5)*

A deeper meaning of the above-quoted verses from Genesis suggests that the husband whom GOD instructed was to "*rule*" over Eve later became her Son

---

[67] Refer to Chapter: "Transposition of Spirit Energy Into Physical Bodies."
[68] Mt: 1:20.

in The Revelation, predestined to "*rule*" over all nations.[69] The exalted ruler that Mary would bring into the world can be correlated in meaning with the allegorical rider on the white horse destined to "*rule*" the world "*with a rod of Iron.*"[70] In his letter to Timothy, Apostle Paul confirms the validity of the above-cited verses by providing another link between Eve and Mary. He reveals that Eve would be saved in childbirth. How else could Eve be saved in childbirth or be absolved of her transgression, except by way of birthing the empowered Ruler and Savior who would, through His atonement, liberate her and all her descendants from the effects of the initial transgression?

> *For Adam was first formed, then Eve. And Adam was not deceived, but **the woman being deceived was in the transgression**. Notwithstanding **she shall be saved in childbearing**, if they continue in faith and charity and holiness with sobriety. (1 Tim. 2:15)*

Verses in the Book of Timothy, in part, reiterate what Prophet Jeremiah long ago prophesied when he referred to Eve as the "*backsliding daughter*" for having transgressed divine laws:

> ***O virgin of Israel**, turn again to these thy cities. How long wilt thou go about, O thou backsliding daughter? For the Lord hath created a new thing on the earth: **A woman shall compass a man**. (Jer. 31:21-22)*

---

[69] Ps. 2:7-12; Rev. 2:27.
[70] Rev. 19:15-16.

In the Old Testament, Prophet Micah prophesied that the ruler was GOD's predestined firstborn, Adam, who would later be born from She who would travail in childbirth. Because of her part in the transgression, Eve was fated to undergo the travail, the physical pain, of childbirth and her husband would rule over her. Clearly Eve did not, during that particular soul incarnation, birthe the ruler of all people. It was destined to take place during Her soul incarnation as Mary when She did travail in the physical pains of childbirth to deliver the ruler, albeit without being subjected to 3rd dimensional laws of copulation:

> *Thou, Bethlehem Ephratah, thou art little among the thousands of Judah; out of thee shall come forth unto Me* **him that shall rule My people He is from everlasting;** *and I will give them up* **until the time she travaileth to bring forth My first born that he may rule all people.** *(Mi. 5:2-3)*

That Eve eventually reincarnated as Beloved Mary becomes even more apparent in The Revelation, in which She is symbolically described as the "*heavenly woman crowned with* **twelve stars,** *clothed with the sun and with the moon at her feet,*"[71] whose '*child' was taken up to GOD and to his throne.*" The symbolic meaning of this verse is derived by again correlating verses in Genesis and The Revelation. In Genesis, we learn that as a result of the transgression, Adam, Eve and all souls who formed the Adamic forerunners and descendants, became clothed with coats of skin; in

---

[71] Symbolically, the sun is scripturally synonymous with male energy; the moon is synonymous with female energy.

other words, confined in dense flesh bodies in the materiality of the earth.[72] Their only escape from fleshed encasement was to reach for the Tree of Life,[73] synonymous with the essence of GOD's Spirit. Thus the woman clothed in the Sun is analogous to Eve who, later after Her soul incarnation as Beloved Mary, became clothed in the brilliant Light of the most Holy Trinity.

The twelve stars adorning Mary's heavenly crown in The Revelation symbolize the twelve tribes of Israel. As previously explained, Mary was the first Mother of all; accordingly, the twelve tribes of Israel later became Her descendants — Her children. The Book of Genesis teaches that Joseph, one of the twelve patriarchs of Israel, dreamed that the sun, moon and eleven stars would one day make obeisance to him. The dream, in part, foreshadowed Joseph's rise to power under the Egyptian Pharoah, and that he would one day save the twelve tribes from a devastating famine. More significantly, however, scriptures correlate the eleven stars with Joseph's eleven brothers and their respective tribes.[74] Joseph, Jacob's son, can rightfully be counted as a star himself which brings the count of the stars to twelve:

> *Behold, I have dreamed a dream more; and behold,* ***the sun and the moon and the eleven stars made obeisance to me.*** *. . . . What is this dream*

---

[72] Gen. 3:2.
[73] The Tree of Life is recorded as being guided by a flaming "Sword" — Michael (Gen. 3:23-24).
[74] Refer to Chapters: "Israel's Divine Genealogical Tree and the Divine Lineage" and "Joseph: A Previous Soul Incarnation of Jesus of Nazareth," which explain Joseph's role in the genealogies. See also Num. 24:16-19.

> *that thou hast dreamed? Shall **I and my mother
> and thy brethren indeed come to bow down our-
> selves to thee** to the earth? (Gen. 37:9)*

This verse defines the sun as the father figure, the moon as the mother figure and the twelve stars as the twelve patriarchs of Israel,[75] who are Eve's descendants. Membership in the twelve tribes of Israel, however, is no longer restricted to those of Jewish descent. Under terms of the New Covenant, all of GOD's children have the potential of becoming at-One again in the twelve heavenly levels of the mystical spirit body of Christ, and heirs according to the promise, as will be discussed in subsequent chapters:

> *For ye are all the children of God by faith in Christ Jesus. For as many of you as have been baptized into Christ have put on Christ. There is neither Jew nor Greek, there is neither bond nor free, there is neither male nor female; for ye are all one in Christ Jesus. And if ye be Christ's, then are ye Abraham's seed, and heirs according to the promise. (Gal. 3:26-29)*[76]

The Book of Genesis and of The Revelation disclose another continuity of expression between Eve and Mary. The enmity that ensued between Eve and the Serpent's seed fomented a battle that spanned numerous generations. The Book of The Revelation reveals that Eve had subsequently incarnated as Beloved Mary to continue the battle against the Ser-

---

[75] The twelve stars are also analogous to the twelve Apostles and the twelve levels of the New Jerusalem as will be discussed in following chapters. Cf. Eph. 2:19-22; Rev. 21:12,14, 19-22.

[76] Gal. 3: 6-29.

pent, also known as the dragon, the Devil and Satan, that afflicted her in the Garden:

> *And the Lord God said unto the **serpent**. . . . **I will put enmity between thee and the woman, and between thy seed and her seed;** It shall bruise thy head and thou shalt bruise his heel. (Gen. 3:14:15)*

> *And **the great dragon, was cast out, that old serpent** called the Devil, and Satan.. . . . . (Rev. 12:9)*

> *. . . **And the dragon was wroth with the woman and went to make war with the remnant of her seed**, which keep the commandments of God and have the testimony of Jesus Christ. (Rev. 12:15-17)*

Mary's name, meaning "*Sea of Bitterness,*" mirrors the suffering She endured and overcame in accordance with GOD's Master Plan for mankind. As was the case with the first Adam, Eve suffered greatly in the earth plane from the beginning in order to be quickened into a state of perfection. Only in a quickened state induced by GOD's Holy Spirit could She effectively assist in reversing the karmic debt of the first transgression. For Her part, Mary, who had attained to a perfected state, immaculately conceived the Savior of this world in accordance with GOD's divine laws. Unlike Her descendants, the mixed seed, Her Son Jesus was the perfect seed born of a virginal birth in holy union with GOD. In this unblemished state, He underwent the sacrificial Atonement and restored the Tree of Life, empowering and liberating His descendants from laws that had kept them earthbound since the original transgression. Mary, therefore, rightfully deserves deep veneration because:

1) She is the first expressed female divinity of GOD on earth, and 2) Her actions assisted in reversing karmic laws activated by the Adamic transgression when She virginally birthed the Ruler. However, it was when the Lord resurrected after His Atonement that Mary, His Binary Soul, was able to regain Her rightful position as the heavenly Mother of All. Accordingly, the intercession and saving grace remains ever with the Lord, because: 1) He is the empowered Son of GOD and Maker of mankind, and 2) His sacrificial Atonement has the power to extricate His descendants from their exile in lower dimensions of existence.

In some of Her messages to the world, Beloved Mary warns mankind that Satan is cleverly scheming to deceive many. That he does so by masquerading as an "*Angel of Light*"[77] to induce false Marian apparitions and other negative spirit manifestations is plausible. For this reason, discernment and the testing of spirits is extremely important. Living a virtuous life based on the Son's two commandments of Love[78] while seeking guidance through GOD's Holy Spirit to know truth, is essential in order to avoid ever-present spiritual snares.[79] Considering the imminence of the Lord's return, Mary's role as an active force against Satan the Serpent becomes more significant. As the now gloriously crowned Queen of the Cosmos and the empowered Mother of all living, She has returned via contemporary apparitions to assist her Son, the crowned Savior of mankind in battling against Satanic influences. In the end, the Serpent who beguiled Her and Adam in the Garden will be crushed and put away for another thousand years, after which

---

[77] 2 Cor. 11:13-14.

[78] Mt. 22:37-40; Jn. 14:15-21.

[79] 1 Jn. 4:1.

time the Devil will be released for a short period on the earth, and thereafter cast into the "*lake of fire*" to burn forever.[80]

EVOLUTION AND CREATION

It is an enigma how the first Son of GOD[81] so gloriously composed of His FATHER's Holy Spirit, fell prey on earth to Satan's web of deceit. This mystery begins to unravel when we go back to the time after the great division of Light and darkness when spirit forces took expression in lower levels of existence. Because scriptures nowhere state that GOD ever conveyed ownership to Satan over any portion of what the Eternal Son had made, it is presumable that this powerful Archangel manipulatively took possession of planet earth where free will prevailed, and installed himself in power. Lucifer, Son of the Morning, and other angels were apparent participants in the evolutionary process by using their imagination, ingenuity and knowledge of DNA to elevate lower vibrational flesh life forms into manlike creatures which they could manipulate for their own purposes.[82] These lower life forms did not possess GOD's Holy Spirit because Satan and his angels had formulated their origins. After having started a biological reproductive pattern of lower life forms, these in time mutated into increasingly more complex flesh creatures which developed into a variety of species. The great dinosaurs and other barbaric primitive forms illustrate what these angels were able to produce under the governance of Satan. His objective

---

[80] Rev. Ch. 20.
[81] Lk. 3:38.
[82] Isa. 14:12-15; 54:16; Ezek. 28:14.

of colonizing the earth with flesh creatures devoid of GOD's Holy Spirit with the intention of establishing his kingdom on earth, supports Paul's earlier-noted explanation that the flesh body existed before the spirit body incarnated on earth. From an evolutionary perspective, this implies that although primitive pre-human beings appeared on the earth eons ago, they only became sufficiently physically well developed to accommodate angelic spirit souls in comparatively recent millennia. Charles Darwin, who wrote at length about the law of evolution, indicated that life forms evolved through natural laws that accommodated survival and adaptation. With this in mind, we begin to realize that Satan's interference in the process of creation is the root cause of the physical imperfections of this world, and accounts for the reason why man was not initially created in his final genetic makeup from the beginning. When one begins to understand how thoughts pattern the mind and the DNA, then it is becomes evident that considerable time was required to upgrade the mental and physical characteristics of the flesh body before it could accommodate higher states of consciousness.

It is theorized that man gradually evolved from a primitive ape-like being into a progressively more intelligent being. Many dispute, however, that though we may have a common ancestor, there is no "*missing link*" to be found between man and ape, because man evolved on a separate path. Yet, that hominids may have evolved from a primordial time predating the ape is allegorically disclosed in the Bible. According to GOD's timetable, a "*day*" in heavenly higher dimensions can be likened to a thousand years on earth.[83] With this in mind, man, created on the 6th day after living forms in the sea were created on the 5th day, fits within the theoretical claims that his flesh body evolved from primordial marine cells through protracted eons of time before eventually mutating into a flesh being able to accommodate more complex spirit souls than other mammals. Phylogeny Recapitulates Ontogeny is a scientific term describing the development of man's flesh body from the time of conception to its full development within the mother's womb. It can be compared to an evolutionary blueprint mapping the course of the human life form as it progresses through the embryonic and fetal stages and is comparable to prehistoric marine life cells progressing through different evolutionary stages. The human gestation period exemplifies this process, beginning with the sperm fertilizing the ovum to produce the zygote, by the multiplication of cells (morulla), to a life form consisting of appendages of fins and gills (embryo sprouting arms and legs) and spine-like tail. Scientists have further discovered that the controlling genes for major structural characteristics, such as head to tail differentiation in developing animals, were common to most animals. In other words, very similar genes govern the same pattern of development in fruit flies, rodents and even human beings. Therefore, that man shares similar controlling genes as other animalistic life forms before diversity takes place, suggests that man may have evolved from the same primordial conditions.

As evolution unfolded, primitive life forms crossed over with other life forms and mutated into new creations. As these emerged, spirit forces took physical

---

[83] Ps. 90:4; 2 Pet. 3:8.

expression in accommodating genes which were rooted in different pre-existent conditions. This describes in over-simplified terms the gradual process of creation through evolution. The concept can somewhat be explained in the cross-cultivation of plants. When a vegetable is genetically modified through cross-cultivation, the final result is a new creation; yet its origin has its root in different pre-existent forms. This developmental pattern is to a lesser degree, observed in the broccoflower — a broccoli crossed over with a cauliflower. The missing link would become further removed from its source of origin if the broccoflower became cross-cultivated with another variety, and so on. After having crossed over numerous times, new varieties would become so different as to be identified as new creations. Unless we possessed knowledge of its initial parental cross-over, we would be hard pressed to find the concrete "*missing link*" of the future offspring of the broccoflower because it was created within the genetical makeup of different pre-existent conditions. Does the existence of the broccoflower's mixed offspring suggest that they evolved on a separate path? No. Rather it suggests that they have complementary genes, which through the process of cross-cultivation produced them as numerous varieties and eventually into new creations. The simplified explanation of genetically modified plants serves to explain how man's flesh body may well have evolved from primitive marine cells, and through mutation of pre-existent conditions, to have ultimately developed into a more advanced hominid possessing a brain sufficiently developed to accommodate a higher state of consciousness — the soul — as in the man, Adam.

Satan, however, resented Adam and Eve because of the Holy Spirit that was in them. What happened next explains how the first generation of Light succumbed to Satanic influences and became entrapped in lower earthly dimensions of existence.

EVE BITES THE APPLE

When the Adamic spirit forces manifested in the earth plane to restore order, Satanic energy permeated the earth's auric field, and all life forms were subjected to its influence. In order to incarnate into flesh bodies in accordance with 3rd dimensional laws, this angelic order, as previously noted, had to first undergo a process of spirit metamorphosis. By that process, the Adamic lineages assumed lower states of consciousness and, like all other life forms in this dimension, became subjected to powerful Satanic impressions which impaired their ability to stave off the bestial earthly desires of the animalistic flesh bodies into which they had incarnated. This brought about a conscious state of vulnerability which the powerful governing Archangel, Satan, used to his advantage. Unable to accept that GOD had given dominion of the earth to Adam, He planned to infiltrate the lineages of Light with the goal of promoting a new race under his rule. For this reason, he sought to sabotage Adam's mission of spiritualizing the earth with lineages of Light by instilling into the first parents an appetite for the desires of the flesh, which militated against GOD's Will.

Because carnality[84] opposes GOD's Spirit, Adam and Eve, vulnerable to the deceitfulness prevalent in lower states of consciousness, innocently allowed themselves to be manipulated by Satan. Under his influence, they committed an act that repelled the Tree of Life — the imprint of the Holy Spirit — the ethereal glue that kept them connected to their angelic form in higher levels of existence. Satan, who wanted to aggrandize his kingdom on earth, deceitfully approached Eve because she was able, in union with him, to propagate a seed of his spirit on earth. And because Eve was at-One with Adam in spirit — as well as bone of his bones and flesh of his flesh[85] — he automatically became implicated in Satan's deceitful plan because the woman was a correlative part of him. In a weakened state of consciousness fueled by desire, Eve was consciously manipulated by the prince of the world to commit a sexual act which fostered lineages of a mixed breed: offspring born in accordance with earthly sexual conceptions. Because Eve's spiritual understanding was cloaked in lower states of consciousness, she was led to believe that by committing this act, she and her descendants would become as gods in a world where Satan, as the covering cherub, had taken control.[86]

The consequences of their actions severely disrupted the manner in which future lineages would multiply on the earth.[87] Scriptures inform us that before the transgression, Adam and Eve were encouraged to

---

[84] Rom. 8:7-11 teaches that the carnal mind is enmity against God because it is not attuned to HIS laws. It must be quickened through Christ in GOD.

[85] Gen. 2:23-24.

[86] Gen. 3:4-5.

[87] Gen. 3:16.

be fruitful and multiply without the painful, physical process of childbirth, which implies that the propagation of Adam's seed had before then been accomplished by other means than earthly copulation. Having repelled the Holy Spirit, the Adamic lineages became encased in physical bodies with the added burden of undergoing earth experiences with limited celestial knowledge and spirit energy. The cumulative ramifications of the fall found expression in subsequent family lineages as they unfolded throughout the generations. Rendered unable to effectively discern the principles of cause and effect, they became increasingly more entrenched in Satanic influences which kept their souls earthbound through repeated life cycles. As time passed, man — still influenced by Satanic temptation — became increasingly limited in heavenly knowledge and eventually began to believe that the earth, including its carnality and its laws, was his destined reality. That immaculate conceptions were the predetermined means by which the earth plane was to be populated was knowledge that was forgotten by man as time unfolded.

Fortunately, another master plan was put in place to help awaken man in order that he could extricate himself from earth laws, so that he might return to his spiritual estate. It was only by reaching again for the Tree of Life — which had been removed from the earth plane because of the infraction,[88] *supra* — that Adam could return to a state of At-One-ness with GOD, and subsequently liberate his descendants from the shackles that had kept them bound in Satanic bondage from the time of the proverbial fall.

---

[88] Gen. 3:22-24

—CHAPTER FOUR—

ISRAEL'S DIVINE GENEALOGICAL TREE AND THE DIVINE LINEAGE

THE ENMITY BETWEEN TWO SEEDS

To effectively fulfill their mission of spiritualizing the earth with lineages of GOD's Light, it was imperative that the Sons of Light remained at-One with their binary mates in order that the sacrosanct seed be kept intact. This undertaking was looked darkly upon by Satan who resented the fact that a highly-spiritualized root race had found expression in a plane of existence where lower life forms were governed under his laws. Because Eve's angelic higher self was the divine female expression of the Son of GOD, Satan was well aware that in higher levels of existence her spirit, in union with the Son, contributed to creation. He was also aware that being the female counterpart of Adam on earth, Eve's offspring were far superior to the animalistic flesh forms at that time prolific on the earth. With the intention of keeping man under his control while aggrandizing his own kingdom on earth, Satan sought to sabotage the Adamic mission by merging Eve's creative forces with his own. Consequently, when Adam and Eve satiated their sexual carnal cravings, induced by Satanic **desires and thoughts**, they became trapped in the materiality of the earth plane, subjected to 3rd dimensional laws. By indulging in physical sexual activities, they inadvertently activated laws that altered their divine creative forces on different levels; it resulted in the "*enmity*" that GOD consequently placed between Satan and Eve's seed:

> And ***I will put enmity between thee and the woman, and between thy seed and her seed;*** *it shall bruise thy head and thou shalt bruise his heel. (Gen. 3:15)*

The carnality of their sexual activity resulted in Eve's firstborn, Cain, the first in the Adamic lineages to be born in accordance with physical laws, and the first to receive the mark of exile.[89] Cain's name became symbolic of the exiled generations that followed. That his spirit was tainted became evident when, out of jealousy, he slew his brother Abel. Although the Adamic forerunners incarnated in a dimension which subjected them to lower states of consciousness, the question arises: how could an offspring born from parents of the Light be capable of committing such a vile act? The answer is found in the "*enmity*" GOD had placed between Satan and Eve's seed. It is apparent that Cain inherited attributes from two opposing spirit sources — overwhelmingly from Satan. Because Cain was born in direct violation of GOD's laws,[90] a dominant portion of the Serpent's spirit incarnated in the soul of Eve's first son. That Cain inherited mental and spiritual attributes from the Serpent's iniquitous spirit explains why he readily succumbed to negative influences. Having recog-

---

[89] Gen. 4:15.
[90] Gen. 3:3,11.

nized the error of their ways, Adam and Eve turned away from Satan's influences and temptations, confessed their iniquity to GOD and consequently drew into materiality a more spiritually advanced soul — Abel — who, unlike Cain, inherited a principal portion of GOD's Spirit.

Desires and thoughts nourish the mind which is alive in every cell of the human body and by them genetic bloodlines were positively and negatively altered to influence future generations. Scientifically, it is well known that energy can be transformed and redirected. Thoughts — energy impulses — are the initiating forces that induce one to feel emotions, form ideals and initiate actions. Thoughts, whether negative or positive, have a direct effect on seven major ductless glands: Gonads, Cells of Leydig, Adrenals, Thymus, Thyroid, Pineal and the Pituitary. The Pituitary gland, commonly known as the "third eye" in esoteric circles, is the master gland of the Endocrine System. In combination with the adjacent Hypothalamus, it is the link between the subjective mental feelings of emotions based in the cortex and the simultaneous body-wide physical and physiological change. This means that everything thought, said and done seeks expression through this higher center, ethereally and physically. One's negative thoughts cause the Pituitary gland to unchain a sequence of hormonal reactions in the bloodstream, thereby causing further imbalances at the mental, physical and ethereal level. Because this major gland works in synergy with the other ductless glands, a negative cycle of cause and effect ensues. In a metaphoric sense, one has allowed, through free will, the "*beast of Revelation*" to take a foothold upon one's consciousness and physical system via this higher center. The "*forehead*" is referred to in the Book of the Revelation to be the area in which GOD will seal HIS faithful during the great spiritual awakening [91] which also coincides with the time of great upheaval.[92] On the other hand, it is also referred to as the area in which the "*beast*" will make his mark.[93] In brief, the Pituitary provides an ethereal doorway through which negative (Satan) and positive (Christ) forces manifest. Like attracts like, and the **mark** on the forehead is analogous to the mark of the Beast or the Seal of the living GOD destined to be imprinted on the glandular door, the Pituitary gland.

The Serpent cleverly infiltrated the biological mechanism of Eve's descendants through her weakened desires and thoughts in accordance with natural laws, associated with lower states of consciousness. This imbalance conditioned the offspring's DNA and it was through the blood (and endocrine secretions) that the tainted seed continued to spread over the earth. Blood is the physical body's life-giving essence, once tainted by lower influences, it paradoxically bound man's soul into materiality. That Satan fathered negative souls on earth in this manner was disclosed ages later by Jesus when He charged a gathering of Jews that their "*father the devil*" had been a "*murderer from the beginning.*" This linked him to Cain, the first tainted offspring born in accordance with lower states of consciousness, the first murderer re-

---

[91] Joel 2:28.
[92] Rev. 9:4-5.
[93] Rev. 13:16-17; Rev. 16:2; Rev. 19:20; Rev. 20:4.

corded in the Bible. As will be seen, Cain continued to father tainted seed upon the earth:

> ***Ye are of your father the devil,*** *and the lusts of your father ye will do.* ***He was a murderer from the beginning,*** *and abode not in the truth because there is no truth in him. (Jn. 8:44)*

Cain Versus Abel:

That Cain was unable to overcome his inherited Satanic character explains why GOD had favored his brother Abel's offering.[94] Abel, a shepherd, presented GOD with a firstling from his flock of sheep which symbolically foreshadowed the coming of the life-giving sacrificial Lamb,[95] the Son of GOD, who would one day redeem the Adamic race from their entrapment in the earth plane. Had Abel not been slain, he may well have fulfilled a key role in the Divine Lineage destined to birthe Jesus, the sacrificial lamb. Cain, on the other hand, presented GOD with fruit from the cursed ground he tilled, which karmically reflected GOD's penalization of the Serpent, Adam and Eve for having transgressed:

> *And the Lord God aid unto the Serpent, Because thou hast done this. . . .* ***upon thy belly shalt thou go, and dust shalt thou eat all the days of thy life.*** *(Gen. 3:14)*

> *And unto Adam he said, Because thou hast hearkened unto the voice of thy wife, and hast eaten of the tree of which I commanded thee saying Thou*

---

[94] Gen. 4:1-7.
[95] Heb. Ch. 10.

> shalt not eat of it: **cursed is the ground for thy sake;
> in sorrow shalt thou eat of it all of the days of thy
> life;** *Thorns and thistles shall it bring forth to thee;
> and thou shalt eat the herb of the field; In the sweat
> of thy face shalt thou eat bread.... (Gen. 3:17-18)*

The fruit of the ground which Cain tilled and presented as an offering, was earth food upon which the chastised physically-earthbound man became dependent for his survival, rather than partaking of the Tree of Life, which was the life-giving "*bread*" the Adamic lineages were predestined to eat during their earthly sojourn. This was later reflected during the Exodus when the children of Israel continued to long for more delectable earthly food. This desire to satiate carnal cravings symbolized that they still had a long arduous journey ahead of them before they could be spiritually quickened to partake of the Tree of Life:

> *I am the bread of Life. Your fathers did eat manna
> in the wilderness and are dead. (Jn. 6:48-49.*
>
> *For the bread of GOD is he which cometh down from
> heaven, and giveth life unto the world and Jesus
> said unto them, I am the bread of life. (Jn. 6:30-35)*

Though Cain was exiled from GOD's presence [96] for the murder of his brother, it appears — based on a seven-generation formula — that GOD made provisions for him by allowing him time to expiate his negative act. Cain's punishment was "*sevenfold.*" [97] The key to interpreting the seven-generation formula is found in the word "*fold*" which, in this context, re-

---

[96] Gen. 4:14.
[97] Gen. 4:15.

fers to individuals forming a particular set of generations. Sevenfold therefore meant that Cain and his descendants would continue to be exiled from GOD's presence and undergo seven generations of life cycles to expunge the negative deed:

> *And the Lord said unto him,* ***Therefore whosoever slayeth Cain, vengeance shall be taken on him sevenfold****. And the Lord set a **mark** upon Cain, lest any finding him should kill him. And Cain went out from the presence of the Lord, and dwelt in the land of Nod, on the east of Eden. (Gen. 4:15-16)*

> *The **words of the Lord are pure words: as silver tried in a furnace of earth, purified seven times**. Thou shalt keep them,* ***O Lord, thou shalt preserve them from this generation, for ever****. The wicked walk on every side, when the vilest men are exalted. (Ps. 12:6-8)*

Lamech Versus Enoch:

Seven generations from Adam, at an important juncture of the family lineages, Lamech, a descendant of Cain, also slew a man. Lamech lamented that if Cain's murder had caused him to be *"avenged sevenfold,"* his — Lamech's transgression — would cause him to be avenged *"seventy times sevenfold."* Based on the seven-generation formula, sevenfold equals 1 set of 7 generations, while seventy times equals 10 sets of 7 generations. Thus, seventy times sevenfold equals 10 sets of 7 generations. The result of Lamech's actions meant that Cain's family branch would continue to be exiled from GOD's presence for seventy generations, all the while accountable to earth laws. According to biblical genealogy, Jesus Christ was born exactly seventy generations after Lamech,[98] which meant that the tainted lineages could only then be redeemed by a Savior whose Spirit was able to unshackle 3rd dimensional laws that had kept them earthbound. Uncannily, history would repeat itself. Exactly seventy generations later (10 sets of 7 generations) — at yet another pivotal time in Cain's lineages — another slaying took place at the hands of Judas Iscariot. Jesus of Nazareth was the victim — the Savior Himself.[99] The Book of Ecclesiastes teaches that there is nothing new under the sun; that which was, will be again.[100] A key reason why Cain's generations perpetuated a negative pattern was that they had no remembrance of former things. They were unable to recognize and rectify past misdeeds except if they were illuminated by the Tree of Life, GOD's Holy Spirit empowered to bring all things to man's remembrance.[101] That Judas was born in the same lineage as Cain and Lamech, fits within the framework of a negative family lineage in which the descendants inherited a tainted spirit. From a reincarnative perspective, these particular individuals who perpetuated the same negative pattern, may well in each case have been the same soul committing the same negative actions:

> *Jesus answered them, Have not I chosen you twelve, and **one of you is a devil**? He spake of Judas Iscariot, the son of Simon, for it was he that should betray him, being one of the twelve. (Jn. 6:70-71)*

---

[98] Lk. 3:23-38.

[99] The events and consequences surrounding Jesus' slaying and inheritance were allegorically prophesied by Him in the parable of the vineyard and the husbandman (Mt. 21:33-39).

[100] Eccl. 1:9-10.

[101] Jn. 14:26.

In the seventh generation of the Adamic lineages, a positive family branch was evolving from the lineage of Adam and Eve's third son, Seth. Unlike his cousin Lamech, Enoch — also a seventh-generation descendant — was a righteous man who walked obediently with GOD for 300 years. That Enoch had overcome all temptations that bind man's soul to this earth sphere of existence is reflected in the following verse, which discloses that he was translated into higher dimensions:

And Enoch walked with God: and he was not; for God took him. (Gen. 5:24)

He then briefly returned to his earth body to advise his children about their spiritual heritage. He counseled them as to how they should live while embodied in flesh on the earth in order that they might eventually be raised up into higher dimensions of existence, rejoined with their higher self portions, and granted a position in GOD's heavenly hierarchy — as had happened to Him.[102] In accordance with GOD's Master Plan for humanity, Enoch, a subsequent soul incarnation of Adam, once again merged in union with the Tree of Life. He would subsequently restore its life-giving spirit to mankind a prophesied seventy generations later when He would appear as Jesus of Nazareth. Following His soul incarnation as Enoch, He returned to the earth plane as Melchizedek — GOD's eternal heavenly ordained

---

[102] Based on the works of 3 Enoch; Hugo Odeberg. Cambridge University Press. Metatron is the heavenly name of Enoch after his transformation and translation into heaven as the Son of GOD.

Priest.[103] As biblical scriptures subtly disclose, He would thereafter return time and again to the earth plane to help guide, move and direct His descendants.

MELCHIZEDEK ESTABLISHES ISRAEL

The saga of man's struggle to free himself from his self-caused earth imprisonment to find his way to the Eternal Heavenly City, the New Jerusalem, winds its way from Adam and Eve's fall through the generations as they unfolded in time. From the Holy Scriptures emerges an explanation of how the negative forces brought about the downfall of man, resulting in the decision of the Son of GOD to reverse that which had transpired when He fell as Adam. Though the mission of spiritualizing the earth with lineages of GOD's Spirit had been foiled by the fallen prince of the earth, one Divine Lineage remained intact which eventually would birthe the last Adam — mankind's Savior.[104] For this reason it was imperative that the godly seed of a specific branch of Israel's Divine Genealogical Tree be preserved. As communicated by the Lord through Prophet Malachi, the generations of the godly seed were to be planted and cultivated by those who had been created as One from the beginning — as binary mates — when He declared:

---

[103] Melchizedek represented the Son of GOD's eschatological priesthood on earth (Gen. 14:18; Heb. Chapters 5 to 9).

[104] Gen. 49:10.

> *And did he not make **One**? Yet **had he the residue of the Spirit**. And wherefore **One**. That he might seek a **godly seed**. Therefore take heed to your spirit, and let none deal treacherously with the wife of thy covenant. (Mal. 2:14-15)*

As Melchizedek,[105] the Son of GOD drew the curtain on the Egyptian Age and replaced it with what became known as the Age of the Hebrews. It was after His earth incarnation as Enoch that He returned in a perfected state as Melchizedek, and chose Abraham and Sarah as the parents who would initiate future generations of the chosen people of Israel. When Abraham met Melchizedek after the battle of the Kings, he knew him to be the Priest of the Most High GOD[106] and paid tithes to Him. It explains why he later immediately recognized Him as Melchizedek and his Lord[107] when he met Him again on the Plains of Mamre. Abraham bowed to the ground in the presence of His Lord who appeared

---

[105] Heb. 7:1-4, Heb. 7:17 Cf. Dead Sea Scrolls: Manuscript B. Fragment 3: (1) [of His grace and peace. Over all the sons of Light] have I been empowered. I asked him [what are your names...?] (2) He [s]aid to me, [my three names are [Michael] and Prince of Light and King of Righteousness"]. The Dead Sea Scrolls Uncovered; Eisenman, Robert and Wise, Michael., Penguin Books, 1992. Correlates with Melchizedek, King of Righteousness holding Christ's Messianic and eschatological priesthood (Heb. Chapters. 5 to 9). *"For this Melchizedek king of Salem, priest of the most High God who met Abraham.....first being by interpretation King of righteousness which is King of Peace...made like unto the Son of GOD abideth a priest continually"(Heb. 7:2-3).*

[106] Heb. Chapters 6, 7, 8.

[107] Gen. 18:1-3; Cf. Heb. Chh. 7 to 8.

to him and Sarah as one of three men — **angels** who appeared in the form of men.[108] Abraham's grandson, Jacob, afterward spoke of just such a redeeming angel to his son Joseph; albeit, no angel has been empowered to "*redeem*" man except Jesus Christ the Son of GOD, who became mankind's Savior:

> *And (Jacob) blessed Joseph, and said, GOD, before whom my fathers Abraham and Isaac did walk,* ***the GOD which fed me all my life long unto this day. The angel which redeemed me from all evil****, bless the lads. . . . (Gen. 48:15-16)*

"*Israel*" can be well described as those angelic souls who compose the twelve branches of the Divine Genealogical Tree. It is they who struggled through the Hebraic Age, repeatedly manifesting on earth in divers times and places from the beginning; even reappearing in this current age. As GOD's, and Christ the Son's, spiritual alterations were wrought in the earth plane, those of Israel changed with them. In a similar fashion, about one third of those to incarnate on earth during the latter days pending the Lord's Return, will continue on into the next coming Age, the Millennium of the First Resurrection. They will form part of a new Adamic race, a root race which will again undertake the mission of re-spiritualizing the earth with lineages of GOD's light — a mission previously foiled by Satan, the fallen prince of this world:

> *And it shall come to pass, that in all the land, saith the Lord, two parts therein shall be cut off and*

---

[108] Angels can metamorphose as humans (Gen. 19:1-2; Heb. 13:2). Paul describes his experience with the Angel of GOD as being the "*I Am*" He served — Jesus' Archangelic Self (Ex. 3:2-6,14; Is.10:-11 cf. Acts. 27:23-24 cf. Jn. 8:58).

die; but the third shall be left therein. **And I will bring the third part through the fire, and will refine them as silver is refined** *and will try them as gold is tried: they shall call on my name, and I will hear them:* **I will say, It is my people:** *and they shall say, The Lord is my God. (Zech. 13:8-9)*

Saying, Hurt not the earth, neither the sea, nor the trees, till we have sealed the Servants of our God in their foreheads. **And I heard the number of them which were sealed: and there were sealed an hundred and forty and four thousand of all the tribes of the children of Israel.** *(Gen. 7:3-4)*

And I (John) looked and lo, a Lamb stood on the mount Sion and with him an hundred and forty and four thousand having his Father's name written in their foreheads. . . . And they sung as it were a new song. . . . and no man could learn that song but the hundred and forty and four thousand. . . . **These were redeemed from among men being the firstfrtuits unto God and to the Lamb.** *(Rev. 14:1-4)*

The divine branch, also known as the Divine Lineage, from which Jesus the Christ would later emerge flowed purposefully through Judah, one of Israel's twelve sons, as biblically foretold. Accordingly, the ebb and flow of the twelve branches of Israel's Divine Genealogical Tree — in particular the Divine Lineage — would be guided, guarded, directed and moved by Melchizedek, the Lord Himself, from heaven above as well as on earth.

Abraham and His Sons/Ishmael Versus Isaac:

Sarah knew that Abraham had been promised a son through whom the godly seed would multiply but as time wore on she was unable to bear him a son. Discouraged, she reasoned that it was her fault that her husband could not father the son upon whom they both pinned their spiritual hopes. Taking the matter into her own hands, and without guidance from the Lord, she reluctantly advised Abraham to father a child with her Egyptian maid, Hagar.[109] The result of the union between these two different seeds produced Ishmael, a wild man whose hand the Lord foretold would be against every man, and every man's hand against him. Sarah had lost faith in the Lord's promise to provide the son for whom she and Abraham had prayed. Her patience had been tested and she had not sufficiently resisted — nor had Abraham — with the result that karmic wheels were set in motion. It was the same kind of negative result Adam and Eve had sustained when they went against GOD's Will in the beginning and Cain was born, which forged the first link in a chain of rebellious generations. The godly seed could not issue from Ishmael, and in accordance with Divine Providence another son would be born through whom the divine heritage would be conveyed.[110] The Lord again intervened in the formation of the lineages when He appeared to Abraham advising him that Sarah, now stricken with old age, would conceive a son who would carry the inheritance. Amused by this declaration, Sarah laughed believing it to be biologically impossible for her to conceive at such an advanced

---

[109] Gen. 16:1-5.
[110] Gen. 17:18-21.

age. In accordance with the Lord's Will, Sarah later bore a son, Isaac, who was destined to play a crucially important role in Israel's divine genealogy.

Abraham, who dwelt among the Canaanites at the time Isaac reached maturity, was concerned that his son would marry outside the appropriate lineage. Accordingly, he instructed his servant to bring Isaac a kindred wife from his own country, and advised him that an angel would guide him in his quest. When the servant arrived in Abraham's country, he paused near a water well where damsels retrieved water. The servant prayed to the Lord that if a woman offered him and his camels a drink of water to satiate their thirst, he would take it as a GOD-given sign that this was the woman Isaac would be guided to marry. As the story unfolded, Rebekah, a fair young maiden, arrived at the water well with pitcher in hand. When Abraham's servant asked her for a drink, she immediately obliged him and without any further request from the servant she drew more water for the camels. As fate would have it, and in accordance with Abraham's wishes, Rebekah was a kindred soul, a descendant in Abraham's brother's lineage. She thereafter left her family and home and followed the servant to another country, where she met and married Isaac. As a highly-spiritualized young woman, Rebekah helped establish future generations of the Divine Lineage.[111] It was through Isaac and Rebekah that Jacob, the father of the twelve tribes of Israel, was born to take his place in the Divine Genealogical Family Tree.

---

[111] Gen. 24:60.

Isaac and His Sons/Esau Versus Jacob:

For a time after their marriage Rebekah was barren but she eventually conceived twins after Isaac entreated the Lord on her behalf. That Satan infiltrated the Adamic DNA with his negative spirit is reflected in the negative and positive twins who struggled in Rebekah's womb. When she asked the Lord why her two unborn children were rebelling against one another, she was told:

> ***Two nations*** *are in thy womb, and **two manner of people shall be separated from thy bowels**; and the one people shall be stronger than the other people; and **the elder shall serve the younger***. *(Gen. 25:23)*

> *And the first came out red all over like an hairy garment; and they called his name Esau. And after that came his brother out. . . . and his name was called Jacob. . . . (Gen. 25:25-26)*

As young adults, the twins' spiritual attributes thereafter reflected in their lifestyles and beliefs. Jacob, the second twin, much more spiritually inclined than his brother, was fully aware that it was the firstborn who stood to inherit the lineal birthright. The Bible relates, however, that Esau who, inherited a greater portion of Satan's spirit, ignored the inestimably great value of the family's inheritance, as was seen when he sold his birthright to Jacob for food to satiate his hunger:

> *Behold, I am at the point to die: and what profit shall this birthright do to me? And Jacob said, Swear to me this day; and he sware unto him; and*

> *he sold his birthright unto Jacob. Then Jacob gave Esau bread and pottage of Lentils; and he did eat and drink, and went his way; thus Esau despised his birthright. (Gen. 25:32-34)*

The Bible leaves no doubt but that in view of the warning Rebekah had received from the Lord, whatever could reasonably be done to prevent the negative son, Esau, from claiming the birthright would prove to be the right thing for her to do. The Lord had forewarned Rebekah of things to come, a prophetic insight which proved to be of extreme importance to her later as she and Isaac carried the future generation of the developing Divine Lineage under the 3 to 4 generation rule.[112]

Circumstances, though, would require her to make some crucially important decisions moving her to react against her husband's will. Rebekah knew the course she needed to follow because the Lord had told her outrightly that Esau was not the son of the promise: it was Jacob. When Rebekah sensed Isaac's imminent death, she took it upon herself to manipulate the paternal blessing of her sons.[113] When the time of the blessing approached, she cleverly disguised Jacob as Esau, the firstborn twin, in order that he might receive the firstborn's blessing. Isaac whose sight had been dimmed by advanced age, did not recognize his second born and blessed him as the first son, as was the traditional custom. Before his passing, Isaac undoubtedly became aware of the mistake Esau had committed when he gave up his birthright for nothing more than a pottage of Lentil, and for this reason kept Jacob's blessing and inheritance intact.

---

[112] Ex. 20:3-5; 34:7; Num. 14:18; Deut. 5:9.
[113] Gen. Chapter 25.

Esau forfeited his birthright, which he afterward grievously lamented without being able to retrieve it.[114] The hatred that arose between the two brothers[115] because of the birthright entitlement reflects the "*enmity*" GOD had placed between Eve and Satan's seed, as a consequence of the Adamic infraction.[116] That Esau inherited a negative spirit is seen in the Lord's message to His Prophet Malachi, in which He emphatically declared that He "*hated Esau*" and would have "*indignation for ever*" against him.[117] Satan's attempt to infiltrate the Divine Lineage had been foiled by celestial guidance. As will be seen, it was through Jacob that the lineage of Light would continue to flow toward its destined goal — the birth of the Son of GOD — Jesus of Nazareth.

Jacob and His Twelve Sons/Reuben Versus Judah:

As Jacob continued to follow the ways of the Lord he was increasingly quickened, as well as protected, guided, directed and moved. The same pattern of devotion to GOD and following HIS Will that had brought about the escalation of spirit force in Abraham and Isaac, culminated in Jacob. He obediently went wherever the Lord sent him, and did what the Lord wanted him to do, having seen the wondrous spiritual results it brought to him and his family. He also had available the benefit of what his immediate ancestors had learned and handed down, which was greatly to his advantage. Under the 3 to 4 generation rule,[118] the spiritualization

---

[114] Heb. 12:16-17.
[115] Gen. 27:41.
[116] Gen. 3:15.
[117] Mal. 1:2-4.
[118] Ex. 20:3-5; 34:7; Num.14:18; Deut. 5:9.

of the lineage had increased step by step, generation by generation. In the third generation of Abraham's lineage, within the Divine Lineage, Jacob's spirit had been quickened by the Lord's Spirit to the extent that the entire lineage from that point was to bear his new GOD-given name — Israel. But of extreme importance, it was not only by his individual accomplishments to that point in his experience that he had reached such an exalted position. His spirituality was founded upon the spiritual gains Abraham/Sarah, and Isaac/Rebekah had made before him, under the rule Jesus would long afterward reveal that everything gained or lost on earth is gained or lost in heaven.[119] The 3 to 4 generation rule is based on this tenet: that the good or evil done by those in a lineage profoundly affects those who come after them in that hereditary line and is manifested at the spiritual, mental and physical level. As before described, Satanic influences inevitably cause a decline in spiritual levels of children born in subsequent generations:

> *Keeping mercy for thousands, forgiving iniquity and transgression and sin; and that will by no means clear the guilty;* ***visiting the iniquity of the fathers upon the children and upon the children's children, unto the third and to the fourth generation****. (Ex. 34: 7)*

Jacob fathered twelve sons with two of his wives, Leah and Rachel, and two of their respective concubines, Bilhah and Zilpah:

> *The sons of Leah, Reuben, Jacob's firstborn, and Simeon, and Levi and Judah, and Issachar, and*

---

[119] Mt. 18:18.

> *Zebulun: The sons of Rachel: Joseph and Benjamin: And the sons of Bilhah, Rachel's handmaid; Dan and Naphtalie: and the sons of Zilpah, Leah's handmaid, Gad and Asher; these are the sons of Jacob, which were born to him in Pandanaram. (Gen. 35:-23-26)*

Reuben, the firstborn, lost his inheritable position in the Divine Lineage destined to birthe Jesus of Nazareth because he had defiled his father's bed. Instead the Divine Lineage was set to flow through another son, Judah, because he prevailed over his brethren.[120] Although the Divine Lineage would be passed down through the Judahn branch, it was Joseph, not Judah, who was later to hold the birthright over the earthly and heavenly family of Israel, as will be discussed.[121]

> *Now the sons of Reuben the firstborn of Israel, (for he was the firstborn; but forasmuch as he defiled his father's bed, his birthright was given unto the sons of Joseph the son of Israel: and the genealogy is not to be reckoned after the birthright.* **For Judah prevailed above his brethren and of him came the chief ruler but the birthright was Joseph's.**). (1 Chr. 5:1-2)

After Reuben came Simeon, then Levi and Judah the fourth son. Because Reuben, Simeon and Levi had committed iniquities, they forfeited the birthright. The burden therefore rested heavily upon the fourth son, Judah, to spiritually conduct the Divine Lineage into future generations.[122] When Jacob

---

[120] Gen. 49:10; 1 Chr. 5:1-2.
[121] Refer to Chapter: "Joseph: A Soul Incarnation of Jesus of Nazareth."
[122] Gen. 49:10.

blessed his sons, Judah received the promise that the Divine Lineage was to flow through his family branch, and that it would not be foreclosed until "*Shiloh*" came.[123] Shiloh was Jesus of Nazareth who did not manifest until many centuries afterward.

We know from Jewish history that the chosen people were strongly entrenched in the practice of raising children in traditional, spiritual ways; one of which was to thoroughly inform them about their past generations.[124] For example, Abraham's reliance upon GOD to guide his trusted servant to find a wife for Isaac, his son of the Lord's promise, was surely taught to those who were afterward born in that lineage. Judah presumably knew that his grandfather Isaac had waited until he was forty years of age to seek a wife, and that he followed a spiritual course to find her. Isaac did not frivolously look for just any woman with whom to have a liaison; he waited patiently to be guided, moved and directed to the wife the Lord knew was patterned for him that he might fulfill the promise given to him.[125] It is a crucially important lesson applicable still today in the formation of man's lineages, albeit he has for the most part abandoned consideration of it. The spirituality of parents and their firm determination to follow the guidance of the Lord and the Holy Ghost is a paramount requirement in the building of spiritualized lineages under the 3 to 4 generation rule. The Bible long ago laid down the fundamental principles by tracing the experiences of those in the fountainhead of the segment of the Divine Lineage commenced by the Lord through Abraham and Sarah.

---

[123] Gen. 49:10.

[124] Ruth 4:11-14.

[125] Gen. Chapter 24.

What is seen in Judah's case is that even though he must have been taught by his father, Jacob, the rudimentary principles involved in seeking the one wife on earth the Lord could have guided him to find — his binary soul[126] as discussed in previous chapters — the Bible records that Judah apparently paid no heed. Scriptures reveal that when he went down from his brethren's place, he simply turned in to a certain Addullamite's house, whose name was Hirah, and took himself a Cannanite wife by the name of Shuah who conceived three sons.[127] But the Lord was displeased with Judah's marital union, which lineage was destined to produce the "*chief ruler.*"[128] Long after these above-described events took place, the Lord through Prophet Malachi admonished Judah because of his actions:

> *Judah hath dealt treacherously and an abomination is committed in Jerusalem; for Judah has profaned the holiness of the Lord which he loved, and hath married the daughter of a strange god (Mal. 2:11)*

Because Judah had failed to wait for Divine Providence to guide him to a wife sufficiently quickened to procreate the next highly-spiritualized generation, the foundations of that lineage were weakened by a hastily chosen wife who failed to meet the Lord's requirements. It became obvious that the lineages would not continue through Shuah when Judah selected a daughter-in-law by the name of Tamar to bear children for his firstborn, Er. Because Er was a

---

[126] Mal. 2:14-15.

[127] Gen. 38:1-5.

[128] 1 Chr. 5:2.

negative spirit who would have tainted the lineages, GOD brought about his demise. When Judah then sent his second son, Onan, in with Tamar to bear a child — as was the custom in those days — GOD showed him no respect and brought about his demise also. This left Shelah, the third son, who was at that time too young to marry. Consequently, Judah shelved that idea until an appropriate time.

Judah and His Sons/Zerah Versus Pharez:

After a bizarre series of events, when Judah failed to marry Tamar to Shelah even though he was of age, Tamar took matters into her own hands. She apparently met the spiritual requirements of a woman who was worthy to play a very significant role in the Divine Lineage. Led by the hand of Divine Providence, her receptive state of spirituality moved her to disguise herself as a harlot to seduce Judah in order to preserve the spiritual sanctity of the Divine Lineage.[129] Her desires and thoughts, albeit not able to be channeled into the kind of actions she would have liked because of circumstances brought about by Judah and Shuah, helped her to accomplish her mission of procreating the next generation of the Divine Lineage. Speculatively, it is even possible that had Judah waited patiently for guidance to a wife of the Lord's choice, in time Tamar might have been guided to him in accordance with laws governing spiritually-designed marriages. The union between Judah and Tamar brought about the conception of twins, who, in a similar pattern as seen in Jacob and Esau, also caused a split in the Divine Lineage.

---

[129] Gen. 38:15-26.

The division between the two brothers was foreshadowed by a dramatic sign given at the time of their births:

> *And it came to pass in the time of her travail, that, behold, twins were in her womb. . . . and when she travailed, the one put out his hand, and the midwife took and bound upon his hand a scarlet thread, saying. This came out first. As he drew back his hand, behold his brother came out: and she said, How hast thou broken forth? This breach be upon thee: therefore his name was called Pharez. And afterward came out his brother, that had the scarlet thread upon his hand: and his name was called Zarah. (Gen. 38:27-30).*

The midwife's traditional understanding of spiritual birthing rules, which conflicted with the reality of the situation, caused her to believe that Zerah was wrongfully dispossessed of his birthright entitlement by his brother Pharez because of their unusual births. Zerah had begun to be born but at the last moment withdrew his hand so that Pharez became the firstborn, causing the midwife to believe Pharez had committed a sin against his firstborn brother. In order to protect who she believed was the rightful son of the birthright, the midwife bound a scarlet thread around Zerah's hand. In time it became patently clear under the 3 to 4 generation rule that Pharez was the positively inclined son destined to promote the Divine Lineage because Zerah proved to be negative.

An examination of the direct lineage of Pharez shows that ten generations after his manifestation in flesh, King David was born[130] and the generations between

---
[130] Ruth 4:18-22.

them, according to the Bible, were composed of highly-spiritualized individuals. This is exemplified in Ruth, David's great-grandmother, who was guided directly to Boaz by way of an astonishing series of events as chronicled in the Book of Ruth. Ruth and Boaz strictly adhered to spiritual rules and laws, remaining steadfast in their faith and belief. After they passed the Lord's testing, they were able to marry and bring Obed into the world. He, in turn, fathered Jesse, who then fathered David. The Bible carefully records the spiritual knowledge, understanding and desires of those who participated in the lineage, and that they were well aware of the spiritual ramifications of what was taking place in the lives of Ruth and Boaz:

> *And all the people that were in the gate, and the elders, said, We are witnesses. The Lord make the woman that is come into thine house like Rachel and like Leah, which two did build the house of Israel: and do thou worthily in Ephratah, and be famous in Bethlehem: And let thy house be like the house of Pharez, whom Tamar bare unto Judah, of the seed of which the Lord shall give thee of this young woman. (Ruth 4:11-12)*

Zerah, the negatively inclined son, had apparently entered into his experience as the result of previous negative life manifestations which had left him at a lower spiritual level. He was doubtless drawn to incarnate as Judah and Tamar's negative son due to the conflicting desires, thoughts and actions of his parents. In every generation, souls wait in other dimensions for an optimal opportunity to incarnate in an infant on earth, whose spiritual condition is appropriate for some prospective parental situation able to provide it with the best available conditions for its further development. The Bible reveals that Zerah — the son around whose hand the scarlet thread was tied — was indeed negatively inclined. When Zerah continued his negative ways, the soul of his son Zabdi — who was in a proportionately negative spiritual condition as the result of previous earth experiences, compounded by his father Judah's negative works — was drawn into the pool of those souls eligible to incarnate at that time and in that situation. Because Zabdi had done even worse than his father Zerah, the next generation of his children was drawn from an even less Lord-quickened pool of souls awaiting their turn to manifest in flesh on the earth. In the third generation Zabdi's son, Carmi, was born and he too failed to heed the warning implicit in the 3 to 4 generation rule and continued in negative ways. In the fourth generation his son, Achan, was born. When he committed the "*accursed trespass*" in violation of the Lord's Will, the Lord decided to terminate that particular branch of the lineage. The 3 to 4 generation rule stands for the proposition that as each generation continues to fall away from the Lord, the souls of the next generations of children born will be drawn from more negative parents, until by the fourth generation the Lord may even see fit to scatter or eliminate that lineage, as demonstrated in the case of Zerah's great grandson, Achan. It is evident that what transpired in Zerah's subsequent generations indicate that individuals in his branch of the lineage had been unable to reverse their negativity, as recorded in the Book of Joshua.[131]

Unlike his brother Zerah, Pharez came into the world endowed with a more quickened spirit, and as

---

[131] Josh. 7:16-18.

Judah and Tamar's positive son he became the one through whom the Divine Lineage would continue to flow. From Pharez, Esrom was born and, in turn, became a son of the inheritance.[132] From this point, the Divine Lineage often took twists and turns to accommodate others who would appropriately assume their rightful position as parents to promote succeeding generations. From the time of the Adamic infraction, positive and negative forces have continually manifested in souls forming the human family. Thus the well being of family lineages remains ever the responsibility of each individual, because the gains or losses of each, in turn, predetermines the course of future generations. The greater the gains, the greater the potential spirituality of those who follow in that lineage; conversely, the more serious the losses, the more afflictions will be imposed on the offspring. What each individual does on earth directly affects those in that family because souls tend to incarnate and reincarnate in the same or close family structures. *"Desire"* is one of the leading factors in bonding together individuals who have strong feelings of whatever kind toward each other. When strong feelings and ties grow up between negatively inclined individuals, they may be drawn to find one another in succeeding earth experiences, inclining them to continue suffering spiritual decreases as a result. When positive changes are made by one family member, all those around such an individual may profit from it. When individuals are attuned to GOD, they help fulfill HIS Master Plan which, in part, involves the same mission as that of our Adamic forerunners: that of spiritualizing the earth with lineages of HIS Light. Though the purpose of the Divine Lineage was to bring about the birth of Jesus Christ of

---

[132] Lk. 3:33.

Nazareth, a pattern exists within its legacy which helps us understand how to spiritually elevate family lineages. As man's spiritual understanding evolves, he will increasingly begin to realize that earth conceptions occurred because of the tampering of Eve's creative forces and that virginal conceptions will again be the means by which soul forces will multiply in the earth plane. Parents who have acquired an understanding of these biblically-defined spiritual laws, and teach them to their children, provide them with a firm foundation upon which future generations can be built.

TABLE 1

The following Table lists the names of the descendants in the first seven generations from Adam. The split between two different seeds is observed in the positive and negative lineages which manifested because of the Adamic deception.

THE SEVEN GENERATIONS OF ENOCH AND CAIN

POSITIVE LINEAGES	NEGATIVE LINEAGES
1. Adam/Eve	1. Serpent/Adam/Eve
2. Seth	2. Cain
3. Enos	3. Enoch
4. Cainan	4. Irad
5. Maleleel	5. Mehujael
6. Jared	6. Methusael
7. **Enoch** *	7. **Lamech** *

Source: Positive Lineages recorded in Lk. 3:23-38.
Negative Lineages recorded in Gen. 4:17-18.
KJV Bible

TABLE 2:

The following Table lists the names of the descendants in the Divine Lineage beginning at the pivotal point from Enoch and Lamech's 7th generation. "*. . . . If Cain shall be avenged sevenfold, truly Lamech seventy and sevenfold.*" *(Gen. 4:24)*

THE DIVINE LINEAGE

10 SETS OF SEVEN COMPLETE GENERATIONS

1ST SET OF SEVEN COMPLETE GENERATIONS

1.	ENOCH
2.	METHUSALA
3.	LAMECH
4.	NOE
5.	SEM
6.	ARPHAXAD
7.	CAINAN

2ND SET OF SEVEN COMPLETE GENERATIONS

| 1. SALA |
| 2. HEBER |
| 3. PHALEC |
| 4. RAGAU |
| 5. SARUCH |
| 6. NACHOR |
| 7. THARA |

3RD SET OF SEVEN COMPLETE GENERATIONS

| 1. ABRAHAM |
| 2. ISAAC |
| 3. JACOB |
| 4. JUDA |
| 5. PHARES |
| 6. ESROM |
| 7. ARAM |

4TH SET OF SEVEN COMPLETE GENERATIONS

| 1. AMINADAB |
| 2. NAASSON |
| 3. SALMON |
| 4. BOAZ |
| 5. OBED |
| 6. JESSE |
| 7. DAVID |

5ᵀᴴ SET OF SEVEN COMPLETE GENERATIONS

| 1. NATHAN |
| 2. MATTATHA |
| 3. MENAN |
| 4. MELEA |
| 5. ELIAKIM |
| 6. JONAN |
| 7. JOSEPH |

6ᵀᴴ SET OF SEVEN COMPLETE GENERATIONS

| 1. JUDA |
| 2. SIMEON |
| 3. LEVI |
| 4. MATTHAT |
| 5. JORIM |
| 6. ELIEZER |
| 7. JOSE |

7ᵀᴴ SET OF SEVEN COMPLETE GENERATIONS

| 1. ER |
| 2. ELMODAM |
| 3. COSAM |
| 4. ADDI |
| 5. MELCHI |
| 6. NERI |
| 7. SALATHIEL |

8TH SET OF SEVEN COMPLETE GENERATIONS

1. ZOROBABEL
2. RHESA
3. JOANNA
4. JUDA
5. JOSEPH
6. SEMEI
7. MATTATHIAS

9TH SET OF SEVEN COMPLETE GENERATIONS

1. MAATH
2. NAGGE
3. ESLI
4. NAUM
5. AMOS
6. MATTATHIAS
7. JOSEPH

10TH SET OF SEVEN COMPLETE GENERATIONS

1. JANNA
2. MELCHI
3. LEVI
4. MATTHAT
5. HELI
6. MARY - virgin mother*
7. JESUS

* It had been prophesied since the time of the Old Prophets that Jesus would be born of a Virgin in the House of David (Is. 7:13-14).

Sources: Genealogies recorded in Lk. 3:23-38
         KJV Bible

PART TWO

—CHAPTER ONE—
PROPHET ISAIAH

Only through the birth of Jesus Christ whose Divine Lineage was wending its way through the generations could mankind be extricated from laws that had bound him to the earth plane since the proverbial fall in the garden. It is said that there is a heavenly providence which cares for fools and children; a sympathetic invisible hand to lovingly protect them as they pass through treacherous earth experiences which may often prove to be devastating. The Bible leaves no doubt but that the hand of providence is actually the hand of the Lord, the Son of GOD, who — after His precipitous fall as Adam — set about the incredibly difficult task of reversing what had resulted. The Bible reveals that man's spiritual evolution from the time of the fall was uphill all the way. The Lord's Spirit mountain extends far up above the earth dimension, and the way to it steep, the climb inescapably trying, exhausting and frustrating.

Men had become vagabonds in the earth, exiled in materiality until they could find a way to be sufficiently quickened by GOD's Holy Spirit able to raise them up through the successively higher levels of consciousness back to their heavenly place. The pathway was purposefully designed as a protracted and often disheartening road back home for all who seek the kingdom of heaven. Man had disobeyed GOD, and he needed to prove his spiritual mettle, because nothing dark and evil is allowed in the Light of Heaven. What he had done on earth needed to be recompensed on earth: for which reason the rule became that all things gained or lost on earth were at the same time gained or lost in heaven; and consequently much was expected of those to whom spiritual increases might be given by the Lord.[133]

Satan sought to close off any avenue the Lord opened which might conceivably lead to salvation. Even the highly spiritualized Hebrew priests and prophets, ordained by the Lord Himself to serve under the Mosaic Law, fell before Satan's negative onslaughts. This evident corruption provided man with incontrovertible proof that an earth testing was taking place, and that it was focused on him. The soul in man is not natural to the earth: only his flesh body is to be considered of an earthly character. As Jesus would long afterward teach, we are to be **in** the earth but not **of** the earth. Apostle John would go even further, instructing that we are not to love the world, nor anything in it; and that anyone who does so does not have the love of GOD the FATHER, because earth life involves lusts of the flesh, the eyes and the pride of life, which are not of GOD, but of the world.[134] The souls in man had gotten themselves trapped in flesh, seemingly inextricably mired in the lower levels of consciousness characteristic of the earth plane.

A New Covenant was needed: one which would provide mankind with a more reliable means by which

---

[133] Mt. 18:18; Lk. 12:48; 1 Cor. 3:6-15.
[134] Cf. 1 Jn. 2:14-17.

they could attain to the Kingdom of GOD. But events had demonstrated that the chosen people of Israel, under the Mosaic law, were yet far from able to realize their heavenly dreams. They continually persisted in militating against GOD's Will even in the face of the absolute requirement that, because their original fall had been caused by disobedience, obedience was first and foremost required of them. But how to remove from them their deeply entrenched belief in the Mosaic Law, and replace it with a revolutionary and radically different New Covenant? The minds of those who would surely come after them would have to be reprogrammed against the grain of all the teachings of their ancestors. Most of the common people were still so undeveloped spiritually they had no means to receive the much higher frequencies of the vibrations of their Lord and Maker. But the Lord developed a way to communicate with them effectively, and in a credible way acceptable to them. From among those who were most spiritually sensitive, He chose prophets who were at that time sufficiently quickened by His Spirit that they were able to hear His voice. They would convey GOD's Word to His chosen people.

Part Two of this work is composed of that which was received by the exalted prophets of Israel who spoke for the Lord, beginning with Isaiah, a distinguished servant of His.

Speaking through Isaiah and succeeding prophets, the Lord begins to foretell the end of the First Covenant and the bringing in of His New Covenant because of Israel's failure to obey Him.

In Prophet Isaiah's time, the Lord the Son of GOD began to speak GOD's Word to the people of Israel through His prophets to recount HIS displeasure with their lowered state of spirituality and to begin to prepare them for what was predestined to come as a result. The following Bible quotations and comments connecting them, provide a summation of Israel's ebbing spiritual condition as of the time the major prophets began to lay the groundwork for the expectations of the chosen people during oncoming generations. The chosen people are defined as they who will constitute the new celestial hierarchy under construction. As noted previously, they have reincarnated since the beginning, through the Hebraic Age, and on into this current age.

The Lord, speaking through Prophet Isaiah soon after He called him, immediately began to reveal His dissatisfaction and sorrow at the sagging spiritual estate of the children of Israel, lamenting:

> *I have nourished and brought up children, and they have rebelled against me. The ox knoweth his owner, and the ass his master's crib: but Israel doth not consider.* **Ah sinful nation, a people laden with iniquity, a seed of evildoers, children that are corrupters: they have forsaken the Lord,** *they have provoked the Holy One of Israel unto anger, they are gone away backward. (Isa. 1:2-4)*

The Lord had imbued his Spirit into His people starting when He had first taken them out of slavery from the land of Egypt under the hand of Moses, when His Spirit in the cloud had guided, guarded, moved and directed them by day and by night as they followed Him to their earthly promised land in Canaan. He had many times attempted to dissuade them from their disobedience, but it had been in vain. Even as Moses and Joshua son of Nun went up to the Holy Mount to receive GOD's commandments, the people — desiring to return to slavery in Egypt rather than overcome the dire conditions of their Exodus — had rebelled. They desired the material trappings of earth rather than to seek GOD and the spiritual pathway He sought to keep them on, in order that He might one day free them from the shackles of their earthly imprisonment. Driven by Satanic forces, they persuaded Aaron to make for them a golden calf, an Egyptian pagan idol. Spiritually blinded in their actions, they were unaware of GOD's dissatisfaction with their materialistic and idolatrous worshiping. When, therefore, the Lord spoke through Isaiah, implying that it would be useless for the people to be stricken any more because they would only revolt against Him the more, it carried the veiled notice that He was contemplating making changes which would offer a better way for them to follow. He made it plain that the chosen people had taken it upon themselves to establish rituals which He the Lord considered useless, or worse:

> *To what purpose is the multitude of your sacrifices unto me? saith the Lord: I am full of the burnt offerings of rams, and the fat of fed beasts, and I delight not in the blood of bullocks, or of lambs, or of he goats. When ye come to appear before me, who hath required this at your hand, to tread my courts? Bring no more vain oblations; incense is an abomination unto me; the new moons and sabbaths, the calling of assemblies, I cannot away with: it is*

> *iniquity, even the solemn meeting. Your new moons and your appointed feasts my soul hateth; they are a trouble to me; I am weary to bear them. (Isa. 1:11-14)*

The Lord left no doubt in his castigation that the rituals propounded by inept priests and false prophets were not of His doing, nor were they anything He favored. He admonished the people that if they would cleanse themselves of their iniquity, ceasing to do evil right before His eyes — if they would learn to do well, seek judgment, relieve the oppressed, care for the orphans and plead for the widow — He would forgive their scarlet sins so they would be as white as snow. Significantly, the Lord foretold that if they persisted in doing evil, they could not expect to maintain contact with Him:

> *And when ye spread forth your hands,* ***I will hide mine eyes from you****: yea, when ye make many prayers,* ***I will not hear****: your hands are full of blood. (Isa. 1:15)*

In this brief comment the Lord laid down a terrible indictment against those responsible for Israel's waning spiritual condition. He no longer thought it feasible to punish Israel because regardless of how He tried them, they preferred to continue in their own earthly desires, thoughts and actions, disobeying His Will. Through Isaiah, He accused the chosen people of having developed a virtually insatiable craving for materiality; of women possessing pompous attitudes and that he was sorely displeased that they had stopped worshiping Him, their GOD.[135] He warned that a day would come when the lofty looks of man

---
[135] Isa. 3:16-24; Isa. 2:7-8.

would be humbled, and the haughtiness of men would be bowed down, and in that day the Lord alone would be exalted.[136] He then uttered a warning applicable to all mankind:

> *Say ye to the righteous, that it shall be well with him: for they shall eat the fruit of their doings. Woe unto the wicked! It shall be ill with him: for the reward of his hands shall be given to him. (Isa. 3:10-11)*

This spelled out the rule Jesus of Nazareth would long afterward describe as the law that whatever one sows, one reaps, the law of karma. Based on this law, their negative ways would lead them to the sword of their enemy which, the Lord prophesied, would leave Jerusalem desolate.[137] Those willing to escape death at the hands of King Nebuchadnezzar were commanded to surrender to their enemy and voluntarily go into exile in Babylon for seventy long hard years. By obeying GOD's Will — by facing suffering associated with seventy years of exile — they were paying the karmic debt they had accrued. By doing so, they were positioning themselves on a higher rung of Jacob's metaphorical ladder leading to higher heavenly levels. When Isaiah heard the Lord calling out, before the exile in Babylon, asking whom He should send to admonish the people of Israel, he replied: *"Here am I, send me."* [138] When Isaiah asked the Lord how long the suffering in exile was to last, He replied:

> *Until the cities be wasted without inhabitant, and the houses without man, and the land be utterly*

---

[136] Isa. 2:11.

[137] Isa. 1:16-20; Isa. 3:25-26.

[138] Isa. 6:8.

> *desolate, and the Lord have removed men far away, and there be a great forsaking in the midst of the land. But in it shall be a tenth, and it shall return, and shall be eaten: as a tell tree, and as an oak, whose substance is in them, when they cast their leaves: **so the holy seed shall be the substance thereof**. (Isa. 6:11-13)*

Only one tenth of all those who entered into exile in Babylon would return afterward to provide the holy seed, the Spirit, of their future generations doing so in the manner in which the seed of the mightiest of trees perpetuate themselves. The future of the Lord's Divine Genealogical Tree was to depend largely upon this one-tenth remainder of the people of Israel. During the course of His instructions to Isaiah, the Lord disclosed another significant revelation.

> ***Behold, I and the children whom the Lord hath given me are for signs*** *and for wonders in Israel from the Lord of hosts, which dwelleth in mount Zion. (Isa. 8:18)*

It would later correlate with another crucially important disclosure noted in the New Testament. The same continuity of expression long afterward written in the Book of Hebrews revealed that He, the Lord who spoke to Isaiah would, in the future, return as Jesus of Nazareth:

> ***Behold I and the children GOD hath given me.*** *Forasmuch then as the children are partakers of flesh and blood, he also likewise took part of the same (i.e. incarnated in flesh); that through death*

> *he might destroy him who had the power of death, that is, the devil. (Heb. 2:13-14)*

In the first Old Testament verse, the Lord quoted GOD the FATHER as having given HIS children to Him. In the second New Testament verse, the Lord and the children given to Him have incarnated in flesh bodies. It was during His earth incarnation as Jesus of Nazareth that the Lord returned once more to bring the scattered children of GOD together at-One again. This was to be accomplished by removing the negative afflictive influences of Satan through the sacred act of Atonement as confirmed by Caiaphas, a high priest who ruled at that time:

> *Nor consider that it is expedient for us, that **one man should die for the people, and that the whole nation perish not.** And this spake he not of himself; but being high priest that year, he prophesied that **Jesus should die for that nation: And not for that nation only, but that also he should gather together in one the children of God.** (Jn. 11:50-52)*

Isaiah was again told that the Son of GOD would Himself manifest in an exalted way in the future:

> *For unto us a child is born,[139] **unto us a son is given:** and the government shall be upon his shoulder: and his name shall be called Wonderful, Counsellor, The Mighty God, The everlasting Father, the Prince of Peace. Of the increase of his government and peace there shall be no end, upon the throne of David, and upon his kingdom, to order it, and to establish it with judgment and with*

---

[139] Meaning born unto Israel; cf. Num. 24:19; Rev. 12:1-5.

> *justice from henceforth even for ever. The zeal of the Lord of hosts will perform this. (Isa. 9:6)*

Jesus of Nazareth was born a Jew, and thus "*unto Israel*," and the above stated titles all applied to Him. As the Son whom GOD has empowered,[140] the increases of His heavenly government continue to be built up. After the Tribulation and the Millennium of the First Resurrection there will be peace without end for those who attain to GOD's Kingdom, of which HE, and the Son the Lamb, are the Light.[141] The Son is referred to as the everlasting Father because He is man's Maker,[142] Savior, Intercessor to GOD the FATHER, and Eternal High Priest in Heaven.[143] The following verses in Isaiah clearly delineate between GOD the FATHER and God the Son whom He empowered:

> *Ye are my witnesses, saith the Lord, and my servant whom I have chosen: that ye may know and believe me, and understand that **I am** he: before me there was no God **formed**, neither shall there be after me. I, even I, am the Lord: and beside me there is no savior. (Isa. 43:10-11)*

The belief grew up among many that the above comment was attributable to GOD the FATHER, but the words themselves belie that interpretation. When the Son of GOD admonished the people, acknowledging Jeremiah to be His servant, He used the term "*I am.*" as the Lord often did when He spoke through His prophets. He further revealed that before Him

---

[140] Jn. 5:21-23.

[141] Rev. 21:22-23.

[142] Eph. 3:9-10; 2 Cor. 6:17-18

[143] Heb. Chapters 5 to 10.

there had been no God formed, nor would there be after Him.[144]

This delineated between GOD the FATHER and the Son HE chose, they were not the same entity. GOD is eternal: there is no credible information known which ascribes HIS birth or development — much less HIS Creation — to anyone other than HIMSELF. It is apparent, then, that the Lord, the Son, who spoke these words to Prophet Jeremiah, *supra*, had to have been himself *"formed"* from GOD's Holy Spirit.[145] The Bible reveals that "*only one Son*" has been Anointed by GOD above all other sons, and that He in turn afforded the Spirit of all other Children of GOD.[146] Accordingly, as the empowered Son of GOD, He is to establish the Kingdom of Heaven with judgment and with justice forever when He returns to take dominion as foretold in the New Testament. These spiritual truths were being foretold in pieces to Jews in Isaiah's time in order that the people would be better prepared to accept the radical changes the Lord would subsequently bring upon the earth.

Through Prophet Isaiah, the Lord foretold a day when there would be peace and tranquility, a time when in His heavenly mountain[147] all would be well

---

[144] Isa. 43:10.

[145] Jn. 4:24 Cf. Jesus taught that He had come into the world as a "*light*" (Jn. 12:46; and cf. 1 Jn. 1:5-7). Apostle Paul taught that Christ would give His light to those who were otherwise "*dead*" in their sin (Eph. 5:14). Beloved John wrote that there would be no need of the light of candles or of the sun in heaven, for the Lord God gives them light (Rev. 22:5; and cf. Rev. 21:22-23).

[146] Jn. 1:1-3; Eph. 4:4-5.

[147] In the prophetic sense, mountains refer to heavenly dimensions of existence.

because the earth would be full of the knowledge of the Lord:

> *And in that day there shall be **a root of Jesse, which shall stand for an ensign of the people;** to it shall the Gentiles seek: and his rest shall be glorious. And it shall come to pass that in that day, **that the Lord shall set his hand again the second time** to recover the remnant of his people, which shall be left, from (many countries), and from the islands of the sea. **And He shall set up an ensign for the nations**, and shall assemble the outcasts of Israel, and gather together the dispersed of Judah from the four corners of the earth. (Isa. 11:10-12)*

Jesse was the father of King David, the root that was to come. Jesus Christ was "*the son of David*" because it had been shown to Jews that He was to be born later in the Judahn lineage which was David's lineage.[148] It was Jesus Christ who "*stood for an ensign*" of the people — He was the "*Shiloh*" around whom the people were to gather after the Judahn generations had led to the earth manifestation of the Son of GOD as Jesus of Nazareth, as foretold by Jacob's blessing to Judah.[149] When it was written that the Lord's "*rest would be glorious.*" it referred to the length of time after His resurrection when He was to dwell above the veil,[150] and of His prophesied return some 2,000 years later on the Cloud.[151] Then he would "*set His hand again the **second time** to recover the remnant of His people*" — a time that coincides with His return to the earth plane as the empowered Messiah. As Jesus, He

---

[148] 1 Chron. 28:4; Jn. 7:42.

[149] Gen. 49:10.

[150] Heb. 6:19-20.

[151] Mk. 14:61-62; Lk. 21:25-28; Acts 1:9-11.

was the prophet of whom Moses spoke as recorded in the Old Testament; however when He returns the second time He will be the glorified and empowered Savior of mankind.[152]

The Lord the Son spoke through Prophet Isaiah to forecast a day when the people of Israel would say to the Lord that they would praise Him, despite His anger with them, because He would turn away His anger and comfort them. They would say:

> *Behold, God is my salvation: I will trust and not be afraid: for the Lord JEHOVAH is my song; He also is become my salvation. (Isa. 12:2-3)*

Without specifically announcing His New Covenant, the Lord through Prophet Isaiah began to furnish clues by which the people of Israel would have a sense of what was coming. He foretold that radical changes were in the offing: that a time would come when the Tree of Life would be extended to the Gentiles by way of the Son:

> *BEHOLD my servant, whom I uphold; mine elect, in whom my soul delighteth;* ***I have put my spirit upon him: he shall bring forth judgment to the Gentiles****. I the Lord have called thee in righteousness, and will hold thine hand, and will keep thee, and give thee for a covenant of the people,* ***for a light of the Gentiles****. To open the blind eyes, to bring out the prisoners from the prison, and them that sit in darkness out of the prison house. (Isa. 42:1,6-7)*

This confirmed that GOD had ordained that the Son was to bring in a New Covenant which would serve as

---

[152] Deut: 18:18-19; Cf. Jn. 12:49; Jn. 14:10; Jn. 11:50-52.

a light to the Gentiles, to open their spiritually blind eyes that they might be released from their imprisoned exile in lower dimensions of existence. Prophet Isaiah later received a further clarification of this message, indicating that the Son was also to "*restore the preserved of Israel,*" the remnant of those who struggled to fulfill GOD's Will:

> *And now, saith the Lord that formed me from the womb to be HIS servant,* ***to bring Jacob again to him****, Though Israel be not yet gathered, yet shall I be glorious in the eyes of the Lord, and my GOD shall be my strength. And HE (GOD) said, It is a light thing that thou shouldest be my servant to raise up the tribes of Jacob,* ***and to restore the preserved of Israel: I will also give thee for a light to the Gentiles****, that thou mayest be my salvation unto the end of the earth. Thus saith the Lord, the Redeemer of Israel, and HIS HOLY ONE, to him whom man despiseth, to him whom the nation abhorreth, to a servant of rulers, Kings shall see and arise, princes also shall worship, because of the Lord that is faithful, and the Holy One of Israel, and HE (GOD) shall choose thee. (Isa. 49:5-7)*

> *The children which thou shalt have, after thou has lost the other, shalt say again in thine ears, The place is too strait for me: give place to me that I may dwell. Then shalt thou say in thine heart, Who hath begotten me these, seeing I have lost my children, and am desolate, a captive, and removing to and fro? And who hath brought up these? Behold, I was left alone, these, where had they been?* ***Thus saith the Lord GOD, behold, I will lift up mine hand to the Gentiles, and set up my***

> *standard to the people: and they shall bring thy sons in their arms, and thy daughters shall be carried upon their shoulders.* (Isa. 49:20-22)

This foretold that the Jews would merge into attunement with the Gentiles in a way that would bring them to a state of At-One-ment with GOD and in which state future generations would be constructed. It opened the way for all on earth to become members of the saved of Israel to eventually be granted places in the heavenly hierarchy.[153]

> *And it shall come to pass that ye shall divide it by lot for an inheritance unto you, and to* **the strangers that sojourn among you which shall beget children among you**: *and they shall be unto you as born in the country among the children of Israel;* **they shall have inheritance with you among the tribes of Israel. And it shall come to pass that in what tribe the stranger sojourneth there shall ye give him his inheritance**, *saith the Lord God.* (Ezek. 47:22-23)

Isaiah then continued to forecast further details of what the Lord the Son would accomplish when He would long afterward appear as Jesus Christ, man's Savior. In the following verses, he related what GOD the FATHER had said to HIS heavenly Son:

> *Thus saith the Lord, in an acceptable time have I heard thee, and in a day of salvation have I helped thee, and given thee for a covenant of the people, to establish the earth, to cause to inherit the desolate heritages; That thou mayest say to the prisoners, Go forth; to them that are in darkness. Shew your-*

---

[153] Jn. 14:1-4; Gal. 3:26-29.

> *self. They shall feed in the ways, and their pastures shall be in high places. (Isa. 49:8-9)*

Isaiah then foretold that the Son — GOD's Servant — would deal prudently with the people, that He would be exalted and extolled and be very high in the heavens. Many would be astonished at Him, His visage would be marred more than any man, his form more than the sons of men, and:

> *So shall He sprinkle many nations; the kings shall shut their mouths at him: for that which had not been told them shall they see; and that which they had not heard shall they consider. (Isa. 52:15)*[154]

He then revealed one of the most amazing prophesies found in the entire Bible. It describes in surprising detail events involving the Lord the Son of GOD when He would much later appear in flesh on earth as Jesus of Nazareth to bring in His New Covenant:

> *He is despised and rejected of men; a man of sorrows, and acquainted with grief: and we hid as it were our faces from him; He was despised, and we esteemed Him not. Surely He hath borne our sorrows: yet we did esteem him stricken, smitten of GOD, and afflicted. But He was wounded for our transgressions, he was bruised for our iniquities: the chastisement of our peace was upon Him; and with His stripes are we healed. All we like sheep have gone astray; we have turned every one to his own way; and the Lord has laid on Him the iniquity of us all.*

---

[154] Cf. Rom. 15:21, in which Apostle Paul quotes this verse in connection with Jesus Christ's New Covenant: *"But as it is written, To whom he was not spoken of, they shall see: and they that have not heard shall understand."*

> *He was oppressed, and He was afflicted, yet He opened not His mouth: He is brought as a lamb to the slaughter, and as a sheep before her shearers is dumb, so He opened not His mouth. He was taken from prison and from judgment: and who shall declare His generation? For He was cut off out of the land of the living: for the transgression of my people was He stricken. And He made His grave with the wicked, and with the rich in His death; because He had done no violence, neither was any deceit in his mouth. Yet it pleased the Lord to bruise Him; HE hath put Him to grief: when thou shalt make His soul an offering for sin, He shall see His seed, HE shall prolong His days, and the pleasure of the Lord shall prosper in His hand. He shall see of the travail of his soul, and shall be satisfied: by His knowledge shall MY righteous servant justify many; for He shall bear their iniquities. Therefore will I divide Him a portion with the great, and He shall divide the spoil with the strong; because He hath poured out His soul unto death: and He was numbered with the transgressors; and he bare the sin of many, and made intercession for the transgressors. (Isa. 53:3-12)*

It is a remarkable undeniable fact that this above prophetic information was given to Prophet Isaiah by the Lord, GOD the FATHER, hundreds of years before HIS Son incarnated in flesh as Jesus of Nazareth.

In Isaiah Chapter 54, it is the Lord the Son who reveals He is Israel's husband, by name the Lord of hosts — the Redeemer the Holy One of Israel; He shall be called the God of the whole earth. [155] He was the same Lord, Son of GOD who said *"the Lord who swore*

---
[155] Isa. 54:5.

that the waters of the Flood of Noah would no more cover the earth."[156] The Lord, the Son, speaking through Isaiah then added:

> *For thou shalt break forth on the right hand and on the left;* ***and thy seed shall inherit the Gentiles,*** *and make the desolate cities to be inhabited. (Isa. 54:3)*

This reflected a time to come when there would be a joining of the people of Israel with the Gentiles:

> *Then shalt thou see, and flow together, and thine heart shall fear, and be enlarged; because the abundance of the sea shall be converted unto thee,* ***the forces of the Gentiles shall come unto thee. Thou shalt also suck the milk of the Gentiles****, and shall suck the breast of kings: and thou shalt know that I the Lord am thy Savior and thy Redeemer, the Mighty one of Jacob. (Isa. 60:5,16)*[157]

These above verses presaged a radical change: the Light of GOD which had rested upon Israel, was to be granted to the Gentiles but it was not simply a matter of the Gentiles being able to share GOD's Light with the chosen people; the Light was to be removed from all who had not abided with GOD the FATHER and the Lord the Son. It would be granted to Jews and Gentiles alike:

---

[156] Isa. 54:8-9. Cf. Gen. 9:11-16.

[157] Cf. Rom. 11:25-27: *"For I would not, brethren, that ye should be ignorant of this mystery, lest ye should be wise in your own conceits; that blindness in part is happened to Israel, until the fullness of the Gentiles be come in. And so all Israel shall be saved: as it is written, There shall come out of Sion the Deliverer, and shall turn away ungodliness from Jacob: For this is my covenant with them when I shall take away their sins."*

all who would accept the radical changes being foreshadowed by the Lord the Son through His Prophets, when and as they came to pass. These verses heralded a unification of all on earth. Jews and Gentiles alike were to attune to one another. Isaiah distinguished between GOD's Spirit Light given to the Son without measure, and material earth's light of the sun and moon:

> *The sun shall be no more thy light by day; neither for brightness shall the moon give light unto thee: but the Lord shall be unto thee an everlasting light, and thy GOD thy glory. Thy sun shall no more go down; neither shall thy moon withdraw itself: for the Lord shall be thine everlasting light, and the days of thy mourning shall be ended. Thy people also shall be all righteous: they shall inherit the land forever, the branch of my planting, the work of my hands, that I may be glorified. (Isa. 60:19-21)*[158]

Isaiah wrote another startling prophecy which strikingly applied not only to the manifestation of the Son of GOD as Jesus of Nazareth — the Prophet foretold by Moses as previously noted[159] — but also subtly foretold His Second Coming, His return as the Messiah:

> *The Spirit of the Lord GOD is upon me; because the Lord has anointed me to preach good tidings upon the meek; He has sent me to bind up the brokenhearted, to proclaim liberty to the captives,*

---

[158] Cf. Rev. 21:22-23: "*And I saw no temple therein for the Lord GOD ALMIGHTY and the Lamb are the temple of it. And the city had no need of the sun, neither of the moon, to shine in it: for the glory of GOD did lighten it, and the Lamb is the light thereof.*"

[159] Deut. 18:15,18.

> *and the opening of the prison to them that are bound. To proclaim the acceptable year of the Lord, and the day of vengeance of our GOD: to comfort all that mourn. (Isa. 61:1-2)*

The Lord the Son gave this prophetic message to and through Prophet Isaiah hundreds of years before He manifested in flesh on the earth as Jesus of Nazareth. The Master is not known to have spoken of His earth mission until about age 30 — not even to have divulged that He was on earth to fulfill that written of Him in Heb. 2:13-18 — to reveal that He was to Sacrifice His earth life in order to bring about the demise of the Devil. But immediately after He emerged from His wilderness testing by Satan,[160] He began to teach in the power of the Spirit, truths which the Bible does not divulge He had ever before spoken. He proceeded to Galilee where He began to teach in the synagogues, and when He came to the city of Nazareth, He stood up to read on the Sabbath day, and read from the Book of Isaiah.[161] He turned to the scroll where the above-cited prophecy by Isaiah appeared, and began to read the first two verses reported in Isaiah Ch. 61. He read down to the last phrase of Isa. 61:2, but stopped at that point and did not read the whole verse. He read, "*To preach the acceptable year of the Lord,*" which referred to His current appearance as Jesus Christ. But He purposefully left out the remainder of Isaiah's prophecy:

> *. . . and the day of vengeance of our GOD; to comfort all that mourn. (Isa. 61:2)*

It was not at that time, in that earth appearance, time for the "*day of vengeance*" — the Tribulation described

---

[160] Lk. 4:1-2.
[161] Lk. 4:14-17.

as the Desolation, the great and terrible day of the Lord, known as Armageddon — which the Bible foretells must come at the end of the current period. Then the Lord will return to take dominion to bring in the Millennium of the First Resurrection.[162] Jesus knew that He was at that time fulfilling the prophecy given through and by Moses,[163] but it was not yet time to present Himself as the Messiah. He was fulfilling His prophesied role as Jesus of Nazareth hundreds of years after Moses' prophecy.[164] For that reason He left out those lines which did not apply at that time, but which would apply when it was time for Him to return in what has become universally known as His Second Coming.

The next following verses in that Chapter are especially revealing in that they foreshadow the time to come to which the first two verses applied. It was the acceptable year of the Lord GOD, whose Spirit was upon Him, the Son, and He was to change the outlook of those who followed Him in that terrible day of turmoil — the Tribulation and Desolation of which the prophets wrote — at which time He would then comfort all who mourned and appoint them to Zion, their eternal heavenly place.[165] He was to escalate

---

[162] Rev. 20:1-6.

[163] Deut. 18:18-19.

[164] Jesus admonished Jews who sought to kill him because He had healed a man on the Sabbath: *"How can ye believe, which receive honor one of another, and seek not the honor that comes from God only? Do not think that I will accuse you to the Father: there is one that accuses you, even Moses, in whom ye trust. For had ye believed in Moses, ye would have believed in me: for he wrote of me. But if ye believe not his writings, how shall ye believe my words?"*

[165] This refers to the city sought by Abraham, Isaac and Jacob, as written in Hebrews Chapter 11.

the spiritual condition of those of Israel who would remain true and loyal to Him; they would become *"trees of righteousness planted by the Lord that He might be glorified."*[166]

The Lord told the people of Israel through Isaiah that because of the iniquities of their fathers, who had burned incense upon the mountains and blasphemed Him upon the hills, He would measure their former work accordingly. It was an expression of the law Jesus would later describe as receiving according to what had been done,[167] the law of karma. He then foretold that which had been shown to Prophet Balaam long before[168] and by implication added that it was drawing near time for *"Shiloh"* to appear and be granted the reins of power held by Judah's tribe until that time:

> *And I will bring forth a seed out of Jacob, and **out of Judah** an inheritor of my mountains: and mine elect shall inherit it, and my servants shall dwell there. (Isa. 65:9)*

To briefly recount, according to Jacob's blessing of Judah, Judah was to hold the sceptre of power in the Divine Lineage and there would be no other lawgiver until *"Shiloh"* came and that after He manifested *"the people were to gather around Him."* Many centuries had passed since Jacob blessed Judah but the Lord in the time of Isaiah confirmed that the unique prophecy still held. It would be the Holy Spirit of the Son of GOD who would subsequently manifest

---

[166] Isa. 61:3.

[167] Isa. 65:7.

[168] *"Out of Jacob shall come he that shall have dominion, and shall destroy him that remains in the city."* (Num. 24:19)

on earth as Jesus of Nazareth, the predestined "*Shiloh*" of Jacob's illuminating blessing of his son Judah.

The Lord promised those who had forsaken Him that they were to be numbered by the sword: removed from among "*the lot of Jacob*"[169] because when He called to them they did not answer, and when He spoke they did not hear but rather did evil before His eyes, choosing to do that which did not delight Him.[170] On the other hand, He uttered a glorious promise to those who would obey Him:

> *For, behold, I create new heavens and a new earth: and the former shall not be remembered, nor come to mind. But be ye glad and rejoice for ever in that which I create: for, behold, I create Jerusalem a rejoicing, and her people a joy. And I will rejoice in Jerusalem, and joy in my people: and the voice of weeping shall be no more heard in her, nor the voice of crying. (Isa. 65:17-19)*

This epic verse referred to the time when the long anticipated event known to many as The Rapture — the Second Coming — takes place. The Jerusalem referred to in this verse is not the earthly city by that name in Israel. It applies to the Eternal Heavenly New Jerusalem sought in faith by Abraham, Isaac and Jacob.[171] The above quoted three verses of Isaiah's leave no doubt but that the Jerusalem of which the Lord spoke is not the earth city we now know but rather will comprise the "*new heavens and new*

---

[169] For the Lord's portion is His people; Jacob is the lot of His inheritance (Deut. 32:9).
[170] Isa. 65:11-12.
[171] Heb. Ch. 11.

earth," supra, He has prepared for those who are His: later described by Jesus Christ when He addressed certain of His followers:

> *Let not your heart be troubled: ye believe in GOD, believe also in me. In my Father's house are many mansions: if it were not so, I would have told you. I go to prepare a place for you. And if I go and prepare a place for you, I will come again, and receive you unto myself; that where I am, there ye may be also. And whither I go ye know, and the way ye know. (Jn. 14:1-4)*

Prophet Isaiah's revelation from the Lord the Son commenced an important series of disclosures by him and the Prophets of his time, aimed at providing spiritual foundations for the changes the Lord planned to make in due time. For example, He revealed that certain ones were to declare His glory among the Gentiles, who would then bring their brethren for an offering unto the Lord out of all nations, as the children of Israel bring an offering in a clean vessel into the house of the Lord.[172] Under the New Covenant, the "*clean vessel*" meant a spiritually clean soul, body and mind, and the "*house of the Lord*" was no longer a stone temple, it was the Spirit of the Lord. This was confirmed much later when some inquiring Jews asked Jesus to give them a sign, which led to the following colloquy:

> *Destroy this temple, and in three days I will raise it up. Then said the Jews, Forty and six years was this temple in building, and wilt thou rear it up in three days? But He spoke of the temple of His body. (Jn. 2:19-21)*

---

[172] Isa. 66:19-20.

The Lord declared that the new heavens and earth He would make would remain before Him, and that *the seed of His would remain.*[173] He foretold that in a very short period — from one new moon to another, and from one Sabbath to another — all flesh would come to worship before Him and that they would look upon the carcases of those who have transgressed against Him.[174] By this the Lord foretold the long awaited and feared Tribulation, the Desolation and Armageddon to come upon the whole earth, the time known also as the great and terrible day of the Lord.[175]

The Lord closed out His Word to Prophet Isaiah by cautioning all who had failed to obey Him to that time — including all who would fail to follow Him and declare His Word in the future — by issuing a warning to all rebellious ones who would be born later:

> *... for their worm shall not die, neither shall their fire be quenched; and they shall be an abhorring unto all flesh. (Isa. 66:23-24; cf. Mk. 9:43-50)*

---

[173] Isa. 66:22.

[174] Isa. 66:24.

[175] "And at that time shall Michael stand up, the great prince which standeth for the children of thy people; and there shall be a time of trouble, such as never was since there was a nation even to that time: and at that time thy people shall be delivered, every one that shall be found written in the book." (Dan. 12:1) And see Mt. 24:21: *"For then shall be great tribulation, such as was not since the beginning of the world to this time, no, nor ever shall be."* Also cf. Rev. 7:14, which describes a heavenly scene: "*And one of the elders answered, saying unto me, What are these which are arrayed in white robes? And whence came they? And I said unto him, thou knowest. And he said to me, These are they which came out of great tribulation, and have washed their robes, and made them white in the blood of the Lamb.*"

—CHAPTER TWO—
PROPHET JEREMIAH

As He had prophesied through Isaiah, the Lord continued to forecast His New Covenant with Prophet Jeremiah, whose book reveals how the Lord the Son sought to establish the terms of His New Covenant, in order that He could directly communicate with His children of Israel, rather than through human prophets.

About the time Jeremiah was attaining to adulthood he was suddenly quickened by the Lord's Spirit into a much higher level of consciousness. The Word of the Lord came to him, revealing:

> *Before I formed thee in the belly I knew thee; and before thou camest forth out of the womb I sanctified thee, and I ordained thee a prophet unto the nations. (Jer. 1:4-5)*

Even before Jeremiah's birth, while his soul was yet in higher dimensions of existence than the earth, in what is known as the spirit world, the Lord knew him. Further, the Lord knew him well enough and thought enough of him to bring to pass and oversee his formation in his mother's womb and to sanctify him and ordain him as a prophet to the nations. It may be presumed from this that the Lord who spoke to Jeremiah was the Son of GOD, because the Bible instructs that He is man's Maker;[176] thus it is clear that He had Made Jeremiah, having formed him in his mother's womb, as above related. The Lord who spoke these words did not say that GOD the FATHER had formed Jeremiah in the womb, but that He Himself had done it: meaning that He as the Son of GOD was man's Maker. David, the "*sweet Psalmist,*" authored many of the Psalms, and presumably supplied the following evidence as to why this was the Son speaking:

> *For the Lord is **a** great God, and **a** great king above all gods. (Ps. 95:3)*

David had made a distinction between GOD the FATHER and a "second Lord," the latter whom he proclaimed to be his Lord.[177] With that in mind, the above verse does not identify the Lord spoken of as **THE** great GOD, but rather as **a** great God and **a** king above all (other) Gods. In brief, the above-cited verse refers to the Son of GOD. Scriptures proclaim that we should all worship and bow down, kneeling before the Lord our maker[178] — His name is the Lord of Hosts; our redeemer the Holy One of Israel [179] — the God of the whole earth shall He be called.[180] The following Psalm further confirms the Son as being the Lord of the Old Testament:

> *For he is our God: and we are the people of his pasture, and the sheep of his hand. Today if ye will*

---

[176] Jn. 1:1-3.
[177] Ps. 110:1.
[178] Ps. 95:6.
[179] Isa. 45:11-12.
[180] Isa. 54.5.

> *hear His voice, Harden not your heart, as in the provocation, and as in the day of temptation in the wilderness: When your fathers tempted me, proved me, and saw my work. Forty years long was I grieved with this generation, and said, It is a people that do err in their heart, and they have not known my ways: unto whom I sware in my wrath that they should not enter into my rest. (Ps. 95:7-11)*

These verses were later inscribed in the Book of Hebrews and unmistakably identify this God as being Christ the Son of GOD:

> *And Moses verily was faithful in all his house, as a servant, for a testimony of those things which were to be spoken after;* **but Christ as a son over his own house; whose house are we,** *if we hold fast the confidence and the rejoicing of the hope firm unto the end. Wherefore (as the Holy Ghost saith, TODAY IF YE WILL HEAR HIS VOICE, HARDEN NOT YOUR HEARTS, AS IN THE PROVOCATION, IN THE DAY OF TEMPTATION IN THE WILDERNESS. WHEN YOUR FATHERS TEMPTED ME, PROVED ME, AND SAW MY WORKS FORTY YEARS. WHERE I WAS GRIEVED WITH THAT GENERATION AND SAID, THEY DO ALWAYS ERR IN THEIR HEART; AND THEY HAVE NOT KNOWN MY WAYS. SO I SWARE IN MY WRATH, THEY SHALL NOT ENTER INTO MY REST). (Heb. 3:5-11)*

The Lord above referred-to was able to sanctify Jeremiah's soul and to ordain him as a prophet through whom He would speak unto the nations, *supra*, which connotes the power of a Maker. And when Jeremiah replied that he could not serve the Lord as one of His prophets because he was at that time only a child, the Lord told him not to say to Him that he was a child, because He would be with him, and that he should go forth to do all that He would command him. In that day and in that time not many on earth were sufficiently spiritualized into a level of consciousness enabling them to receive the much higher vibrational "*voice*" of the Spirit of the Lord. He chose to work through and by those who had been able to do so and who strove to serve GOD. The sum of this is that we understand Jeremiah to have undergone previous earth experiences in which he had fitly demonstrated his desire to obediently serve the Lord, for which reason He chose him to be a prophet to the nations. When the Lord's Word came to Jeremiah he immediately began to receive prophetic impressions. One prominent disclosure was that He, the Lord the Son, would utter His judgments against those who had done wickedly and forsaken Him, burning incense unto other gods and worshiping the works of their own hand.[181] The Lord then foretold that certain kings, priests and people would be against him, but that he would be protected against their afflictions: that they would fight against him and his prophesies, but they would not prevail against him, for the Lord was with him to deliver him from them.[182]

It is evident that in Jeremiah's time Israel was seriously rebelling against the Lord; even those in power, the priests and many people. He was working through prophets He knew could be trusted and relied upon

---

[181] Jer. 1:16.
[182] Jer. 1:17-19.

to do His Will regardless of danger to themselves, to warn the people of the disastrous results of their failing to adhere to GOD's Will.

The Lord through Prophet Jeremiah continued to pave the way for His New Covenant, even outlining it and explaining certain key changes to be wrought by it. He began by sending Jeremiah to *"cry in the ears of Jerusalem"* a recounting of times past when the people of Israel were holy, so their enemies were devoured. Yet the people had turned against the Lord and gone far from Him, walking after vanity and being vain.[183] The Lord accordingly disclosed the current state of His relationship with His chosen people:

> *Hath a nation changed their gods, which are yet no gods? But my people have changed their glory for that which doth not profit. Be astonished, O ye heavens, at this, and be horribly afraid, be ye very desolate, saith the Lord. For my people have committed two evils; they have forsaken me the fountain of living waters, and hewed them out cisterns, broken cisterns, that can hold no water. (Jer. 2:11-13)*

He then accused them of having brought their problems upon themselves by forsaking the Lord their GOD when He led them by the way.[184] Plainly the sheep of Israel were in trouble with the Lord their shepherd: yet being forgiving, He continually strove to keep them sheltered in His protective fold. He asked them to consider who would help them when trouble came? Who

---

[183] Jer. 2:1-10.

[184] Generally speaking, people resist change. While souls reside in their heavenly home it apparently seems to them an easy task to descend into the earth dimension to fulfill that which they come here to accomplish.

would come forth to help a people who had elected to set up and rely upon idols and false gods of their own choice? other than their Lord. He chided them: "*let those gods of their choice rise up to save them in a time of trouble — the people of Judah who had as many gods as they had cities!*"[185] He warned them that the invisible spirits which actually provided the force behind their visible material wooden and stone idols were not of the Lord at all, but were negative spirits preying on the people's spiritual ignorance and false beliefs.[186]

After the Lord called Jeremiah and promised to protect him even though many, including priests and prophets, would be against him, *supra*, he immediately put him to work. He first excoriated the leaders of Israel and the people, flatly accusing them of ways that were intentionally evil. He devoted considerable effort to bringing to Israel's attention a list of their spiritual defilements and then again began to foreshadow radical changes to come because of their disobedience—the seventy-year exile:

> *And it shall come to pass, when ye shall say, Wherefore doeth the Lord our GOD all these things unto*

---

[185] Jer. 2:28.

[186] As we later learn from the experience of Apostle Paul, negative forces he had unwittingly let into his consciousness had as much as taken control over him, to the extent that he was going about persecuting Jesus' followers. Paul afterward "saw the light" of the Lord on the Damascus Road, and was converted and made the last Apostle Christ is known to have chosen. That Apostle later confessed he was a chief sinner, blasphemer, persecutor and injurious, but that he obtained Christ's mercy because he had done it ignorantly in unbelief (1 Tim. 1:12-15). He had then turned his life around and gone off teaching and preaching Christ the Son's Gospel.

> *us? then shalt thou answer them, Like as ye have forsaken me, and served strange gods in your land, so shall ye serve strangers in a land that is not yours. (Jer. 5:19)*

At the time of the fall, GOD sentenced both, the Serpent and Adam, into exile in the earth advising them it would last all the days of their earth confinement.[187] When the Son of God — who had fallen as Adam and was sentenced to the earth plane to partake of that dimension all the days of his life — he was in effect condemned to remain on earth to "*eat bread*" until he died in that earth experience, because GOD had exiled him to the earth plane. But GOD the FATHER is merciful and HE did not close the door on those whom HE had exiled; they would be able to receive GOD's Quickening Spirit sufficiently to be released from earth bondage if and when they would return to HIM by remaining obedient to HIS Son's will.

Speaking through Prophet Jeremiah, the Lord left no doubt about His feelings toward those without

---

[187] Gen. 3:14, 17-19. A brief examination of the governing principle of man's exiles reveals that he is set apart from GOD on those occasions when he disobeys HIS WILL, and is therefore exiled. In such cases, the Lord moves people from a land of their own in which they rule themselves, and enforces their confinement in a strange place among others who hold them in bondage. We see this exemplified in all biblically-recorded exiles, starting when Adam and Eve disobeyed GOD's specific command not to do certain things, and accordingly GOD cut off HIS Holy Spirit from man and confined him to the earth until such time as he would turn himself around and cease being disobedient.

understanding. He declared His disparagement toward those who refused to do what they should:

> *But this people have a revolting and a rebellious heart; they are revolted and gone. Neither say they in their heart, Let us now fear the Lord our GOD, that gives rain, both the former and the latter rain, in his season: he reserves unto us the appointed weeks of the harvest. Your iniquities have turned away these things, and your sins have withheld good things from you. For among my people are found wicked men: they lay wait, as he who sets snares; they set a trap, they catch men. As a cage is full of birds, so are their houses full of deceit: therefore they are become great, and waxen rich. Shall I not visit for these things? saith the Lord: shall not my soul be avenged on such a nation as this? A wonderful and horrible thing is committed in the land: The prophets prophesy falsely, and the priests bear rule by their means; and my people love to have it so: and what will ye do in the end thereof? (Jer. 5:23-31)*

The obvious negative spirit influencing men to behave as the Lord knew they were, was due to the insidious penetrating desires, thoughts and intentions of Satan, who has battled against the Son from the beginning. It was the force that inclined Adam and Eve to go against GOD's Will, and still today influences souls incarnated in flesh on the earth to do their own will rather than the Lord's Will. Disobedience to HIM and the Son HE chose is intolerable to HIM, and extremely hazardous to any soul's well being.

Through Prophet Jeremiah the Lord promised — as recorded in Chapter Six — that a desolation would come upon those of His people who rejected Him:

> *Be thou instructed, O Jerusalem, lest my soul depart from thee; lest I make thee desolate, a land not inhabited. (Jer. 6:8)*

That this was the Son speaking is evident from the fact that He threatened to withdraw His Spirit from the people of Israel — which He could do because He was their Maker — they were composed of His Spirit.[188] Step by step He was leading them to understand that changes were in the offing which would lead to a new and different pathway His people were to follow. He admonished Israel through Prophet Jeremiah that the people from the least of them to the greatest were given to covetousness: that the prophets and priests were dealing falsely with the people GOD had given Him.[189] After disclosing His displeasure, He declared:

> *Hear, O earth: behold, I will bring evil upon this people, even the fruit of their thoughts, because they have not hearkened unto my words, nor to my law, but rejected it. (Jer. 6:19)*

The Lord left no lingering doubt that He was less than impressed by the ways of Israel at this point; the people having bent before the onslaught of negative forces of the Devil. But what emerges as important to our understanding is that the Lord has the power to control the fruits of the thoughts of those

---

[188] Job 35:10; Ps. 95:6; Prov. 22:2; Isa. 45:11-13; 51-13; esp Isa. 54:5; Jer. 33:2; Hos. 8:14.

[189] Jer. 6:13; Cf. Heb. 2:13-16.

who array themselves against Him, as well as to give helpful thoughts and even His Spirit power, to those who do His Will. The history of Israel during the Hebraic Age indicates that when the people followed the Lord's will they were able to overcome all the enemies who stood before them, as exemplified in the collapse of the walls protecting the City of Jericho.[190]

The Lord spoke again through Jeremiah, asking the people to amend their ways and actions by not oppressing others, by executing judgment between a man and his neighbor and by not walking after other gods they did not know.[191] And He added:

> *But go ye now unto my place which was in Shiloh, where I set my name at the first, and see what I did to it for the wickedness of my people Israel. (Jer. 7:12)*

The Book of Joshua[192] emphasizes the spiritual importance of Shiloh in that period but when Israel failed to do the Lord's Will, He brought about its desolation. Jeremiah was told to advise the people they should not pray for that people, nor lift up cries

---

[190] After Jericho fell, when Joshua son of Nun sent a small force against the mountain fortress, Ai, and it failed, he threw himself to the ground, knowing that something was amiss: and events showed that it was due to a negative act by one of his men (Josh. Ch. 7).

[191] Jer. 7:1-11.

[192] Josh. Chapter 18.

[193] Jer. 7:16.

on their behalf for He would not hear them[193] and He further lamented:

> *The children gather wood, and the fathers kindle the fire, and the women knead their dough, to make cakes to the queen of heaven, and to pour out drink offerings unto other gods, that they may provoke me to anger. (Jer. 7:18)*

The people of Israel were not heeding the Lord's Will. They were straying off into other ways, emphasizing the importance of the queen of heaven, and making offerings to other gods. Therefore the Lord spoke harshly to them, reminding them that they were guilty of having established practices and rituals which He had not commanded them at all:

> *Thus saith the Lord of hosts, the God of Israel; Put your burnt offerings unto your sacrifices, and eat flesh. **For I spake not unto your fathers, nor commanded them in the day that I brought them out of the land of Egypt, concerning burnt offerings or sacrifices.** But this thing commanded I them, saying, **Obey my voice and I will be your God, and ye shall be my people: and walk ye in all the ways I have commanded you, that it may be well unto you.** But they hearkened not, nor inclined their ear, but walked in the counsels and in the imagination of their evil heart, and went backward not forward. Since the day that your fathers came forth out of the land of Egypt unto this day I have even sent unto you all my servants the prophets daily rising up early and sending them: Yet they hearkened not unto me, nor inclined their ear, but hardened their neck: they did worse*

---

[194] Gal. 3:24-25; Rom. 5:13.

> *than their fathers. Therefore thou shalt speak all these words unto them; but they will not hearken to thee: thou shalt also call unto them, but they will not answer thee. But thou shalt say unto them, this is a nation that obeyeth not the voice of the Lord their God, nor receiveth correction: truth is perished, and is cut off from their mouth. (Jer. 21-28)*

These passages revealed that what the Lord really desired of His people was that they obey His voice. We begin to see here the Lord's growing impatience with the chosen people, which would inevitably lead to a New Covenant. The First Covenant had been intended to provide a basic form of GOD's Law as man's "*schoolmaster*" because sin cannot be imputed when there is no law.[194] It follows that without man's acceptance of responsibility under GOD's Law, spiritual increases cannot be granted to him; as Jesus taught.[195] The Lord had given a preliminary basic inscribed version of His Law on the Holy Mount to Moses and Joshua, but it was being neither respected nor heeded by many of the people. Consequently earth testing was weeding out those who were not following the Way He was making passable for them.[196]

---

[195] Mt. 18:18.

[196] Heb. 5:11-14. As late as the time of Apostle Paul, people had not well responded to the Lord's basic spiritual instructions — long after the oracles of GOD had been made known on the earth — so that even at that late time, when they should have been teaching the deeper spiritual mysteries, they were still "*drinking milk*" rather than consuming the "*strong meat*" of spiritual knowledge and understanding.

That the Lord had not commanded the priests of Israel to become involved in burnt offering rituals had been revealed by Prophet Isaiah,[197] thereby emphasizing its importance. The Lord's design for His people was being made increasingly clear through His prophets. He had become so discouraged with those who were disobeying Him that He warned Jeremiah that none should pray for their good:

> *When they fast I will not hear their cry; and when they offer burnt offerings and an oblation, I will not accept them: but I will consume them by the sword, and by the famine, and by the pestilence. (Jer. 14:12)*

Jeremiah responded, saying that the prophets were pacifying the people, telling them they would not see the sword, nor have famines but would have peace. But the Lord accused the nefarious negative prophets of not having been sent by Him — that He had not even spoken to them — yet they were prophesying false visions and divinations, doing so deceitfully. He foretold that those prophets would themselves be victims of the sword and famine and that the people who accepted their prophesies would be cast out into the streets of Jerusalem.[198] It later took place when the Romans overran Jerusalem and so totally devastated it that not one stone of the original foundation was left standing. Still today Jews do not have reliable knowledge about where the original foundations of the city were laid. That changes were necessary was echoed in all the Lord's Words. He outrightly told the people what must transpire and why:

---

[197] Isa. 1:11-15.
[198] Jer. 14:13-15.

> *Thou hast forsaken me, saith the Lord, thou art gone backward: therefore will I stretch out my hand against thee, and destroy thee; I am weary with repenting. And I will fan them with a fan in the gates of the land; I will bereave them of children, I will destroy my people, since they return not from their ways. (Jer. 15:6-7)*

But the Lord left open a door for those who would not let themselves be drawn away from Him:

> *Verily it shall be well with **thy remnant**; verily I will cause the enemy to entreat thee well in the time of the evil and in the time of affliction. (Jer. 15:11)*

In a string of messages given through His prophet, He promised the people that if they would return to Him, then He would **bring them again** that they might stand before Him, removing the precious from the vile: but, He cautioned, they must return to Him and not to their idols and other gods.[199] At this time the seventy-year exile was drawing ever nearer, and the Lord began to issue more warnings through and by Jeremiah. The struggle between the forces of good and evil was intense, negative spirits continually afflicting the children of Israel, luring and tempting them to follow devilish ways at the expense of overcoming the spirit forces that strove to sink them in a spiritual mire of darkness. Jeremiah asked the Lord if He would deal with the negative recalcitrant ones who would choose to remain in the city rather than enter into exile according to GOD's Will at the time when Nebuchadrezzar, the king of Babylon, would make war against them; to which He replied:

---

[199] Jer. 15:19.

> *Behold, I will turn back the weapons of war that are in your hands, wherewith ye fight against the king of Babylon, and against the Chaldeans, which besiege you without the walls, and I will assemble them in the midst of this city. And afterward I will deliver Zedekiah king of Judah, and his servants, and the people and such as are left in this city from the pestilence, from the sword, and from the famine, into the hand of Nebuchadrezzar king of Babylon, and into the hand of their enemies, and into the hand of those who seek their life: and he shall smite them with the edge of the sword; he shall not spare them, neither have pity, nor have mercy. (Jer. 21:4-7)*

The Lord then specifically foretold what was to take place for those who would follow His Will, and for those who did not:

> *Behold, I set before you the way of life, and the way of death. He that abideth in this city shall die by the sword and by the famine, and by the pestilence: but he that goeth out, and falleth to the Chaldeans that besiege you, he shall live, and his life shall be unto him for a prey. (Jer. 21:8-9)*

The Lord knew that His support for the powerful Nebuchadrezzar would insure his victory over the people of Israel. It was His Will that the chosen people be punished for their unbelief and lack of faith and their failure to straitly follow His Commandments. He knew that if they remained to fight in the city they would all be exterminated by the superior forces of their enemy. The Lord had prepared a test designed to weed out the unfaithful and disobedient among His chosen people. Those who did His Will were destined to be saved from the debacle confronting them. As has been the standard of man's testing from the beginning, those who would do His Will by accepting exile rather than attempting to avoid His punishment would continue as the remnant of His people, deserving of His mercy. That this was a crucial decision for those caught on the horns of the dilemma confronting them becomes evident when it is considered that an accurate prediction that these events were to take place had long been before written into the Holy Scripture. The prophecy not only foretold the particular occurrence to come, it identified the one who would at that time have dominion over Israel who would bring it to pass. It was the Lord who even at the time the events were to take place spoke through Prophet Jeremiah: it was the Lord of Israel the Son of GOD. Balaam was the prophet who had long before foretold this extremely important event:

> ***Out of Jacob shall come he that shall have dominion***, *and shall destroy him that remaineth of the city.* (Num. 24:19)

It is now understood that a soul portion of the Son of GOD incarnated again as Joseph son of Jacob. Of Him, Prophet Balaam wrote:

> *I shall see him, but not now I shall behold Him, but not nigh:* ***there shall come a Star out of Jacob*** *and a Sceptre shall rise out of Israel.* (Num. 24:17)

Israel was duly sent into its seventy-year exile as the Lord had foretold through His prophets, and He took occasion to forecast remarkable changes to come afterward. After commenting that He was against the pastors who fed His people,[200] He admonished them that because they had scattered His flock and driven them away:

> *I will gather the remnant of my flock out of all countries whither I have driven them, and will bring them again to their folds; and they shall be fruitful and increase. And I will set up shepherds over them which shall feed them: and they shall fear no more, nor be dismayed, neither shall they be lacking, saith the Lord. (Jer. 23:3-4)*

That this applied to that which would befall Israel after the seventy-year exile is evident from the fact that the Lord promised to set up shepherds over them. A history of what transpired after the exile is written in the Books of Nehemiah and Ezra, which disclose that the Lord did set up reliable shepherds over the people. The Lord's next following comments, however, projected ahead hundreds of years to a time when **GOD** would set up **One** Shepherd[201] over all who would ever afterward believe in and follow Christ, the Son **GOD** created and anointed above all other sons of **GOD**:

> *Behold, the days come, saith the Lord, that I will raise unto David a righteous Branch, and a King shall reign and prosper, and shall execute judgment and justice on the earth. In his days, Judah shall be saved, and Israel shall dwell safely: and this is his*

---

[200] Jer. 23:1-2.
[201] And other sheep I have, which are not of this fold: them also I must bring, and they shall hear my voice: and there shall be one fold, and one shepherd (Jn. 10:16).

> *name whereby he shall be called, THE LORD OUR RIGHTEOUSNESS. Therefore, behold, the days come, sayeth the Lord, that they shall no more say, the Lord liveth which brought up the children of Israel out of the land of Egypt; But the Lord liveth, which brought up and which led the seed of the house of Israel out of the north country, and from all countries whither I had driven them; and they shall dwell in their own land. (Jer. 23:5-8)*

The Son of GOD was indeed the Lord who had brought the children out of the land of Egypt under the guiding hand of Moses. He was the Spirit in the Cloud that guided, moved and directed the people of Israel during their extraordinary Exodus out of captivity in Egypt.[202] He was the same Lord who spoke through and by Prophet Jeremiah in the above-quoted verses. He was the same Lord, the BRANCH of the Tree of Life whom GOD promised to raise unto David in a day to come. It was predestined to transpire in the Lineage of David, which was the lineage of Judah.[203]

In Jeremiah's time the people, despite the Lord's continual protestations, were ignoring His Will, instead following those who were misleading them. Many ignored His prophets and continued to go

---

[202] Moreover, brethren, I would not that ye should be ignorant, how that our fathers were under the cloud, and all passed through the sea: And were all baptized unto Moses in the cloud and in the sea; and did all eat the same spiritual meat; and did all drink the same spiritual meat: for they drank of that spiritual Rock that followed them: and that Rock was Christ. But with many of them GOD was not pleased: for they were overthrown in the wilderness (1 Cor. 10:1-5).

[203] Gen. 49:10; Jer. 23:5; Mt. 1:1; Lk. 18:38; Jn. 7:42.

their own way. When they had fallen away to the extent that many would not adhere to the Mosaic Law in which the Lord had seen fit to indoctrinate them, He began to make provisions for a radical change on the earth. Nevertheless He continued to sort through His people, removing those who were not yet measuring up, while at the same time keeping His door open to any who would repent, change their ways and return to Him.[204] Excerpts from His message to the people by way of Prophet Jeremiah reflect His discouragement with those who had fallen away after He selected Abraham and Sarah to commence their all-important segment of the Divine Lineage. Many of His people were being rendered spiritually helpless before the continual onslaught of the Devil's divisive ways, often perpetuated by some of the prophets and priests of that time. It reached such a critical point that the Lord saw fit to make the following comments through His faithful servant, Prophet Jeremiah:

> *I have heard what the prophets have said, who prophesy lies in my name, saying, I have dreamed, I have dreamed. How long shall this be in the heart of the prophets that prophesy lies? Yet, they are prophets of the deceit of their own heart; Which think to cause my people to forget my name by their dreams which they tell every man to his neighbor, as their fathers have forgotten my name for Baal. The prophet that hath a dream, let him tell a dream; and he that hath my word, let him speak my word faithfully. What is the chaff to the wheat? saith the Lord. Behold, I am against the prophets, saith the Lord, that steal my words every one*

---

[204] As later detailed, the Son of GOD through His Prophets kept the door open: and cf. Jn. 10:1-30.

> *from his neighbor. I am against the prophets that use their tongues and say, He saith. I am against them that prophesy false dreams, and do tell them, and cause my people to err by their lies, and by their lightness; yet I sent them not, nor commanded them: therefore they shall not profit this people at all, saith the Lord. (Jer. 23:25-32)*

After addressing these words to Israel, the Lord then reiterated that He would look after those who would willingly go into captivity in the land of the Chaldeans to voluntarily accept the punishment of the exile He had decided to mete out to them as part of His testing:

> *For I will set mine eyes upon them for good, and I will bring them again to this land: and I will build them, and not pull them down; and I will plant them, and not pluck them up. And I will give them an heart to know me, that I am the Lord; and they shall be my people, and I will be their God: for they shall return unto me with their whole heart. (Jer. 24:6-7)*

That the people who voluntarily went into exile were sentenced to suffer for seventy years because of their disobedience was confirmed by the Lord through Jeremiah:

> *And this whole land shall be a desolation, and an astonishment; and these nations shall serve the king of Babylon seventy years. (Jer. 25:11)*

It was subsequently disclosed in the writings of Prophets Ezra and Nehemiah that even after the seventy-year exile was fulfilled many of the people had not yet by that time brought themselves to do the Lord's Will. By the time of the Latter Days Prophets it had become apparent that regardless of how zealously the Lord strove to bring his flock into His Fold and keep them safely protected there, they had become too unbelieving, spiritually scattered and caught up in other beliefs to respond to His pleadings that they turn back their own desires, thoughts and ways in favor of doing GOD's Will. They had become blinded, even as David had foretold.[205] Their egoistic unbelief had drowned them, lowering their Spirit vibrations so drastically they were no longer able to hear GOD's Word, much less fulfill the Will of the Son, who is the Word of GOD. By committing those into exile who would voluntarily accept it, He opened a door of escape for them, while closing it, at least for a time, to those who would refuse to submit to His Will.

When the pre-New Covenant exile came, many would elect to die in Jerusalem rather than follow the path the Lord had set out for them. It became apparent that He was systematically sorting out those who had become negatively inclined due to Satanic influences and were following their own impaired will. As for the Lord, He left no doubt of His intentions, admonishing through Prophet Jeremiah that Nebuchadnezzar the king of Babylon was His servant, and that those who refused to bring themselves under his rule would be consumed by his hand; whereas those and their children who would go into captivity and survive would

---

[205] *"Let their table become a snare before them: and that which should have been for their welfare, let it become a trap. Let their eyes be darkened, that they see not; and make their loins to continually shake. Pour out thine indignation upon them...."* (David's Palm 69:22-25).

one day return to their homeland.[206] These would still be considered the remnant of Israel.

The Lord promised that the holy vessels remaining in the captured house of Judah in Jerusalem, would be carried into Babylon and held safely until He visited the people, after which He would see that they were restored to their place.[207] When one prophet, Hananiah, claimed that the Lord of hosts, the God of Israel, had told him that He had broken the yoke of the king of Babylon, and that within two years the Lord would return all the vessels to their place, it turned out to be untrue. As the Lord foretold to Jeremiah,[208] Hananiah died within a year after having uttered his false prophesy.[209] It demonstrated that those who attempt to influence others as the result of their own false impressions or spirit receptions from *"other gods"*

---

[206] *"And now have I given all these lands unto the hand of Nebuchadnezzar the king of Babylon, my servant...and all nations shall serve him...and it shall come to pass that the nation and kingdom which will not serve (him), and that will not put their neck under the yoke of the king of Babylon, that nation will I punish, saith the Lord, with the sword, and with the famine, and with the pestilence, until I have consumed them by his hand. Therefore, hearken not to your prophets, nor to your diviners, nor to your chanters, nor to your sorcerers, which speak unto you, saying, Ye shall not serve the king of Babylon. For they prophesy a lie unto you, to remove you far from your land; and that I should drive you out, and you should perish."* (Jer. 27:6-10).

[207] Jer. 27:21-22.

[208] This fulfilled Deut. 18:20, which had foretold that any prophet who spoke in the Lord's name, which He had not commanded him to speak, or who spoke in the name of other prophets, would die as a result.

[209] Jer. 28:15-17.

were not to be countenanced. Even more importantly, it foretold the end of the days of human prophets and priests influenced by negative spirit intrusions they too easily accepted into consciousness and acted upon to the detriment of those they strove to serve on behalf of the Lord.[210]

The Son was preparing His people for the New Covenant He had already decided to bring into the earth plane. He had gradually and inexorably set apart those of His children who would do His Will from those who would not. The former were to become the remnant or the preserved of Israel. He began to spell out the terms of the New Covenant through Prophet Jeremiah:

> *Thus saith the Lord of hosts . . . unto all who are carried away captives, whom I have caused to be carried away from Jerusalem into Babylon. Let not your prophets and your diviners, that be in the midst of you, deceive you, neither hearken to your dreams which ye cause to be dreamed, for they prophesy falsely unto you in my name: I have not sent them, saith the Lord. After seventy years be accomplished in Babylon I will visit you, and perform my good work toward you, in causing you to return to this place. For I know the thoughts that I think toward you, thoughts of peace, and not of evil, to give you an expected end. Then shall ye call upon me, and ye shall go and pray unto me, and find me when ye shall search for me with all your heart. (Jer. 29:4-13)*

---

[210] Cf. Heb. 5:1-3, asserting that earth priests are compassed with infirmity, and so need to purify themselves before they can hope to purify those who suffer from negative influences as they do. It was for that reason that GOD Anointed one Son as man's Eternal High Priest who had been perfected in the earth plane.

In these verses the Lord foreshadowed what was to come by commanding the people to no longer pay heed to those who He knew would seek to divert them from the pathway He had set them on. Step by step He was guiding, moving and directing Israel toward the proclamation of His New Covenant.

The Book of Jeremiah[211] records the Lord's promise to punish all those priests and prophets who had spoken against His sending the people into captivity. In particular He criticized Shemaiah, who had prophesied a lie, for which he and his seed were to be punished, including that none of his children should dwell among the people of Israel, nor behold the good the Lord would do for them, because he had taught rebellion against the Lord. Shemaiah's negative ways brought him under the 3 to 4 generation rule which spells out that if a man rebels against GOD's Will, the Lord will hold it against his descendants for 3 to 4 generations;[212] except if they repent their ways, and not again turn back to them.[213] This rule would become a principle feature of the New Covenant.

The Lord then told Jeremiah that He would bring his people out of captivity in the north country, and return them to Jerusalem: that He would cause them to walk by the rivers of waters in straight ways so they would not stumble. They were on the way to their

---

[211] Jer. Chapter 29.

[212] Ex. 20:3-5; Ex. 34:7; Num. 14:18; Deut. 5:9.

[213] That this rule not only held in Jeremiah's time, and was preached by John the Baptist (Mt. 3:1-2), but was a key part of Jesus Christ's Gospel, is found in many New Testament writings: for example Mt. 4:17; Mk. 1:15; Lk. 13:3,5,30; Acts 3:19; Rev. 2:5; Rev. 2:22; Rev. 3:3,19.

New Covenant. The Lord then made known through Prophet Jeremiah that He had scattered Israel, but would gather the people again as a shepherd gathers his flock; that He had redeemed Jacob from the negative Archangel Satan, who was still at that time stronger than Jacob.[214] He then foretold an event predestined to take place many centuries later when King Herod would call for the slaying of all male children under the age of two years, in a desperate attempt to eliminate the one whom prophesies had foretold was to be ruler over Israel, thereby posing a threat to his power:

> *Thus saith the Lord; a voice was heard in Ramah, lamentation, and bitter weeping; Rachel weeping for her children refused to be comforted for her children, because they were not. (Jer. 31:15)*

> *Then Herod, when he saw that he was mocked of the wise men, was exceeding wroth, and sent forth, and slew all the children that were in Bethlehem, and in all the coasts thereof, from two years old and under. . . . Then was fulfilled that which was spoken by Jeremy, the prophet, saying, IN RA-MA WAS THERE A VOICE HEARD, LAMENTATION, AND WEEPING AND GREAT MOURNING, RACHEL WEEPING FOR HER CHILDREN, AND WOULD NOT BE COMFORTED, BECAUSE THEY ARE NOT. (Mt. 2:16-17)*

In accordance with prophecies, Jesus of Nazareth would be born — foretold to come as *"Shiloh"* in the lineage of Judah— in the lineage of David. Born in the city of Bethlehem, He was indeed to one day be the heavenly ruler over all GOD's Creation. Herod had in vain re-

---

[214] Jer. 31:10-11.

built the stone temple in Jerusalem for the third time: it was the Son of GOD, incarnated as Jesus Christ, who was man's predestined eternal Spirit temple.

The Lord promised through Jeremiah that in days to come those who had followed His Will would no more say that their fathers *"had eaten a sour grape "* — which the Lord had given them and they had found it unpalatable — or say that the children's teeth were "*set on edge*" because of the bitter pill their Lord had compelled them to swallow by accepting exile in Babylon.[215] These comments were leading to the Lord's extraordinary divulgence through Prophet Jeremiah of a time to come when He would bring about a radical change upon the earth. The First Covenant had expended its usefulness, and man's means of attaining to the higher heavenly dimensions was in need of upgrading. As the Lord's prophets were proclaiming, many priests and prophets were going their own way, not instructing the people according to GOD's Will, but rather according to their own imaginations. Conditions had become spiritually disastrous.

The seventy-year exile had preserved those who would do the Lord's Will ahead of their own, and they were to be granted better conditions and circumstances. He spoke to these of a time to come when they would each have a direct relationship with Him. They would no longer be subjected to the often distorted whimsical ideas and imaginations of other human would-be intercessors, whose erroneous instructions and prophesies the people were often unable to distinguish from those sent by their Lord.[216] This was to be replaced with an illuminating

---

[215] Jer. 31:30.
[216] Isa. 54:5.

New Covenant which was meticulously described by the Lord through Prophet Jeremiah:

> *Behold the days come, saith the Lord, that I will make a new covenant with the house of Israel, and with the house of Judah: Not according to the covenant I made with their fathers when I took them by the hand to bring them out of the land of Egypt; which my covenant they brake, although I was an husbandman unto them, saith the Lord: But this shall be the covenant that I shall make with the house of Israel; After those days, saith the Lord, I will put my law in their inward parts, and write it in their hearts; and will be their God, and they shall be my people. And they shall teach no more every man his neighbor, and every man his brother, saying, Know the Lord: for they shall all know me, from the least of them, saith the Lord: for I will forgive their iniquity, and I will remember their sin no more. (Jer. 31:31-34)*

It is of more than passing significance that the Lord's New Covenant was to be made with the house of Israel, and that He would put His Law in their inward parts, and write it in their hearts, and would be their God, and they were to be His people. The Lord specifically applied this change to the chosen people, notifying them that it would come into effect at a later time. Very importantly the chosen people were to accept the Lord's mandated conditions and governing rules. It presaged a juncture of the Spirit which had been granted to the people of Israel, with that of those Gentiles who would be found acceptable to the Lord, to form one single spiritual mainstream of souls bound for the heavenly New Jerusalem. In ways quite unimaginable even to those loyal Jews who had served the Lord the Son from the beginning of earth incarnations, they were destined to play crucially important roles in what was to come when this predestined spiritual merger took place.

The New Covenant was not to apply until the Lord the Son of GOD manifested as Jesus of Nazareth. The Bible specifically spells out that early in Jesus' Ministry, when He sent out His twelve Apostles, He commanded that they were not to go the way of the Gentiles, but they were rather to go only unto the lost sheep of the house of Israel.[217] But later He expanded upon that restriction, advising them He also had other sheep which were not of the same fold, whom He must also bring: that they would hear His voice and there would be one fold, and one shepherd.[218] It meant that those of the Old Covenant would become accountable to the terms of a new and better Covenant, as was long afterward explained in the Book of Hebrews.[219]

The long term significance of the seventy year exile, as the prophets foretold it and as the Bible confirms it, was that by their experience in captivity in Babylon the loyal children of Israel were shown the importance of remaining true to their Lord, able to bring themselves into accord with whatever changes He ordained for them. They knew from what He had foretold through Prophet Jeremiah that radical changes were coming and, although they had no idea what alterations would be wrought, they looked for-

---

[217] Mt. 10:5-6.
[218] Jn. 10:16.
[219] Hebrews Chapters 8 and 9.

ward expectantly, knowing that His Will was always to be obeyed. The bringing in of the New Covenant was predestined to come to pass in astonishing ways, provoking a broad range of conflicting reactions among Jews and Gentiles alike. In Jeremiah's time nobody on earth could possibly have conceived what was to confront mankind when the changes were made.

—CHAPTER THREE—
PROPHET EZEKIEL

The word of the Lord came expressly upon Ezekiel the priest, son of Buzi, in Chaldea in the fifth year of king Johoiachin's captivity.[220] It was attended by a bizarre spiritual rebirth experience, albeit not atypical of some of man's reported contacts with entities in the spirit realm. Ezekiels's visions are detailed in Chapter One of his book, the closing verse of which is reminiscent of what took place when GOD made HIS covenant with Noah:[221]

> *As the appearance of the bow that is in the cloud in the day of rain, so was the appearance of the brightness round about. This was the appearance of the likeness of the glory of the Lord. And when I saw it, I fell upon my face, and I heard a voice of one that spake. (Ezek. 1:28)*

After Jeremiah recovered from the shock of the infusion of Spirit in him, the Lord set him on his feet and directly addressed him.[222] He straitly told Ezekiel that He was sending him on a mission to the children of Israel, a rebellious people who had defied Him to that very day. He called them impudent and

---

[220] Ezek. 1:1-3.
[221] Gen. 9:11-16.
[222] Ezek. 2:1-2.

stiff-hearted, and declared that regardless of whether or not they would hear or heed Ezekiel, they would at least know there was a prophet among them.[223] He gave his prophet *"a book he was to eat"* which he found to be as sweet as honey.[224]

The Lord again indicated His displeasure with His people, particularly noting His depleted confidence in them. He confided that though He was not sending Ezekiel to a people who spoke a different language, which he might not be able to understand, that even had He actually done so even strangers would be more likely to hearken to him than the people of Israel at that time:

> *But the house of Israel will not hearken unto thee; for they will not hearken unto Me: for all the house of Israel are impudent and hardhearted. Moreover He said unto me, Son of man, all my words that I shall speak unto thee receive in thine heart, and hear with thine ears. (Ezek. 3:7,10)*

At this time the children of Israel were still in captivity in Babylon, and the Lord commanded His prophet to go speak to them, regardless of whether or not they would hear or forbear.[225] Ezekiel was whisked away in Spirit to deliver the Lord's message:

> *Then the spirit took me up, and I heard behind me a voice of a great rushing, saying, Blessed be the*

---

[223] Ezek. 2:3-5.

[224] Ezek. 3:1-3. Cf. Isa. 7:22, which correlates with Beloved John's having asked the angel who spoke to him to *"give him the little book,"* which he found it to be in his belly bitter, but in his mouth sweet. He was then told he must prophesy again to many peoples (Rev. 10:9-11).

[225] Ezek. 3:11.

> *glory of the Lord from His place. I also heard the noise of the wings of the living creatures that touched one another, and the noise of the wheels over against them, and a noise of a great rushing.*[226] *So the spirit lifted me up, and took me away, and I went in bitterness, in the heat of my spirit; but the hand of the Lord was strong upon me. (Ezek. 3:12-14)*

A crucially important spiritual principle was then revealed to Ezekiel which relates to the law of *karma* — the rule Jesus described as the requirement that one must reap as has been sown. As was seen in the case of Jonah, that harsh rule can cause a prophet to carefully consider his decision as to whether or not to put himself at risk by going out of his way to confront people who were quite content doing their own will. The Lord told Ezekiel that He had *made him a watchman* unto the house of Israel, for which reason he was to listen to His Word and then warn the people of Israel accordingly:

> *When I say unto the wicked, Thou shalt surely die; and thou givest him not warning, nor speakest to warn the wicked from his wicked way, to save his life; the same wicked man shall die in his iniquity; but his blood will I require at thine hand. Yet if thou warn the wicked, and he turn not from his wickedness, nor from his wicked way, he shall die in his iniquity; but thou hast delivered thy (own) soul. (Ezek. 3:18-19)*

---

[226] This description of Prophet Ezekiel's is strongly suggestive of a description of the "*heavenly chariot*" which swept Prophet Elijah up from the earth in full view of Prophet Elisha (2 Ki. 2:11-12).

Prophet Ezekiel thus found himself in a precarious position. The Lord had called him as one of His Watchmen, charged with the responsibility of conveying His Word directly to those He sought to protect from suffering death at their own hands because of their failure to do GOD's Will. This can be readily perceived as hazardous to the health of a prophet boldly confronting a hardhearted iniquitous stranger admonishing him that his life is in peril unless he forthwith makes radical changes for the better! Such responsibility severely tests the faith, belief, will and courage of anyone called upon to serve the Lord.[227]

This above-quoted charge to Ezekiel was considered so important that the Lord reiterated it, sketching it out in even more precise detail:

> *Again, When a righteous man doth turn from his righteousness, and commit iniquity, and I lay a stumbling block before him, he shall die: because thou hast not given him warning, he shall die in*

---

[227] For example, Prophet Balaam had reached a level of consciousness which enabled him to enter into a trance state, in which he heard the words of GOD, and knew the knowledge of the Most High (Num. 24:16). But when he was charged by the Lord to confront Balak and advise him to tell his people not to seek the counsel of idols and strange gods, he — perhaps out of fear of reprisals — advised him the opposite, for which reason the Lord long afterward revealed through Beloved John the Lord's scathing rebuke of Balaam, because he had taught Balak to cast a stumbling block before the children of Israel; to eat things sacrificed unto idols, and to commit fornication (Rev. 2:14). Those who set out to serve the Lord are required to do so with the courage to speak His Truth.

> *his sin, and his righteousness which he hath done shall not be remembered; but his blood will I require at thine hand. Nevertheless if thou warn the righteous man, that the righteous sin not, and he doth not sin, he shall surely live, because he is warned; also thou hast delivered thy soul. (Ezek. 3:20-21)*

Next following verses describe how the Lord worked with Ezekiel as His prophet, which still today remains important because under the New Covenant each individual follower of the Lord's is now his/her own prophet, so to speak. His followers receive information directly from the Holy Ghost the Spirit of Truth and other Comforter sent by GOD in the name of Christ the Son.[228] Ezekiel related the Lord's command to him:

> *And the hand of the Lord was there upon me; and He said unto me, Arise, go forth into the plain, and I will there talk with thee. Then I arose, and went forth into the plain: and, behold, the glory of the Lord stood there, as the glory which I saw by the river of Chebar: and I fell on my face. Then the spirit entered into me, and set me upon my feet, and spake with me, and said unto me, Go, shut thyself within thine house. But thou, O son of man, behold, they shall put bands upon thee, and shall bind thee with them, and thou shalt not go out among them: And I will make thy tongue cleave to the roof of thy mouth, that thou shalt be dumb, and shalt not be to them a reprover: for they are a rebellious house. But when I speak with thee, I will open thy mouth, and thou shalt say unto them, Thus saith the Lord God; He that heareth, let him hear; and he that forbeareth, let him forbear: for they are a rebellious house. (Ezek. 3:22-27)*

---

[228] Jn. 14:15-17,26; 15:26; 16:7,12-15.

The Lord commenced to make known what He had in mind as punishment for the people of Israel for their having militated against His Will. He promised that those who had escaped the exile would, because of their abominations, fall by the sword, famine and by pestilence;[229] and intimated that He would not retain them as a part of the remnant of His children:

> *Destruction cometh; and they shall seek peace, and there shall be none. Mischief shall come upon mischief, and rumor shall be upon rumor; then shall they seek a vision of the prophet; but the law shall perish from the priest, and counsel from the ancients. The king shall mourn, and the prince shall be clothed with desolation, and the hands of the people of the land shall be troubled: I will do unto them after their way, and according to their deserts will I judge them; and they shall know that I am the Lord. (Ezek. 7:25-27)*

Ezekiel related what happened when the Lord showed him visions revealing the abominations of the people:

> *Then said He unto me, Son of man, hast thou seen what the ancients of the house of Israel do in the dark, every man in the chambers of his imagination? For they say, The Lord seeth us not; the Lord hath forsaken the earth. Therefore will I also deal in fury: mine eye shall not spare, neither will I have pity: and though they cry in mine ears with a loud voice, yet will I not hear them. (Ezek. 8:12,18)*

He then promised to gather those of the exile from the countries where they had been scattered, remove

---

[229] Ezek. 6:11.

all detestable abominations from them, give them one heart, and put a new spirit in them. But He promised those who continued in their old ways that He would recompense their negative ways upon their own heads.[230] Thus the Lord's sorting of His people continued. Those who did His Will were proportionately quickened by His Holy Spirit, preserving them as part of the remnant He would eventually save out; whereas those who chose to remain rebellious were being gradually left behind in their less spiritual states of consciousness. He promised that there would be no more any vain visions nor flattering divinations within the house of Israel, because He would speak, and that the word He spoke would come to pass.[231] And He specified His reasons for the radical changes which were to be inculcated into the terms of His New Covenant:

> *O Israel, thy prophets are like the foxes in the deserts. Therefore, thus saith the Lord God, Because ye have spoken vanity and seen lies, therefore, behold, I am against you, saith the Lord. And mine hand shall be upon the prophets that see vanity, and that divine lies: they shall not be in the assembly of my people, neither shall they be written in the writing of the house of Israel, neither shall they enter into the land of Israel; and ye shall know that I am the Lord God. (Ezek. 13:4, 8-9)*

What stands out in these passages is that the Lord was constantly sorting His sheep: separating the prophets who spoke the truth from those who did not. Lacking a sufficiency of the Lord's Spirit, they were too often under the mis-impression they were

---

[230] Ezek. 11:17-21.

[231] Ezek. 12:24-25.

in touch with GOD. But they were in fact too often unknowingly transmitting to others what they received from other gods and the spirits that spoke to them when they sought information incautiously. They were often prophesying the product of their own imaginations — or even worse the thoughts of the Devil.[232] As a result, discernment between negative and positive spirit transmissions was of crucial importance: the Devil Himself could speak to them and they were unaware of the difference. And because their spiritual condition depended upon the extent to which they were able to acquire GOD's Holy Spirit to quicken them, and because they were unable to acquire IT except they would believe in Him and fulfill His Will before their own, the matter became a two-edged sword to them. It was becoming clearer that the Old Covenant was failing.

The New Covenant The Lord contemplated when Prophet Ezekiel wrote would remove all need for the use of information conveyed by human individuals whose levels of spirituality spanned a broad spectrum from negative to positive. The Lord through Prophet Ezekiel thus disclosed the reasons why He would turn over Israel as with a plow, removing His people from their reliance upon those who prophesied concerning Jerusalem, and who saw visions of peace for her when in fact there was no peace in sight at that time:[233]

> *Because with lies ye have made the heart of the righteous sad, whom I have not made sad; and*

---

[232] Cf. 2 Cor. 11:14, which conveys Apostle Paul's teaching: *"For such are false Apostles, deceitful workers transforming themselves into the Apostles of Christ. And no marvel, for Satan himself is transformed into an angel of light."*

[233] Ezek. 13:16.

> *strengthened the hands of the wicked, that he should not return from his wicked way, by promising him life: therefore ye shall see no more vanity, no divine divinations: for I will deliver my people out of your hand: and ye shall know that I am the Lord. (Ezek. 13:22-23)*

The New Covenant was taking shape. The Lord would deliver the people of Israel from the influences of false prophets and priests who did not have the Spirit of GOD in them. He was continually striving to spiritually quicken His sheep, maintaining them in a fit condition that He could one day bring them all into a single heavenly fold [234] Ezekiel was admonished by the Lord that men in every land needed to be extremely careful not to trespass against Him grievously, because if they did:

> *Then will I stretch out mine hand upon it, and will break the staff of the bread thereof, and will send famine upon it, and will cut off man and beast from it. (Ezek. 14:13)*

The Lord who gave this warning long ago through Prophet Ezekiel to the people of Israel is the same Lord the Son of GOD whose Holy Spirit is represented by the Holy Bread of life and light by which

---

[234] In John 10:16 Jesus declares, *"And other sheep I have, which are not of this fold: them also I must bring, and they shall hear my voice; and there shall be one fold, and one shepherd."* By this He referred to the Gentiles, whom He was also to bring. Apostle Paul later explained: *"For as many of you as have been baptized into Christ have put on Christ. There is neither Jew nor Greek, there is neither bond or free, there is neither male nor female: for ye all are one in Jesus Christ. And if ye be Christ's, then are ye Abraham's seed, and heirs according to the promise."* (Gal. 3:27-29)

souls are quickened into immortality. It was earthly manna which sustained the people of Israel during their Exodus: but souls are saved by the spiritual bread of Jesus Christ's flesh given in sacrifice, as symbolized in the Holy Sacrament, the Eucharist.[235]

When Jesus correlated His Two Commandments with all the law and with the prophets,[236] He in effect correlated principles of the Mosaic Law with those of His Law, which was GOD's Law. He codified the law under which the Hebrews had been bound, and concentrated it into a new, improved and much more advanced form, and expressed it in His New Covenant. The Law of Moses was a preparation, ineffective for purposes of salvation. No soul is saved by rituals and sacrifices of the blood of animals. The purpose of the Mosaic Law was to set the foundations for a better way predestined to be afterward given to mankind.[237]

The Lord explained[238] the workings of the 3 to 4 generation rule, which He had given to and through Moses,[239] and which was to remain a governing principle under the New Covenant. The Lord decreed that if a man fathers a son who, seeing his father's sins, considers them and elects not to repeat them, that son shall surely live. The soul that sins shall die,

---

[235] Jn. 6:58.

[236] *"Thou shalt love the Lord thy GOD with all thy heart and with all thy soul, and with all thy mind. This is the first and great commandment. And the second is like unto it, Thou shall love they neighbor as thyself. On these two commandments hang all the law and the prophets."* (Mt 22:36-40)

[237] *For the law made nothing perfect, but the bringing in of a better hope did; by the which we draw nigh unto GOD. (Heb. 7:13-28)*

[238] Cf. Ezek. Ch. 18.

but the son shall not bear the iniquity of the father, and neither shall the father bear the iniquity of the son. In each case, the righteousness of the righteous shall be upon him, and the wickedness of the wicked shall be upon him. If the wicked will turn from his sins, and keep the Lord's statutes from that time, and do what is lawful and right, he shall not die — his transgressions shall not be mentioned unto him: in his righteousness that he has done, shall he live.[240] But when a righteous man turns away from his righteousness, and commits iniquity, and dies in them — expires while in that negative state — for his iniquity that he has done shall he die. And when the wicked man turns away from his wickedness that he has committed, and does that which is lawful and right, he shall save his soul alive.[241]

But, the Lord lamented:

> *Yet saith the house of Israel, The way of the Lord is not equal. O house of Israel, are not my ways equal? are not your ways unequal? Therefore I will judge you, every one according to his ways. Repent, and turn yourselves from all your transgressions; so iniquity shall not be your ruin. Cast away from you all your transgressions; and make you a new heart and a new spirit: for why will ye die, O house of*

---

[239] The Lord disclosed His 3 to 4 generation rule to and through Moses in Ex. 20:3-6; Ex. 34:7; Num. 14:18; and Deut. 5:9. The principle as written in Ex. 20:3-6: *"I the Lord thy God am a jealous God, visiting the iniquity of the fathers upon the children unto the third and fourth generation of them that hate me; and showing mercy unto thousands of them that love me, and keep my commandments."*

[240] Ezek. 18:14, 20-22.

[241] Ezek. 18:26-27.

> *Israel? For I have no pleasure in the death of him that dieth, saith the Lord God: wherefore turn yourselves and live. (Ezek. 18:29-32)*

This verse captures the spirit of the Lord's requirements from day one, after man's exile in the earth plane following the fall of Adam and Eve and all who had entered into the earth plane with them. There has never since been a day when good men and women have not been quickened by the Lord's Holy Spirit, or when evil ones did not suffer spiritual losses for the evil they have done.[242] Step by step, life after life, each incarnated soul is to express its desires to move closer to GOD the FATHER, and to Christ the Son, albeit they exist in dimensions unseen by flesh eyes. The main difference between Ezekiel's time and the period since Jesus Christ's Atonement on the Cross, is that souls in the time of the prophets were required to live virtually perfect lives under the Law of Moses. If in any serious way they failed to do so, there was no immediate effective relief for them: they were condemned to return in another body in a subsequent earth experience, and try again to eliminate self-incurred negative stains they had accumulated. An additional problem was that under the Mosaic Law, during each successive earth experience a soul not only might be unable to reduce its karmic burdens, but instead incur more.

Under Jesus Christ's New Covenant, His Grace is made available to those who accept Him as their Savior: provided only they repent their negative ways, forgive all others their trespasses, and then do not return to a negative state. Their <u>karmic obligations are by Grace once and for all removed</u> from their

---
[242] Mt. 18:18.

karmic disposition; which was not possible under the Mosaic Law:

> *For the law was given by Moses, but grace came by Jesus Christ. (Jn. 1:17)*

Without the Lord the Son's Grace, the cycles of reincarnation were all but impossible to avoid, because in each succeeding earth experience souls were still confronted by powerful negative forces they generally found to be still as impossible to overcome as they had in their previous earth lives. By the Lord's Sacrifice on the Cross on behalf of all those who remained as yet insufficiently perfected, those who would obediently follow Him and His New Covenant were no longer under the Law of Moses, but rather, under His Grace.[243] As for those who choose not to believe in Him and follow Him: if Jews, they remain under the Law of Moses if they profess it. Those who remain among the heathen are under no law at all, but are subject to GOD's edict to the Son that He *"break them with a rod of iron, dash them in pieces like a potter's vessel."* [244]

What is seen in Ezekiel's time is that the Lord was preparing those who would set themselves to follow Him and His Will in order that He could proportionately escalate them from their comparatively lower spiritual state toward a higher level of consciousness, while bringing them into a state of At-One-ness with Him, and thus with GOD. It could not be accomplished under the Old Covenant, which relied upon dissonant earth priests and prophets; problems which would be eliminated by the New Covenant, which was individualized to fit each soul, permitting direct

---
[243] Cf. Rom. 5:12-21.
[244] Cf. Psalm 2:7-9.

contact with GOD by the intercession of HIS eternal heavenly Priest, the Son of GOD, established after the order of Melchizedek.[245]

The above quoted verses of Prophet Ezekiel focus on some of the earliest spiritual principles still applicable today under the New Covenant. Those who obey GOD's Will and Christ the Son's Will, doing good on the earth and not evil, are quickened by GOD's Holy Spirit as it has been made available by Christ the Son of GOD. Those who do evil without at some point repenting and changing their ways tend to fall farther back into spiritual darkness life after life on earth, until they learn who their Lord and Maker is, and obey Him and His New Covenant.

Ezekiel recounted that when certain elders came and sat before him to enquire of the Lord, His Word came to the Prophet, admonishing that if the elders had come to enquire of Him, He would not be enquired of by them because of the abominations of their fathers; and He replied in a way that explained in historical terms why He was to bring in His New Covenant:

> *In the day when I chose Israel, and lifted up mine hand unto the seed of the house of Jacob, and made myself known to them in the land of Egypt, saying, I am the Lord your God; in the day when I lifted up mine hand to bring them into a land that I had espied for them, flowing with milk and honey, then said I to them, Cast ye away every man the abominations of his eyes, and defile not yourselves with the idols of Egypt: I am the Lord your God. But they rebelled against me, and would not hearken unto me: they did not every man cast*

---

[245] Cf. Gen. 14:18; Heb. Chh. 7-8.

away the abominations of their eyes, neither did they forsake the idols of Egypt: then I said, I will accomplish my anger against them in the midst of the land of Egypt.[246] *But that my name's sake might not be polluted, I brought them out of the land of Egypt, and brought them into the wilderness. And I gave them my statutes, and shewed them my judgments, which if a man do, he shall even live in them. But the house of Israel rebelled against me in the wilderness: they walked not in my statutes, and they despised my judgments, which if a man shall do, he shall even live in them; and my sabbaths they greatly polluted. But I wrought for my name's sake, that it should not be polluted before the heathen, in whose sight I brought them out. But I said unto their children in the wilderness, Walk not in the statutes of your fathers, neither serve their judgments, nor defile yourselves with their idols. I am the Lord your God; walk in my statutes and keep my judgments and do them. Notwithstanding they rebelled against me . . . and I said I would pour out my fury upon them. Wherefore I gave them also statutes that were not good, and judgments by which they should not live. (Ezek. 20:5-25)*

The Lord sought to preserve His people in a sufficiently spiritualized mode that He could quicken them into higher levels of consciousness. But the way

---

[246] This verse confirms that when Joseph and his brothers were established in Egypt to multiply their numbers, it was mandated by GOD as a form of exile. They were removed from Canaan as Abraham had been shown in a dream they would be (Gen. 15:13); and they later were returned to Canaan from Egypt as Abraham's second dream had foretold (Gen. 15:16).

He had laid down for them actually had little if anything to do with ritualistic animal sacrifices and burnt offerings. He desired that they fulfill GOD's Will, which is also the Son's Will: yet they instead perpetually sought to satisfy their own earthly desires. The result was that their thoughts and actions were subjected to the negative influences of Satan the Devil and his angels, who regard the earth as their own. Thus the Lord spoke through Ezekiel of a new pathway into which He would lead those who would follow Him:

> *I will cause you to pass under the rod, and I will bring you into the bond of the covenant: and I will purge out from you the rebels, and them that transgress against me: I will bring them forth out of the country where they sojourn, and they shall not enter into the land of Israel: and ye shall know that I am the Lord. (Ezek. 20:37-38)*

The Lord here again promised to purge the people; to separate those who would do His Will from those who would not. They would have to "*pass under the rod*" of severe testing in order to delineate those who would follow and obey Him, from those who preferred to do their own will to suit themselves. Those who passed testing would be drawn to His Holy Spirit Mountain at the height of Israel. He would gather all the remainder of the house of Israel to serve Him and He would accept them; albeit He would require their spiritual offerings.[247]

The Lord then foretold through Ezekiel that He would one day make an end to the negative influ-

---

[247] Ezek. 20:38-40; cf. 1 Pet. 2:5.

ences of Satan; the Devil who continually brought chaos into the earth plane:

> *And thou, profane wicked prince of Israel, whose day is come, when iniquity shall have an end, Thus saith the Lord; Remove the diadem, and take off the crown: this shall not be the same; exalt Him that is low, and abase him that is high. I will overturn, overturn, overturn it: and it shall be no more, until He come whose right it is; and I will give it to Him. (Eze. 21:25-27)*

This forecasted that the Lord the Son would manifest in flesh as Jesus of Nazareth in His spiritually perfected state to overcome the Devil, and — having nothing of the Devil's spirit in Him — encourage all who believe in Him and follow Him to have no fear, because He had overcome the temptations of earth for all who would be His.[248]

Ezekiel then expounded upon the Lord's attitude toward Tyrus and His reasons for it[249] including certain details relating to one of the Devil's negative sons in flesh, a king of Tyrus:[250]

> *Son of man, take up a lamentation upon the king of Tyrus, and say unto him, Thus saith the Lord God; Thou sealest up the sum, full of wisdom and perfect in beauty. (Ezek. 28:12)*

The Lord here commanded His Prophet Ezekiel to *take up a lamentation* upon the king of Tyrus, who at that time was a living man on the earth. But although

---
[248] Lk. 4:1-14; Jn. 14:30; 16:33.
[249] Ezek. Chh. 26 to 28.
[250] Cf. Ezek. Chapters 26 - 28.

the message was directed through Ezekiel to the king of Tyrus, the remainder of the Lord's admonishment leaves no doubt but that He referred to Satan's spirit as the controlling mental spiritual influence in the king:

> *Thou hast been in Eden the garden of GOD; every precious stone was thy covering (etc.).* **Thou art the anointed cherub that covereth; and I have set thee so: thou wast upon the (heavenly) holy mountain of GOD;** *thou hast walked up and down in the midst of the stones of fire.* [251] *Thou was perfect in thy ways from the day that thou wast created, till iniquity was found in thee. By the multitude of thy merchandise (i.e. material possessions) they have filled the midst of thee with violence, and thou hast sinned: therefore I will cast thee as profane out of the mountain of GOD:*[252] *and I will destroy thee,* **O covering cherub,** *from the midst of the stones of fire.*[253] *Thine heart was lifted up because of thy beauty, thou hast corrupted thy wisdom by reason of thy brightness: I will cast thee to the ground, I will lay thee before kings, that they may behold thee. Thou has defiled my sanctuaries by the multitude of thy iniquities, by the iniquity of thy traffic; therefore will I bring forth a fire from the midst of thee, it shall devour thee,*

---

[251] Cf. Job 1:7: "*And the Lord said unto Satan, Whence comest thou? Than Satan answered the Lord, and said, From going to and fro in the earth, and from walking up and down in it.*"

[252] This came to pass as Ezekiel foretold at 21:25-27, and as reported at Rev. 12:7-12.

[253] Christ the Son of GOD fulfilled this destruction of the negative powers of Satan the Devil when He incarnated as Jesus of Nazareth and was Crucified on the Cross, as had been foretold of Him at Heb. 2:13-18.

> *and I will bring thee to ashes upon the earth in sight of all them that behold thee.* **And they that know thee among the people**[254] *shall be astonied at thee: thou shalt be a terror, and never shalt thou be any more. (Ezek. 28:13-19)*

From these above verses, it is understood that a soul portion of the spirit of Satan incarnated on the earth as the king of Tyrus in the time when the Lord spoke to and through Prophet Ezekiel; which explains why the Son of GOD so outspokenly addressed that nation and Satan.[255] It is important to keep in mind that the spirit-children of Satan represent those who were born in the generations of Cain and chose to remain negatively inclined. Those who have remained in GOD's Light, known as *"Israel,"* are the children in the spiritual lineage of Jacob — the children GOD gave to the Son — many of whom have opposed Satan from the beginning.[256] Through the centuries untold numbers of the Lord's children have crossed back and forth across the border between good and evil, thereby becoming in effect *mixed seed.* But the Lord has left the door open for any of them to return to Him, as He repeatedly promised through His prophets.

The Lord through Ezekiel emphasized the failure of the Levitical Priests to live up to GOD's requirements.[257] Apostle Paul afterward ascribed this fail-

---

[254] This related to Satan's earth appearances "*among the people*" — he appeared in a number of earth incarnations from the time he was Cain until he was Judas Iscariot in Jesus' time.

[255] Ezekiel Chapters 26-28.

[256] Ex. 17:13-16; Deut.32:3-9; John 8:31-47.

[257] Cf. Ezek. Chh. 22, 24 to 32 and 34 to 37.

ure to human nature, explaining that high priests selected by man are ordained in things pertaining to GOD to offer gifts and sacrifices to GOD — to have compassion for those who have ignorantly gone off the way — but they themselves are compassed with infirmity.[258] Accordingly, a people reliant upon temporal human priests as their source of purification — priests whose spiritual state is susceptible to negative intrusions — risk being cut off from GOD's Holy Spirit. Therefore, when Christ the Son was ordained as man's eternal heavenly Priest, for those who would accept Him and His New Covenant doctrine, there was no longer a need for reliance upon imperfect human priests susceptible to negative intrusions.[259] In accordance with that principle, Ezekiel detailed some of the Lord's reasons for His dissatisfaction with those who were at that time shepherding His chosen people of Israel, and by implication indicating why He was planning to bring in His New Covenant to replace the old one:

> *Son of man, prophesy against the shepherds of Israel, prophecy, and say unto them, Thus saith the Lord unto the shepherds; woe be to the shepherds of Israel that do feed themselves! should not the shepherds feed the flocks? (Ezek. 34:2)*

He accused the priests of having permitted His sheep to be scattered, alleging that they took the best for themselves while not looking out for His flock;

---

[258] Heb. 5:1-3.

[259] The matter is summed up in the single verse Heb. 7:25. Referring to Jesus Christ, it is written: *"Wherefore He is able also to save them to the uttermost that come unto GOD by Him, seeing He ever lives to make intercession for them"* (Cf. 1 Tim. 2:1-6; Heb. 9:15-24; Heb. 10:11-14).

and they failed to strengthen the diseased or heal the sick, and had not retrieved those sheep which had been scattered and lost.[260] The Lord then foreshadowed a time when earth priests would no longer be needed or appropriate:

> *Thus saith the Lord God; Behold, I am against the shepherds; and I will require my flock at their hand, and **cause them to cease from feeding the flock**; neither shall the shepherds feed themselves any more: for I will deliver my flock from their mouth, that they may not be meat for them. For thus saith the Lord, I, even I, will both search my sheep, and seek them out. As a shepherd that seeketh out his flock **in the day that he is among his sheep that are scattered; so will I seek out my sheep**, and will deliver them out of all places where they have been scattered in the cloudy and dark day. (Ezek. 34:10-12)*

This virtually spelled doom for the Levitical Priesthood, which would be replaced by GOD's ordination of One Eternal heavenly Priest on the Order of Melchizedek.[261] It applied to the time to come when the Lord the Son of GOD would Himself incarnate in flesh as Jesus of Nazareth to gather His sheep. As foretold through Prophet Ezekiel in the above quoted verses, the Lord foretold that He would gather His people, His sheep, from the countries where they had been scattered. Ezekiel[262] refers to those who were to safely return from the seventy-year exile, whom the Lord would bring out from the

---

[260] Ezek. 34:3-6.

[261] Heb. Chh. 5 to 10; and esp. Heb. Chapter Seven, and Ps. 110:1,4-6.

[262] Ezek. 34:13.

people and gather them again in Jerusalem. But the next verse speaks of high mountains, an allusion to the Holy Mount in Heaven:

> *I will feed them in a good pasture, and upon the high mountains of Israel shall their fold be: there shall they lie in a good fold, and in a fat pasture shall they feed upon the mountains of Israel. I will feed my flock, and I will cause them to lie down, saith the Lord GOD. (Ezek. 34:14-15)*

The Lord the Son then reiterated that He Himself would seek that which was lost and bring again that which was driven away, bind up that which was broken, and strengthen that which was sick. On the other hand, He promised to destroy the fat and the strong; to feed them with judgment,[263] thereby placing another plank in The Way He was preparing for the New Covenant He would bring in hundreds of years later. He promised to judge between the fat cattle and the lean cattle, and to save His flock so they would no longer be a prey to iniquity.[264] He further described the terms of His futuristic New Covenant:

> *And I will make with them a covenant of peace, and will cause the evil beasts to cease out of the land: and they shall dwell safely in the wilderness, and sleep in the woods. And I will make them and the places round about my hill a blessing; and I will cause the shower to come down in his season; there shall be showers of blessing. And the tree of the field shall yield her fruit, and the earth shall yield her increase, and they shall be safe in their land, and shall know that I am the Lord, when I have broken*

---

[263] Ezek. 34:16.
[264] Ezek. 34:16-22.

> *the bands of their yoke, and delivered them out of the hand of those that served themselves of them.*[265] *And they shall no more be a prey to the heathen, neither shall the beast of the land devour them; but they shall dwell safely, and none shall be afraid . . . neither shall they bear the shame of the heathen any more. Thus shall they know that I the Lord their God am with them, and that they, even the house of Israel, are my people, saith the Lord God. And ye my flock, the flock of my pasture, are men, and I am your God, saith the Lord God. (Ezek. 34:26-31)*

The Lord then further described to Ezekiel the spiritual cleansing effects of His New Covenant:

> *I will take you from among the heathen, and gather you out of all countries, and will bring you into your own land. Then I will sprinkle clean water upon you and ye shall be clean: from all your filthiness, and from all your idols will I cleanse you. A new heart also will I give you, and a new spirit will I put within you: and I will take away the stony heart out of your flesh, and I will give you an heart of flesh. And I will put my spirit within you,*[266] *and cause you to walk in my statutes, and ye shall keep my judgments, and do them. (Ezek. 36:24-27)*

---

[265] This is an example of how biblical passages often apply simultaneously to the earth plane and to the spirit dimensions. The Lord promised to break the bands of the yoke of Israel from those unspiritual priests and prophets who victimized them on earth: and at the same He promised to break the negative spiritual bands which trapped them in the earth plane, caught like flies on flypaper in the Devil-imposed cycles of reincarnation.

[266] Suggested here are aspects of the New Covenant foreseen by Prophet Jeremiah at 31:31-34.

Then the Lord described the secure ties by which He would one day bind the people of Israel to the New Covenant, even hinting of the process of reincarnation in a way that people of that time might comprehend its basic principles. The hand of the Lord carried Ezekiel in the Lord's Spirit, and set him down in the midst of a valley full of bones, which he caused the prophet to pass by and view. He asked Ezekiel if those bones could live, to which Ezekiel answered that the Lord knew. The Lord then said to those bones:

> *Behold, I will cause breath to enter into you, and ye shall live. And I will lay sinews upon you, and will bring up flesh upon you, and cover you with skin, and put breath in you, and ye shall live: I will put breath in you, and ye shall live. (Ezek. 37:5-6)*

A shaking then took place, and Ezekiel beheld the bones coming together with flesh and skin on them but there was no breath in them.[267] The Lord then commanded Ezkiel to say to the wind:

> *Thus saith the Lord God: Come from the four winds, O breath, and breathe upon these slain, that they may live. So I prophesied as He commanded me, and breath came into them, and they lived, and stood upon their feet, an exceeding great army.*[268]

---

[267] Ezek. 37:8.

[268] Cf. Rev. 11:11-12: *And after three days and a half the spirit of life from GOD entered into them, and they stood upon their feet; and great fear fell upon them which saw them. And they heard a great voice from heaven saying unto them, Come up hither. And they ascended up to heaven in a cloud; and their enemies beheld them.* Prophet Ezekiel had been shown that those of the Lord's, although dead in the flesh, would be raised up in spirit on that last day (Rev. 7:14-17; Jn. 6:38-54).

> *Then He said unto me, Son of man, these bones are the whole house of Israel: behold, they say, our bones are dried, and our hope is lost: we are cut off for (from) our parts. Then, thus saith the Lord, I will open your graves, and cause you to come up out of your graves, and bring you into the land of Israel . . . I shall put my spirit in you, and ye shall live, and I shall place you in your own land: then shall ye know that I the Lord have spoken it, and performed it, saith the Lord. (Ezek. 37:9-14)*

In these verses the Lord foretold that the people of Israel were to one day return in flesh, which, as later discussed, they did.[269] In the end time, *Israel* is not to be comprised solely of those Jews who have through the centuries incarnated and reincarnated with those who hold to their belief in the Mosaic Law of the First Covenant. The Bible instructs that those *of Israel* are, and will be, those who have done GOD's Will, and the Will of the Son HE Chose above all other heavenly sons. Those who understand laws governing reincarnation are better able to perceive that all souls have made their way through many earth incarnations. For example, some who were Egyptians later converted and became Jews when they manifested during the Hebraic Age. Later many reentered into flesh in the earth plane in Muslim, Buddhist and other families and set out following the teachers and prophets of their choice. Still others, even among Jews who converted from their deeply entrenched Mosaic Law, became devout followers of Jesus Christ.

The Lord disclosed to Prophet Ezekiel that His New Covenant would bring together the tribes of Israel, merging them into a single congregation composed

---

[269] This prophecy correlates with Mal. 3:16-18.

of all who would follow Him as true sheep of His flock. These would willingly join with others seeking spiritual attunement with one another, so all those who followed the Lord the Son would be bundled together:

> *Moreover, thou son of man, take thee one stick, and write upon it, For Judah, and for the children of Israel his companions: then take another stick and write upon it, For Joseph, the stick of Ephraiam, and for all the house of Israel his companions. And join them one to another into one stick; and they shall become one in thine hand. (Ezek. 37:16-17)*

> *Behold, I will take the stick of Joseph, which is in the hand of Ephraim,[270] and the tribe of Israel his fellows, and will put them with him, even with the stick of Judah, and make them one stick, and they shall be one in mine hand. (Ezek. 37:19)*

The Prophet was given certain instructions he was to convey to the people of Israel:

> *Behold I will take the children of Israel from among the heathen, whither they be gone, and will gather*

---

[270] Gen. 48:5 reveals that when Jacob blessed his children, he adopted Joseph's two sons Ephraim and Manasseh, and set them above his own first two sons Reuben and Simeon, whose ways had been seriously afflicted by Satan as described in the Book of Genesis. When Joseph placed his right hand on Ephraim's head, and his left hand on Manasseh's head, Joseph complained because Manasseh had been firstborn and according to Hebraic Law he was to hold the birthright. But Jacob declined to change his decision, instead advising Joseph that although the descendants of both sons would become great nations, Ephraim would exceed his brother (Gen. 48:8-20).

> them on every side, and bring them into their own land, and I will make them one nation in the land upon the mountains of Israel; and one king shall be king to them all.[271] and they shall no longer be two nations, neither shall they be divided into two kingdoms any more at all. And David my servant shall be king over them; and they shall have one shepherd: they shall walk in my judgments, and observe my statutes, and do them. And they shall dwell in the land that I have given unto Jacob my servant, wherein your fathers have dwelt; and they shall dwell therein, even they and their children, and their children's children for ever: and my servant David shall be their prince forever. Moreover **I will make a covenant of peace with them; it shall be an everlasting covenant with them:** and I will place them, and multiply them, and will set my sanctuary in the midst of them for evermore. **My tabernacle also shall be with them**: yea, I will be their God, and they shall be my people. And the heathen shall know that I the Lord do sanctify Israel when my sanctuary shall be in the midst of them for evermore. (Ezek. 37:21-27)

In these verses the Lord speaks of a change from the earthly tabernacle to a heavenly one: as explained in the Book of Hebrews, the sanctuary will no longer be found in earth temples. These verses also refer to the new heavens and earth the Lord promised through Prophet Isaiah He would create to replace the former; which will not be remembered, nor even come to mind.[272]

> But **Christ being come an high priest** of good things to come by **a greater and more perfect**

---

[271] This referred to Jesus Christ, as confirmed in such biblical verses as Mt. 21:4:-9. Cf. Zech. 9:9.

[272] Is. 65:17.

> ***tabernacle***, *not made with hands, that is to say, not of this building. . . . And for this cause he is the mediator of the new testament, that by means of death, for the redemption of the transgressions that were under the first testament, they which are called might receive the promise of eternal inheritance. (Heb. 9:11-15)*

The clock was ticking toward the time for the New Covenant to be activated. In the interim the rituals and practices of Jews continued, destined to be maintained for a while. In the twenty-fifth year of the Babylonian exile,[273] the Lord showed Ezekiel visions of His plan for the City He had in mind to be built. It obviously did not describe the Eternal Heavenly New Jerusalem, because no sacrifices are to be conducted in that Heavenly Place, of which GOD and Christ the Son the Lamb of GOD are the Light.[274] Ezekiel was shown the plan for the temple which was to be reconstructed in Jerusalem under the leadership of Zerubbabel and Jeshua son of Josedech when there would be the momentous return to Jerusalem.[275] The city had been overcome and put to the torch, left desolate and spiritually fallow during Israel's seventy-year exile in Babylon. The Lord then spoke to Ezekiel of the *Heavenly* New Jerusalem, described by the Prophet:

> *He brought me back to the way of the gate of the outward sanctuary, which faced the east, and was shut, and was to be kept shut because the Lord the God of Israel had entered by it. It is for the prince, the prince, He shall sit in it to eat bread before the Lord; He shall enter by the way of the*

---

[273] Ezek. 40:1.

[274] Rev. 21:22-23.

[275] Ezek. Chapters 40-43.

porch of that gate, and shall go out by the way of the same. (Ezek. 44:1-3)

The Son of GOD was the Prince of Israel written of by Prophet Daniel.[276] When it was written, *supra,* that the Lord God of Israel had entered into the Heavenly City by the east gate, it foretold that the Son of GOD as the risen Christ would enter in by the porch of that east gate to eat bread (i.e. spiritual bread) before GOD the FATHER, as was later confirmed in the Book of Hebrews [277] as having taken place. As for the New Jerusalem, the spiritually corrupted were forbidden from entering that spiritual sanctuary.[278] The Lord brought the Prophet again to the door of the Spiritual House, the New Jerusalem, from which waters issued out from under the threshold toward the east, from the **right** side of the House, it being understood that water represents Spirit. After describing how His Spirit would have fruitful effects

---

[276] Dan. 10:13 reveals that Michael, one of the chief princes (at that time), came to help Beloved Gabriel in his efforts to overcome the prince of Persia. Dan. 10:21 discloses that the only one who knew and shared the deeper spiritual truths with Gabriel was Michael, who was (at that time) Israel's prince.

[277] Heb. 9:24 discloses: *"For Christ is not entered into the holy places made with hands, which are the figures of the true; but into heaven itself, now to appear in the presence of God for us."* Heb. 6:18-20 states that we may lay hold on the hope set before us: which hope we have as an anchor of the soul, both sure and steadfast, and which entereth into that within the veil; whither the forerunner is for us entered, even Jesus; made an high priest forever after the order of Melchizedek. (Cf. Heb. 7:9-28 and Heb. 10:11-20; and note Ps. 110:1,4-6)

[278] Ezek. 44:6-9; 1 Cor. 15:50.

upon this Heavenly place, the Lord ordered that it be divided by lot according to the twelve tribes of Israel.[279] But He added a codicil of crucial importance to those mixed spiritual seed on the earth who would afterward find and follow the Lord the Son:

> *And it shall come to pass, that ye shall divide it by lot for an inheritance unto you,* **and to the strangers that sojourn among you,** *which shall beget children among you: and they shall be unto you as born in the country among the children of Israel;* **they shall have inheritance with you among the tribes of Israel.** [280] *And* **it shall come to pass that in what tribe the stranger sojourneth, there shall ye give him his inheritance,** *saith the Lord God. (Ezek. 47:22-23)*

This command by the Lord foretold that a time would come when space was to be made available in heaven for everyone on earth who would fulfill His requirements. Positions in His heavenly hierarchy were, under His New Covenant, to be granted according to the

---

[279] Ezek. 48:29.

[280] Cf. Eph. 3:3-7 in which Apostle Paul, who received the Lord's Truth directly (Gal. 1:11-12), and disclosed: *"How by revelation He made known unto me the mystery; Whereby when ye read ye may understand my knowledge in the mystery of Christ,* **which in other ages was not made known unto the sons of men,** *as it is now revealed unto His Holy Apostles and Prophets by the Spirit: That the Gentiles should be fellow heirs, and of the same (i.e. Spirit) body, and partakers of HIS promise in Christ by the Gospel: Whereof I was made a minister, according to the gift given unto me by the effectual working of His Power."* Paul's spiritual enlightenment came as the result of the promise Jesus had made, reported in Jn. 14:15-17;26; 15:26; and 16:7,12-15.

works of each individual whether they had formerly been a Jew, Gentile or heathen.[281] As will be seen, principles of reincarnation were to play a critically important role in what took place when *Shiloh* appeared. As the prophets continued to receive further information relating to the New Covenant, a clearer outline of its pattern and purpose began to emerge.

The names of the Twelve tribes and their leaders and the heavenly areas to be granted to them, as understood at that time, were revealed to Ezekiel.[282] The Lord revealed the location of each of the heavenly gates constructed as entries into the New Jerusalem. Twelve gates were built, one for each of the twelve tribes. Those Gentiles whom the Lord the Son saw fit to quicken by His Holy Spirit were to be granted heavenly space, some in a surprising way only to be revealed when the New Covenant was brought in. The three heavenly gates looking to the north were to be those of Reuben, Judah and Levi.[283] At the south side of the heavenly city the gates of: Simeon, Issachar and Zebulon. On the west side the gates of: Gad, Asher and Naphtali. On the east side the gates of: Joseph, Benjamin and Dan. As will be seen, this arrangement was subject to change as the centuries passed and each individual who played roles in the developing heavenly scenario accomplished, or failed to accomplish, what the Lord asked of those who were His.

---

[281] Cf. Gal. 3:8: *"And the scripture, forseeing that God would justify the heathen through faith, preached before the gospel unto Abraham, saying, In thee shall all nations be blessed."*

[282] Ezek. Ch. 48.

[283] Ezek. 48:31.

Ezekiel's prophesies were illuminating and revelatory in many respects, as was borne out by events that took place after his time. His book closes with a verse which confirms that the gates he described apply to the eternal heavenly New Jerusalem:

> *It was round about eighteen thousand measures: and the name of the city from that day shall be, The Lord is there. (Ezek. 48:35)*

—CHAPTER FOUR—
PROPHET DANIEL

Daniel understood the meaning of visions and dreams, indicating that he had already attained to a comparatively high spiritual state as the result of some excellent previous earth experiences. The Lord was thus able to communicate with him by way of visions to divulge prophetic events which were predestined to come. Of particular importance is Daniel's vision of the latter days as a period during which souls will be purified by GOD's Holy Spirit made available by the Son of GOD[284] in accordance with His New Covenant; as foretold in Jeremiah 31:31-34.

During the second year of Nebuchadnezzar's rule, the king began to experience disturbing dreams of an ominous nature. Jeremiah had reported that Nebuchadnezzar was the Lord's servant;[285] but the Bible records that the kings's manner and ways had become negative, and it was being reflected in the character of his dreams. Though the king recalled that he had experienced one particular dream, he could not recall any of its details. He called in his magicians, astrologers and sorcerers

---

[284] Jn. 14:26; Jn.16:12-15.
[285] Jer. 27:6-10.

to interpret it because he found it especially disturbing to his spirit.[286] As a man of great power, he admonished them that if they were unable to recount his dream he would find it expedient to have them cut in pieces and their houses converted into dunghills;[287] a threat bearing incredibly alarming prospects. It is often difficult for a man to recall specific dreams of his own, much less bring to his mind the dreams of others. The king, however, thoughtfully promised that if anyone was able to recount the dream for him, and interpret it, royal favors would be heaped upon him. This doubtless left the Chaldean seers in a state of shock. Contemplation of the reward was fine, but they earnestly entreated the king to consider that no king or ruler ever asked such things of a magician or astrologer because no man on earth is able to accomplish it — that only gods could do such things, and gods do not dwell in flesh.[288]

This development was not met with kindly feelings by the king, who ruled with great power and authority, and was unaccustomed to receiving such incompetent responses to his demands. Agitated into a state of fury, he deemed it expedient to destroy all the wise men of Babylon; among whom was Daniel. But even as the king's men set about their mission of exacting the lives of these unfortunate seers, Daniel remained unperturbed. He retired to his house and entreated his three companions to seek the mercies of GOD in heaven concerning this perilous situation that they might

---

[286] Dan. 2:1-3.

[287] Dan. 2:1-5.

[288] Dan. 2:6-11.

[289] Dan. 2:11-18.

not perish along with all the other wise men of Babylon.[289] Then the secret of the king's dream was revealed to Daniel in a night vision, and he blessed GOD in considerable detail. He proceeded without delay to request an audience with the king, and, it having been granted, sagely advised him that only God in heaven is able to reveal the meaning of such secretive mysterious matters.[290] Daniel was then able to disclose to the king details of his dream, and the meaning of it; which overwhelmed his royalty. Nebuchadnezzar then made Daniel a great man, not only pressing upon him many gifts, but also establishing him ruler over the whole of Babylonia, not to mention chief of the governors over all the wise men of his realm.[291]

Daniel's interpretation of the king's dream demonstrated his spiritual acumen as a prophet whom the Lord selected to reveal details of events which would ultimately lead to the establishment of a new heavenly kingdom:

> *And in the days of these kings shall the God of heaven set up **a kingdom, which shall never be destroyed**: and the kingdom shall not be left to other people but it shall break in pieces and consume all these kingdoms, and **it shall stand forever**. (Dan 2:44)*

This foretold that a day was to come when the New Covenant to afterward be brought in, as foretold by Prophet Jeremiah, would lead to the establishment of an eternal heavenly kingdom.

---

[290] Dan. 2:19-28.
[291] Dan. 2:31-49.

As a chosen prophet of GOD, Daniel would subsequently undergo trials which would demonstrate that His continuing faith protected him from negative forces. For example, when it was reported to the king that three of Daniel's acquaintances, Shadrach, Meshach and Abednego, were refusing to worship a golden idol his majesty had set up, he considered their abject refusal to obey his order such an abomination that he promptly fell into another rage. He had personally selected that idol, and commanded that anyone who failed to worship it would be cast into a furnace to be reduced to ashes. It was a royal decree, for which reason he adamantly declined to alter it. It turned out to be another test of faith and belief to be confronted and overcome by the three unfortunates. They were forthwith cast into a fire, which the king, not taking any chances, had thoughtfully ordered heated seven times hotter than its usual temperature. After this had been fulfilled, the king took a look at the results, and could not believe what his eyes were seeing. Incredulous, he asked whether or not he had in fact commanded that these servants be cast into the fire, and was assured that he had:

> *He answered, and said, Lo, I see four men loose, walking in the midst of the fire, and they have no hurt; and the form of the fourth is like the Son of God. (Dan. 3:25)*

When the men emerged from the furnace unscorched by the heat, the king was more than a little impressed. He ordered that the three were no longer required to serve nor worship any god other than their own; but Nebuchadnezzar's time was limited as Daniel learned when a voice was heard from heaven declaring that the kingdom was departed from him.[292]

Another example of Daniel's spiritual abilities was demonstrated during a great feast when Nebuchadnezzar saw handwriting on the wall. It caused his countenance to change and he once again called aloud for his astrologers and soothsayers, ordering them to decipher the writing for him, again promising great rewards for a correct interpretation. The queen spoke up to remind the king that Daniel had an excellent spirit, knowledge, understanding and interpretations of dreams. Daniel was of course once again brought forth, and he interpreted the words of the handwriting on the wall. *MENE*, he explained, meant that God had numbered Nebuchadnezzar's kingdom, and finished it. The word **TEKEL** meant that the king had been weighed in the balance and was found wanting. And *PERES* meant his kingdom was to be divided and given to the Medes and Persians.[293]

When Darius, King Nebuchadnezzar's successor came into power Daniel was again tested. He was

---

[292] Dan. 3:28-29. Dan 4:1-32 explains that King Nebuchadnezzar was to be punished for relying upon his own royal position while overlooking the more exalted powers of the Lord upon whom he actually depended; the Lord who had made it possible for the king to successfully overcome the people of Israel, and exile them seventy years in Babylon. Dan. 4:33-35 relates that at the end of his travail the king changed his ways, conceding, among other things, that *"... all the inhabitants of the earth are reputed as nothing..."*

[293] Dan. 5:25-28.

cast into a den of lions, from which peril he once again emerged unscathed.[294] It was being made patently clear that the prophet's unflinching belief, trust and faith in God was shielding him from the disastrous spiritual afflictions of Satan, whose negative force continued to wreak destruction upon man. At the same time, the intrepid Daniel's ability to be in touch with the Lord's Spirit in vastly higher planes than earth was standing him in good stead, and because of His total belief in GOD he was able to receive remarkably accurate dreams and visions. And his experiences were demonstrating the remarkable spirituality of Daniel in ways which would build up his confidence that what the Lord was speaking through him was accurate and reliable.

The Lord revealed through Daniel one of the most illuminating of the Hebrew Bible's forecasts of the First Coming of the Son of GOD, incarnated as Jesus Christ. After a number of dreams and visions,[295] Daniel saw yet another vision foretelling an extraordinary event which was to come:

> *I beheld till the thrones were cast down, and the Ancient of Days did sit, whose garment was white as snow, and the hair of HIS head like the pure wool: HIS throne was like the fiery flame, and HIS wheels as burning fire.*[296] *A fiery stream issued and came forth from before HIM: thousand thousands ministered unto HIM and ten thousand times ten thou-*

---

[294] Dan. 6:7-24.

[295] Dan. 7:1-8.

[296] Cf. Ezek. 1:15; which suggests that the figure speaking to Daniel was the same God who spoke to Noah (Gen. 9:11-16). And cf. Rev. 20:4, which is linked to the thrones envisioned by Daniel in Dan. 7:9.

> *sand stood before HIM: the judgment was set, and the books were opened. (Dan. 7:9-10)*

These above verses describe GOD seated on HIS Heavenly Throne at the time of Judgment, HIS ministering angels all around HIM. But as foreshadowed in the above verses, HE would not conduct judgment HIMSELF: HE would appoint the Son HE had chosen to fulfill it. At that time, Satan was covering angel over the earth, as previously discussed, and Daniel was shown what was to become of him and his angels:

> *I beheld then because of the great words which the horn spake: I beheld even till the beast was slain, and his body destroyed, and given to the burning flame. As concerning the rest of the beasts, they had their dominion taken away: yet their lives were prolonged for a season and a time. (Dan. 7:11-12)*

This *"horn"* that spoke to Daniel revealed that the Beast (Satan) was to be destroyed. This comports with Heb. 2:13-18 and other New Testament verses leaving no doubt but that the one-time sacrifice of Jesus Christ the Son was to ultimately terminate the Devil's influences in the earth. However, Daniel received word that the lives of the negative angels were to be preserved for a season and a time: a *"time"* being a thousand years on the earth[297] and a *"season"* a comparatively brief period. This agrees with other predictions subsequently written in the Bible. The Millennium of the First Resurrection, revealed in The Revelation,[298] foretells that a thousand years will follow the Lord's return to take dominion, during which the influence of Satan and his angels will be removed

---
[297] Ps. 90:4.
[298] Rev. 20:1-6

from the earth. Having already been confined to the earth by Michael and His Angels, they are to be removed even from the earth plane for a thousand years.[299] Yet as Daniel was shown, and as confirmed in The Revelation, their lives are to be prolonged for a season and a time.[300]

Daniel continued to receive a forecast of what is to transpire when the Ancient of days sits, the Judgment is set, and the heavenly books described in the Bible[301] are opened:

> *I saw in the night visions, and, behold, one like the Son of man came with the clouds in heaven, and came to the Ancient of days, and they brought Him near before HIM. And there was given Him dominion, and glory, and a kingdom that all people, nations, and languages should serve Him: His dominion is an everlasting dominion, which shall not pass away, and His kingdom that which shall not be destroyed. (Dan. 7:13-14)*

The heavenly figure referred to above is of course the Son of GOD to whom GOD has given HIS Holy Spirit without measure, and empowered to conduct Judgment.[302] Christ's heavenly kingdom is to be eternal and everlasting: the new heavens and earth which He has prepared for all who are His, as before related. The people in the house of Jacob were inexorably moving forward generation after generation as a core of all the souls incarnated on earth. They were continuously afflicted by Satan and his angels who

---

[299] Rev. 12:7-12; 20:1-6.
[300] Dan. 7:12; Rev. 20:7-8.
[301] Mal. 3:16; Rev. 20:15; 21:27.
[302] Jn. 3:34; 5:21-23.

sought to derail the Lord's sheep from their heavenly pathway. The people of Israel were being sifted as wheat for the very reason that they afforded the spearhead of the earth's population striving to find their way back into the heavenly dimensions from which they had long before strayed.[303] Every step of the way the Lord was shepherding those who were, or would become, His sheep.

It is clear from the above verses that the people of Israel during the Hebraic Age generally ranked above the level of spiritual knowledge and understanding of the earth's population at that time. Their spirit force was the result of the 3 to 4 generation spiritual escalation started in Abraham and Sarah, gaining further through Isaac and Rebekah, and becoming an exalted force in Jacob, Rachel and Leah.[304] They were to carry forward their spiritual condition, multiplying on the earth to provide flesh vessels into which increasing numbers of developing spirits would be able to incarnate. The reason why the Lord spoke

---

[303] Cf. Amos 9:9-10 and Mt. 3:11-12: the whole of Israel has been, and is still being, sifted, and the good grains sorted out and preserved in the place Christ the Lord the Son of GOD is preparing for those who are his (Jn. 14:1-4). The process has been ongoing since the Son of GOD, after His fall as Adam, returned as Enoch and set about Making The Way Passable into Heaven for all who had fallen, or ever would fall. It is through the workings of the reincarnation process by which those who — like Apostle Paul — had once been dedicated Jews, see the Light of GOD and Christ, and convert from the Old Testament (which has faded away, Heb. 8:13) to the New Covenant the Lord foretold through Prophet Jeremiah at 31:31-34.

[304] Ruth 4:11.

so firmly by and through His prophets was that He observed in all ages that His people were frequently slow to invoke their belief and trust in Him, and to obey Him. He continually admonished them to discern good from evil and do good, promising to forgive the sins of those who would do so, but the process was constantly disrupted because of human frailty, plus the power of Satanic spirits ever trying to block their way.

The Old Covenant and the Mosaic Law were designed to facilitate man's spiritual escalation, but in time it proved to be no longer a viable vehicle. The Lord through His prophets continually warned His people that too many misguided individuals were taking it upon themselves to assume the mantle of prophets and priests in their own right, mistakenly believing the Lord was speaking through them when in fact they did not have the Lord's truth in them at all. The Hebraic Age then gradually began to grind to a halt, having outgrown its usefulness. The only secure way to sustain the spiritualizing process was by way of a New Covenant.

Some of the spiritual insights the Lord conveyed to Prophet Daniel had not before been known or recorded on the earth; in particular what was to take place under the New Covenant. For example, Daniel was advised that the Son of man — the Son of GOD — was to be granted jurisdiction and everlasting dominion over a kingdom in which all people, nations, and languages should serve Him. He was shown that in the future certain negative individuals, referred to as beasts, would arise in the earth; but that despite them the saints would take the kingdom and possess it forever. Daniel was told that another more formidable beast with great power, different from the others, would arise and make war against the saints. The Lord would prevail against them until the *"Ancient of days"* would award judgment to the saints of the most High GOD, after which they would possess the kingdom. One particular beast would come and wear out the saints of the most High,[305] trying to change times and laws, and the saints would be given unto this negative one's hand for a time, times and half a time. But, Daniel was told, the judgment *"shall sit,"* the saints predestined to take away the Devil's dominion and consume it and destroy it [306] In summation Daniel was told:

> *And the kingdom and dominion, and the greatness of the kingdom under the whole heaven, shall be given to the people of the saints of the most High, whose kingdom is an everlasting kingdom, and all dominions shall serve and obey him. (Dan. 7:27)*

The thrust of these above verses is that the Lord revealed in general terms to Prophet Daniel — for the most part through the Archangel Gabriel — long before it transpired that the Son of GOD manifested in flesh would sacrifice Himself on the Cross, and be transformed by GOD's Holy Spirit and translated to GOD's Right Hand in Heaven. There He would be empowered to perform Judgment for GOD: to act for GOD in all matters according to GOD's Will.[307] All this and more was outlined to Prophet Daniel long before it was time for it to come to pass.

---

[305] Cf. Apostle Paul's teaching of the inevitability of this event (2 Thess. Ch. 2).
[306] Dan. 7:17-26.
[307] 1 Pet. 3:18; Jn. 3:34; 5:21-23.

The remarkable revelations given to and through Daniel were not yet finished. When he saw certain visions[308] he was confused, unable to understand their meaning. When he sought to comprehend them, an even higher spirit source than the Archangel Gabriel supervened, and commanded Gabriel that he should make Daniel understand the visions he had been unable to interpret. Gabriel then advised Daniel that the visions he had seen applied to "*the time of the* end,"[309] and that he, Gabriel, would make him to understand "*what was to be in the last part of the indignation.*"[310] He left no doubt but that the end would come at the time appointed. Thus mankind was warned that a certain time has been allotted for earthbound souls to seek the Lord's redemption: to overcome evil while continually striving to attain to as spiritually perfected a condition as possible. The Lord Himself as Jesus of Nazareth would long after repeat this instruction through The Revelation given to Apostle John.[311] The Archangel Gabriel then proceeded to detail to Daniel the

---

[308] Dan. 8:1-14.

[309] Dan. 8:16-17.

[310] The Holy Bible contains many references to GOD's Indignation at those who reject His Word; among them are Deut. 29:28; Ps. 69:19-28; Ps. 78:47; Ps. 102:7-11; Isa. 26:20-21; Ezek. 21:28-32; Heb. 4:24-31; and Rev. 14:9-11. One verse that briefly catches the fullness of the Indignation is Jer. 10:10: *But the Lord is the true GOD, and an everlasting king: at His wrath the earth shall tremble, and the nations shall not be able to abide His Indignation.* This is the Desolation on the earth revealed to Prophet Daniel at 9:13. It corresponds to the Tribulation written of by Daniel (Dan. 12:1-4); Armageddon; and *"the great and terrible day of the Lord."*

[311] Rev. 3:10-12,21.

meaning of his vision relating to the Indignation, *supra*, which was obviously drastic because the Prophet fainted and was sick for several days, after which he arose and went about the king's business: but nobody else understood the vision.

One of the most unusual, and at the same time enigmatic, prophecies given to and through Daniel, the meaning of which has baffled many religious scholars through the centuries, is found in four verses which involve seventy weeks.[312] Included in these verses is the phrase that seventy weeks had been *"determined upon thy people and upon thy holy city, to finish the transgression, and to make an end to sins, and to make reconciliation for iniquity . . . and to anoint the most Holy."* Calculating these verses in prophetic terms establishes the appearance of Jesus Christ very near to the time when John the Baptist began preaching his doctrine of water baptism at the Jordan River.

On another occasion, after a period of fasting, Daniel lifted up his eyes to behold a man clothed in linen whose body was like beryl, his face had the appearance of lightning, his eyes as lamps of fire, and his arms and feet like polished brass. At the time of this occurrence Daniel was in a deep slumber facing the ground, and the Angel's hand touched him and set him upon his knees and upon the palms of his hands, and said:[313]

> *O Daniel, a man greatly Beloved, understand the words that I speak unto thee, and stand upright: for unto thee am I now sent. And when he had spoken this word to me, I stood trembling. Then*

---

[312] Cf. Dan. 9:24-27.
[313] Dan. 10:9-10.

> said he unto me, Fear not, Daniel: for from the first day that thou did set thine heart to understand, and to chasten thyself before thy God, thy words were heard, and I am come for thy words. But the prince of the kingdom of Persia withstood me one and twenty days: but lo, Michael one of the chief princes, came to help me, and I remained there with the kings of Persia. Now I am come to make thee understand what shall befall thy people in the latter days: for yet the vision is for many days. (Dan. 10:11-14)

At that point, Daniel set his face to the ground again and became dumbstruck, but one like the sons of men — whom Daniel recognized as his Lord — touched his lips. Daniel opened his mouth and spoke to the one who stood before him, and lamented that he had no strength because, he asked, how could a servant of the Lord's talk with his Lord? Then there came again to Daniel the Archangel Gabriel, having the appearance of a man, who touched him and strengthened him, and said:

> Knowest thou wherefore I come unto thee? And now will I return to fight with the prince of Persia: and when I am gone forth, lo, the prince of Grecia shall come. But I will show thee that which is noted in the scripture of truth: **and there is none that holds with me in these things, but Michael, your prince.** (Dan. 10:21)

This confirmed that Daniel's heavenly prince was Michael, who at that time was known to Gabriel to be one of the chief heavenly princes, and further that there were certain deep spiritual mysteries known only to Gabriel and Michael. Gabriel then continued to make Daniel understand what was to befall Israel in the latter days, as above noted.[314] He disclosed that he, Gabriel, had in the first year of king Darius' reign stood to confirm and strengthen Daniel, and that he would show Daniel what was to one day take place; including the taking of power by the anti-Christ, the Beast of the Revelation, who would attempt to thwart the New Covenant of Christ the Son's:

> *And the king shall do according to his will; and he shall exalt himself, and magnify himself above every god, and shall speak marvelous things against the God of gods, and shall prosper till the indignation be accomplished: for that is determined shall be done. Neither shall he regard the God of his fathers, nor the desire of women, nor regard any god: for he shall magnify himself above all. Thus shall he do in most strongholds with a strange god, whom he shall acknowledge and increase with glory: and he shall cause them to rule over many, and shall divide the land for gain. He shall stretch out his hand also upon the countries: and the land of Egypt shall not escape. But he shall have power over the treasures of gold and of silver, and over all the precious things of Egypt: and the Libyans and the Ethiopians shall be at his steps. But tidings out of the east and out of the north shall trouble him: therefore he shall go forth with fury to destroy, and utterly make away many. And he shall plant the tabernacles of his palace between the seas in the glorious holy mountain; yet he shall come to his end, and none shall help him. (Dan. 11:36-39, 42-45)*

---

[314] Dan. 10:11-14.

Beloved Gabriel then conveyed an illuminating disclosure to Daniel:

> **And at that time shall Michael stand up, the great prince which standeth for the children of thy (Daniel's) people:** *and there shall be a time of trouble such as never was since there was a nation even to that same time: and at that time thy people shall be delivered, every one that shall be found written in the book.* [315] *And many of them that sleep in the dust of the earth shall awake, some to everlasting life, and some to shame and everlasting contempt. And they that be wise shall shine as the brightness of the firmament; and they that turn many to righteousness as the stars forever and ever. But thou, O Daniel, shut up the words, and seal the book, even to the time of the end: many shall run to and fro, and knowledge shall be increased. (Dan. 12:1-4)*

Gabriel had previously advised Daniel that Michael was his prince, *supra*, and Daniel was instructed that in the critical time of deliverance of souls from earth into Heaven, Beloved Michael would stand up to be recognized for who He is. Further, that it would come at the time of the Lord's Indignation, when all negative ungodly souls are to be removed from the earth in order that the Millennium of the First Resurrection may proceed without ob-

---

[315] Cf. Isa. 26:20-21: *"Come my people, enter thou into thy chambers and shut thy doors about thee: hide thyself as it were for a little moment, until the indignation be overpast. For, behold, the Lord cometh out of his place to punish the inhabitants of the earth for their iniquity: the earth also shall disclose her blood, and shall no more cover her slain."* (And cf. 1 Sam. 2:2-10).

struction. Satan is to be put away during that period.[316] Those who undergo spiritual rebirth by way of a near death experience in the Light find their spirit-selves, their souls, in a place of paradise without any negativity whatever. In that Light, everything and everyone is filled with love, truth and righteousness. That heavenly condition has been brought into existence because Satan and his angels of darkness have been confined to the earth plane, and are unable to exert their negative influences in the higher dimensions of existence. On the other hand, those who undergo dark near death experiences find themselves in, or precariously on the edge of, a dark pit from which cries are issuing, pleading for help.[317] The Latin phrase *res ipsa loquitor* applies: "the thing speaks for itself." Daniel was further told by Gabriel that many who sleep in the dust of the earth — who have died in the flesh in the past — shall awaken, some to eternal life, and some to shame and everlasting contempt.[318] The latter will reap the result of their negative unspiritual behavior during their incarnate earth experiences on earth.[319] Daniel was

---

[316] Rev. 20:1-3.

[317] Jesus explained this situation by parable at Lk. 16: 19-31, confirming that a great gulf has been set between heaven and hell, so that those in either place are separated so they cannot cross over. When a soul in hell asked Abraham to help his family by advising them of the horrible conditions so they would change their ways, he was told: "*If they hear not Moses and the prophets, neither will they be persuaded, though one rose from the dead.*"

[318] This is the spiritual meaning of the bones, representing the souls which are to be revivified by the power of the Christ Spirit as detailed in Ezek. 37-1-14.

[319] 2 Cor. 5:10.

then instructed to seal the book until the time of the end when many would run to and fro, and knowledge would be increased. We have seen man's knowledge, especially in material developments, increased exponentially in recent decades. The prophet next looked and beheld two others, one standing on each side of the banks of a river.[320] One of the two asked a man clothed in linen who was upon the waters of the river:

> *How long shall it be to the end of these wonders? (Dan. 12:6)*

> *And the man clothed in linen who was upon the waters of the river swore by God that it would be for a time, times and half a time; and **when He shall scatter the power of the holy people**, all these things shall be finished. (Dan. 12:7)*

The time, times and half a time represent the 3 ½ thousand years from the time Moses and Joshua received the Law of Moses on the Holy Mount, until the end of the two thousand years of the current Age of the Gentiles. Calculated in the prophetic sense, a day in heaven is as a thousand years on earth.[321] It was 1500 years from the time GOD's basic Law was given to mankind through Moses, until the Son of GOD manifested in flesh as Jesus of Nazareth. And it has been nearly 2000 more years since the time of His First Coming — a total of 3,500 years, or in the prophetic sense, *3 ½ times.*

Daniel did not understand the meaning of the revelation related by the man clothed in linen, *supra*, so

---

[320] Dan. 12:5. Cf. Ps. 46:4-6.
[321] Ps. 90:4.

he asked what shall be the end of these things? to which Gabriel replied:

> *Go thy way, Daniel: for the words are closed up till the time of the end. Many shall be purified and made white and tried; but the wicked shall do wickedly: and none of the wicked shall understand; but the wise shall understand. And from the time that the daily sacrifice shall be taken away, and the abomination that maketh desolate set up, there shall be a thousand two hundred and ninety days. Blessed is he that waiteth, and cometh to the thousand three hundred and five and thirty days. But go thou way till the end be: for thou shalt rest, and stand in thy lot at the end of the days. (Dan. 12:9-13)*

This last comment — that Daniel would *stand in his lot* at the end of the days — meant that after his earth experiences were finished he would occupy a place granted to him by the Lord the Son of GOD. Jacob's lineage is *"the lot"* of the Lord the Son's inheritance.[322] Daniel's revelations then ended, he having by his total belief and faith in GOD learned many important spiritual truths, some of which are only today starting to be well understood. He was followed in time by more prophets whose writings continued to forecast the coming of the Lord the Son's New Covenant.

---

[322] Deut. 32:8-9.

—CHAPTER FIVE—

OTHER LATTER DAY PROPHETS OF THE HEBRAIC AGE

This chapter highlights some of what was written by the prophets who wrote after Daniel's time. Only those portions of their prophecies appear herein which have a significant application to the coming of the New Covenant which the Lord promised through Prophet Jeremiah, *supra*.

PROPHET HOSEA

The Lord revealed to and through Prophet Hosea circumstances and conditions which would exist during the seventy-year exile which was to come; a dual prophesy which also concurrently applied to the Age of the Gentiles which would succeed and encompass the Age of the Hebrews:

> *For the children of Israel shall abide many days without a king, and without a prince, and without a sacrifice, and without an image and without an ephod, and without teraphim:* ***Afterward shall the children of Israel return, and seek the Lord*** *their God, and David their king; and shall fear the Lord and His goodness in the latter days. (Hos. 3:4-5)*

As will be seen, the children of Israel did return in a surprising way, as foretold by the Lord through Prophet Hosea. He advised those who would return to Him what He would do on their behalf:

> *After two days will He revive us: in the third day He will raise us up, and we shall live in His sight.* Then *shall we know, if we follow on to know the Lord: his going forth is prepared as the morning; and he shall come unto us as the rain, as the latter and former rain unto the earth. (Hos. 6:2-3)*

The Lord Himself as Jesus of Nazareth underwent the process of transforming change some hundreds of years after having foretold it through Prophet Hosea. Remarkably, long before Jesus provided His example on the Cross, He as the Lord the Son in heaven described through Prophet Hosea the three-day spirit-quickening process that follows death of the flesh body. In effect his action said: Follow me and my teachings, because I am going to sacrifice my earth life on your behalf, and I will return so you can see and will know I have been able to cross over from heavenly life into temporal earth flesh, then back into eternal life in GOD's LIGHT.[323] He demonstrated the process all souls are to pass through who are able to attain to the Kingdom of Heaven by following Him and His New Covenant Gospel. As a result of the peoples' provocations against Him, the

---

[323] Jesus disclosed: "*Therefore doth my Father love me, because I lay down my own life, that I might take it again. No man taketh it from me, but I lay it down of myself. I have power to lay it down, and I have power to take it again. This commandment have I received of my Father.*" (Jn. 10:17-18)

Lord announced His intention to again punish Israel:

> *Israel is swallowed up: now shall they be among the Gentiles* as a vessel wherein is no pleasure. (Hos. 8:8)

This was a startling announcement forecasting what was to take place when Jesus Christ brought in His New Covenant. After Jerusalem would be overcome about 70 A.D., Israel's fortunes would sag into a protracted stifling eclipse during which Jews would be scattered throughout the world. Literally swallowed up among the Gentiles, they were to undergo another earthly exile on a grander scale than they had ever before experienced; except for man's exile in the earth following the fall of Adam and Eve. Some would resolutely cling to their faith and belief in the Mosaic Law, as had those who had voluntarily endured the previous seventy-year exile in Babylon. But times were changing on the earth, and that which was required of the people in one age would not necessarily be required of them in an oncoming one. There is no development, for better or for worse, without change; and there is always the ever-present danger of falling back rather than moving forward, to be avoided at all costs. The Old Covenant was predestined to be replaced by a new one, and the burden of changing to fit into it fell upon all souls incarnated on the earth. Through Hosea the Lord divulged:

> *My GOD will cast them away, because they did not hearken unto HIM:* **and they shall be wanderers among the nations.** *(Hos. 9:17)*

> *Sow to yourselves in righteousness, reap in mercy; break up your fallow ground: for it is time to seek the Lord, till He come and rain righteousness upon you. Ye have plowed wickedness, ye have reaped iniquity; ye have eaten the fruit of lies: because thou didst trust in thy way, in the multitude of thy mighty men. (Hos. 10:12-13)*

In these two messages the Lord urged the people to turn their backs on iniquity and walk with GOD, as had Enoch before them, so the Lord would come and rain righteousness upon them. Israel had followed the ways of their mighty men and been led into trouble: for which reason the Lord had designed His New Covenant.

PROPHET AMOS

Prophet Amos's time was apparently one of peace and plenty — even luxury — in which conditions the germs of moral and spiritual decadence breed prolifically. Such has been the experience of man through all history: whenever he has enjoyed the most material fruits he has ended up in the worst kind of trouble.

The Lord speaking through Amos laid down a compelling indictment against mankind's misconduct at that time. He reminded His people that He had brought them up from the land of Egypt and led them forty years through the wilderness to possess the land of the Amorites: yet they had commanded His prophets not to prophesy; in return for which He promised to treat them accordingly.[324] He reminded Israel of the mildew and pestilence He had sent upon them, add-

---
[324] Amos 2:9-16.

ing that He had overthrown some of the people as GOD had overthrown Sodom and Gomorrah,[325] but even so they had not returned to Him.

He emphasized through His Prophets that He was exerting pressure upon all who rejected GOD's Will: who selfishly did evil for their own gain. In fact He was, generation after generation and age after age, reducing the numbers of GOD's children who would ultimately be chosen as *His remnant* from among those He was calling. He was providing opportunities to those incarnated in flesh in the earth plane to do good works, so at the end of the days they would stand *"in the lot of Jacob"* to be among those drawn up into the Eternal Heavenly City. He contemplated a New Covenant, which required His people to be spiritually pure, and because they had heaped negativity upon themselves it was required of them to suffer in order that they would learn to follow the way He was preparing for them:

> *Forasmuch therefore as your treading is upon the poor, and ye take from him burdens of wheat: ye have built houses of hewn stone, but ye shall not*

---

[325] Proof that it was the Son of GOD speaking to His Prophets, not GOD the FATHER himself, is found in the above reference to Sodom and Gomorrah. It was the Lord the Son of GOD who spoke through His Prophets, the Word of GOD the FATHER. The Son admonished Israel that it was GOD who had overthrown Sodom and Gomorrah (not saying He the Son had done so): but, He noted, even so those the Son had overthrown by mildew and pestilence had not returned to Him. This clearly defined GOD and the Son as two separate SPIRIT entities, one empowered above the other; as David had written in his Ps. 110:1 (*"The Lord said unto my Lord…"*)

dwell in them; ye have planted pleasant vineyards, but ye shall not drink wine of them. For I know your manifold transgressions and your mighty sins: they afflict the just, they take a bribe, and they turn aside the poor in the gate from their right. Seek good, and not evil, that ye may live: and so the Lord, the God of hosts, shall be with you, as ye have spoken. (Amos 5:11-14)

The Lord then spoke through Amos to warn those who were aligned against Him that they risked being cut off:

Woe unto you that desire the day of the Lord! To what end is it for you? The day of the Lord is darkness, and not light. As if a man did flee from a lion and a bear met him; or went into a house, and leaned his hand upon a wall and a Serpent bit him. Shall not the day of the Lord be darkness, and not light? Even very dark, and no brightness in it? I hate, I despise, your feast days, and I will not smell in your solemn assemblies. Though ye offer me burnt offerings and your meat offerings, I will not accept them: neither will I regard the peace offerings of your fat beasts. (Amos 5:17-22)

In these verses the Lord again foreshadowed the end of ritualistic bestial offerings, which would be terminated by His New Covenant. Amos revealed the Lord's intense feelings against those of Israel who would not follow Him, and His promise that no matter where they might seek a retreat He would find them and remove them. The Lord through His Prophet asserted that he is the one who has His chambers in Heaven from whence He controls the Universe. He declared His overruling providential control of the nations, asserting that He would sift the people as corn is sifted in a sieve, but would not utterly destroy Jacob; that is, His chosen people. He vowed that as He tried Israel He would reduce their numbers, but would preserve a remnant of His people, free of the kind of sinners who boldly asserted that despite their negative ways evil would not overtake them.[326] These would be among those of whom it had been promised that they would return — they would reincarnate in a certain time which lay yet ahead of them.

PROPHET MICAH

Prophet Micah received considerable enlightenment from the Lord about the coming Tribulation, and how it would affect His New Covenant. Micah prophesied:

> *Hear, all ye people; hearken, O earth, and all that therein is: and let the Lord God be a witness against you, the Lord from His Holy Temple. For, behold, he cometh forth out of His place, and will come down and tread upon the high places of the earth. (Mi. 1:2-3)*

The Lord had already correlated this catastrophic event to the time of the Indignation and Armageddon: Prophet Isaiah had spoken of it.[327] Through His prophets the Lord was unceasingly warning of this predestined catastrophe designed to afflict all who reject GOD's Will. Many of the chosen people of Israel had gone astray, and they were being repeatedly advised that they needed to straighten their ways — a warning still in effect on the earth. Those who chose not to

---

[326] Amos 9:1-10.
[327] Isa. 26:20-21.

obey the Lord were to be judged for their destructive deeds and pay a particular spiritual price:

> *Therefore night shall be unto you, that you shall not have a vision: and it shall be dark unto you, that you shall not divine; and the sun shall go down over the prophets, and the day shall be dark over them. Then shall the seers be ashamed, the diviners confounded: yea, they shall all cover their lips; for there is no answer of GOD. (Mi. 3:6-7)*

This message of the Lord's foreshadowed a radical change from the Old Covenant to the new one foretold through Jeremiah, in which prophets would no longer speak for the Lord because each individual would receive GOD's Word directly through the Spirit. Micah foretold that the sun was to go down over the prophets: they would not receive communications from their Lord. The Prophet noted that the destruction which was to come — *"when Zion would be plowed as a field, and Jerusalem would become heaps, would be for Israel's sake."*[328] Such an idea must have been found unconscionable to Israel at the time the prophesy was given: how could the people possibly gain when, as events were to unfold, Jerusalem and the temple would be destroyed by the Romans about 70 A.D?

But the Lord explained to Micah that in the last days it would come to pass that the mountain of the house of the Lord would be established in the top of the mountains — the heavenly New Jerusalem — and it would be exalted above the hills; *"and the people would flow into it."*[329] This referred to the time to come when the Lord the Son of GOD will take dominion at the

---

[328] Micah 3:12.

[329] Micah 4:1.

time of His Second Coming, and bring in His New Covenant:

> *And many nations shall come, and say, Come, and let us go up to the mountain of the Lord, and to the house of the God of Jacob; and He will teach us of His ways, and we will walk in His paths: for the law shall go forth from Zion, and the word of the Lord from Jerusalem.*[330] *And He shall judge among many people, and rebuke strong nations afar off; and they shall beat their swords into plowshares, and their spears into pruning hooks: nation shall not lift up a sword against nation, neither shall they learn war any more.*[331] *But they shall sit every man under his vine and under his fig tree; and none shall make them afraid: for the mouth of the Lord of hosts hath spoken it. (Mi. 4:2-4)*

The Lord through Micah then defined the difference between those who would elect to go their own way, following their own gods, and those who:

---

[330] The Lord had already spoken of this through Prophet Isaiah at 2:2-3, including: *And many people shall go and say, Come ye, and let us go up to the mountain of the Lord, to the house of the God of Jacob; and He will teach us of His ways, and we will walk in His paths: for out of Zion shall go forth the law, and the word of the Lord from Jerusalem.* This refers to the New Covenant brought in by the Lord the Son of GOD, which provides a direct way to reach GOD by the Intercession of Christ, man's Heavenly High Priest (Heb. Chh. 5-10, esp. Heb. 7:25).

[331] Cf. Isa. 2:3; and Lk. 24:47 as links connecting the revelations of the Hebrew Prophets forecasting the New Covenant, to the essence of the New Covenant as it was subsequently brought in by Jesus of Nazareth.

> *Will walk in the name of the Lord our God forever and ever. (Mi. 4:5)*

And through Micah, He foretold a day to come when Jews were to be merged with the Gentiles:

> *Arise and thresh, O daughter of Zion: for I will make thine horn iron, and I will make thy hoofs brass: and thou shall beat in pieces many people: and I will consecrate their gain unto the Lord, and their substance unto the Lord of the whole earth. (Mi. 4:13)*

Israel is here referred to as the horn to be made like iron by the Lord, who would consecrate to Himself the spiritual gains accumulated by those who would be His. Their spiritual substance would be consecrated — sanctified — unto the Lord of the whole earth: *"man's maker and husband: the Lord of hosts and man's redeemer the Holy One of Israel, the God of the whole earth He is called."* [332] This meant that every soul sanctified by the Son would become a spiritual part of Him, by which He would be their Spirit Church. By spirit-quickening process, all souls who become Christ the Son's are sanctified *"in"* Him, and by Him *"in"* GOD.[333] Apostle Paul well described the inevitable merger of all people of the world who would accept

---

[332] Isaiah 54:5.
[333] This principle is found in a series of verses: Jn. 5:19; 10:38; 14:10-11; and Deut. 18:18-19.

the Lord the Son of GOD.[334] The process of screening out those of the Lord's from the heathen — which began to take place early in man's incarnations [335] — was predestined to continue until final judgment. Those who find, follow and obey the Lord the Son of GOD; whether they be Jew, Gentile or of whatever extraction: will be saved by Him. As written, all who call upon the name of the Lord shall be saved.[336]

---

[334] Gal. 3:6-29 lays down the terms of the merger of Jews with Christians and all other peoples of the earth as the Lord intended it. These verses explain in detail why it was ordained from the beginning but was gradually opened to those on the earth who through the ages increased in spiritual knowledge and understanding. That which was seeded in Abraham and Sarah grew up through Isaac, Jacob, Joseph and those who maintained the Divine Lineage and the Spiritual Tree of Life which it represented. As Paul explains, all who are blessed in faith are blessed with faithful Abraham: and the just are not justified by the Law of Moses but by faith. Apostle Paul taught that the Mosaic Law is not of faith, so that the man who does them must live within that Law. He explains that Christ redeemed us from the Law in order that the blessing of Abraham might subsequently be applied to the Gentiles. Before faith came, we were kept under the Law, it being our schoolmaster, which we no longer needed after salvation by faith came, because we are all the children of GOD by faith in Jesus Christ. Those who are baptized into Christ have put on His Spirit, so there is no longer Jew nor Greek; those who accept Him as their Lord are all one in Him. And, Paul concludes, if we be Christ's, then we are Abraham's seed, and heirs according to the promise. All this was foreshadowed in Mi. 4:13.

[335] Deut. 32:8-9; Mi.4:5.

Micah's next prophecy followed right in the footsteps of the above writings. The Lord advised him of the particular place on the earth where the Son of GOD, Jesus of Nazareth, was to be born many years later, as well as important details of what was to transpire:

> *Now gather thyself in troops, O daughter of troops: he hath laid siege against us: they shall smite the judge of Israel with a rod upon the cheek. But thou, Bethlehem Ephratah, though thou be little among the thousands of Judah, yet out of thee shall He come forth unto me that is to be* **ruler** *in Israel; whose goings forth have been from of old, from everlasting. Therefore will He give them up, until the time that she which travaileth hath brought forth: then the remnant of His brethren shall return unto the children of Israel. (Mi. 5:1-3)*

When these monumental verses given by the Lord to and through Prophet Micah are examined point for point, it is seen that they revealed in Micah's time events predestined to take place long afterward when the Son of GOD incarnated as Jesus of Nazareth. When it was written that "*he had laid siege*" against us, it referred to Satan. The word Satan means "*adversary*," and he and his angels had laid siege against the Lord the Son from the time He was Adam. The children of Israel had been separated from the heathen, and the Lord's portion of them became His people: Jacob became the lot of His inheritance. When it was inscribed by Prophet Micah that *"they shall smite the judge of Israel with a rod upon the cheek,"* [337] it forecasted the scourging long afterward maliciously vented upon

---

[336] Acts 2:21.

[337] Micah 5:1.

Jesus of Nazareth as reported in the New Testament.[338]

With equal illumination, Micah foretold that Bethlehem — although not great when measured alongside all of Judah — would nevertheless be the place from which was to come forth unto GOD the one of HIS Choice who was one day to rule over Israel.[339] And it was added that *"His goings forth have been from of old, from everlasting."* It is now understood that the Lord's first earth incarnation in flesh was as Adam and His second as Enoch, after which He reappeared on earth as Melchizedek, Joseph son of Jacob, Joshua son of Nun, Asaph in David's time, Jeshua son of Josedech and in other appearances before He manifested as Jesus of Nazareth to fulfill all prophecies due at that time. His goings forth had indeed been from of old, from everlasting.

Micah's remarkable prophecy went even further, noting that *"He (the Son) would give up those of His until the time that she which travaileth hath brought forth: then the remnant of his brethren shall return unto the children of Israel."*[340] This foretold that a remnant of those of Jacob's who had not fallen beneath the onslaught of

---

[338] Mt. 27:30 – esp. verse 30 – spell out that when Jesus was arrested He was mocked and afflicted (as Isaiah had foretold in Isa. Ch. 53, esp. verse 7) and his enemies then *"spit upon Him, and took the reed, and smote Him on the head."* Mk. 15:19-20 records the same events.

[339] Micah 5:2. Matthew confirmed the validity of this revelation given through Prophet Micah, declaring: *"And thou Bethlehem, in the land of Judah, art not the least among the princes of Judah: for out of thee shall come a Governor, that shall rule my people Israel."* Cf. Lk. 2:4-7.

[340] Micah 5:3.

Satan's negative spirit forces were predestined to return at a later time in the company of a remnant of others of the children of Israel. The Lord through Prophet Isaiah had already set the basis for such an occurrence involving those of Jacob who had escaped the Devil's clutches,[341] and Prophet Malachi would also later foretell it, as will be described.

In the Hebrew Bible the Lord is many times quoted as having threatened to consume certain disobedient people.[342] The next devastating event to confront the people of Israel was to be trod down by the power of the Roman armies: which on its surface appeared to diminish the peoples' spirit force for many centuries. Actually, though, as foretold through Prophet Micah, a predestined transforming spiritual escalation was taking place. Jews continued to incarnate in flesh on the earth, their flocks scattered world wide in accordance with biblical prophecies, but they were building up a tremendous spiritual force. The destruction of Jerusalem and the temple represented yet another exile for them; but there was much more involved in this exile than in those which had gone before. The Lord the Son of GOD in Heaven was guiding, moving and directing all spiritual aspects of what was to become of His children of Israel who had done His Will from the time of Abraham. He planned to separate them out from the rest of the earth's sheep, shepherd them into a flock of His own by way of His New Covenant, and preserve them as His remnant.

---

[341] Isa. 10:20-23.

[342] *"And the Lord spoke unto Moses and unto Aaron, saying, Separate yourselves from among the congregation, that I may consume them in a moment."* (Num. 16:20-21) Also see Josh. 24:20; 1 Ki. 1:10; Neh. 9:32; Pss. 27:30; 59:13; Jer. 8:13; Ezek. 4:16-17; 20:13-14; Dan. 7:26.

The time was nearing for "*Shiloh*" to come, as had been long before foretold,[343] and the world was being prepared for it. Dramatic changes were falling due: the New Covenant was in its birth throes. Life after life on earth, each soul had, under the negative influences of Satan, lived through a number of earth experiences, each time gaining or losing spiritually. Under the Law Jesus would reveal,[344] all their gains or losses on earth were profoundly affecting their heavenly positions. Earth testing was reducing the numbers of those who were spiritually "*of Israel*," and yet as time wore on many were quickened by His Spirit and escalated upward toward their Lord the Son; and thus toward GOD. On the other hand, the spirit of those who did not follow GOD's Will was proportionately depleted. This process through many centuries was separating those who truly were of Israel from those who were not. Some remained true to the Son their Lord whereas others fell away under the afflictions of the Devil and his angels.

In the same way that the children of Jacob — of Israel — had been in the beginning separated from the heathen on earth,[345] a second separation had been gradually but inexorably taking place through the centuries. The people of Israel were themselves undergoing a separation. The Lord's Prophets had repeatedly warned that those who did not do His Will would suffer for it. Their every desire, thought and action was recorded during each of their earth experiences, and whatever they did, or failed to do, became a determining factor in deciding who would remain "*of Israel*" at the end of the Hebraic Age. It is

---

[343] Gen. 49:10.
[344] Mt. 18:18.
[345] Deut. 32:8-9.

beyond coincidence that when Jacob had blessed his sons long before Micah's time he had advised them that his blessings applied to that which would befall them in the last days of the Hebraic Age.[346]

The Lord GOD foretold through Prophet Micah that out of Bethlehem would come forth unto HIM the one who would be ruler over Israel: but the term "*Israel*"was not intended to be loosely construed to refer to all Jews. It did not carry national implications, but rather was restricted to a remnant consisting of those individuals whose faith, belief and obedience to their Lord had enabled them to survive the weeding out process of earth testing. The people of Israel's spiritual destiny was to be altered by the Roman armies when they destroyed Israel and Jerusalem, after which the people were scattered over the earth, reincarnating in many different nations. They were passing through a phase of severe testing, but it was destined to result in a new and better Covenant.

Micah was told that the remnant of Israel would be in the midst of many people, including the Gentiles, even as a young lion [347] Their incarnations at the end of the Hebraic Age continued, each soul returning in a succession of flesh bodies in accordance with the missions it needed to fulfill.

The Lord reiterated through Prophet Micah that He had a controversy with his people, whom He had brought up out of the land of Egypt and redeemed from being the servants of those who had enslaved them, and that He had sent before them Moses, Aaron and Miriam. He posed questions to them which patently suggested that their pursuit of heaven was tak-

---

[346] Gen. 49:1.

[347] Micah 5:7-8.

ing an ineffective course. He asked whether they should come before Him with burnt offerings or with yearling calves? or would the Lord be pleased if they sacrificed thousands of rams, or ten thousand rivers of oil?[348] He declared that what He asked of them was simply:

> *To do justly, and to love mercy, and to walk humbly with thy God. (Mi. 6:8)*

The Lord then admonished Micah that good men had about perished from the earth. There were, He admonished, none upright; that they lay in wait for blood and hunt every man with a net that they may earnestly do evil with both hands. Princes and judges were asking for a reward, even great men had mischievous desires, and together they were weaving evil.[349] He then added a few more hints of what was to take place when He brought in His New Covenant, advising that in Micah's time no man could trust a friend, nor put confidence in a guide, because a man's enemies were the men of his own house, and they could not be relied upon. Men needed worthy advisors, not negatively inspired men who would try to lead them astray, which moved Micah to write:

> *Therefore I will look unto the Lord; I will wait for the god of my salvation: my God will hear me. Rejoice not against me, O mine enemy: when I fall I shall arise; when I sit in darkness, the Lord shall be a light unto me.[350] I will bear the indignation of the Lord, because I have sinned against Him, until He plead my cause, and execute judgment for me: He will bring me forth to the light, and I shall behold His righteousness. (Mi. 7:7-9)*

---

[348] Micah 6:1-7.

[349] Micah 7:2-3.

[350] Cf. Jn. 12:46; Eph. 5:14; 1 Pet 2:9; Rev. 21:23.

This hinted of a time when those of Israel would no longer look to human prophets nor priests but would be in direct touch with their Lord: which was precisely what He had in mind for them. When they repented evil and began to do good He would plead their cause as their Eternal Heavenly Intercessor.[351] He would bring them to the Light of GOD. This expressed the spiritual formula of Christ the Son's New Covenant as the Lord had forecasted it through Prophet Jeremiah,[352] albeit in the time when Micah prophesied the time for it to come to pass lay yet several hundred years in the future.[353]

Prophet Micah then closed His remarks, noting that the Lord pardons iniquity, delights in mercy, and forgives the transgressions of the remnant of His heritage.[354] The Prophet then called upon the Lord, saying:

> *Thou wilt perform the truth to Jacob, and the mercy to Abraham, which thou hast sworn unto our fathers from the days of old. (Mi. 7:20)*[355]

---

[351] Hebrews 7:25.

[352] Jeremiah 31:31-34.

[353] That this was the meaning of Mi. 7:7-9 was long afterward confirmed by a recorded comment of priest Zacharias, father of Elizabeth who was the mother of John the Baptist, recorded at Lk. 1:67-80: which verses include: "*Blessed be the Lord God of Israel; for He hath visited and redeemed His people...to give knowledge of salvation unto His people by remission of their sins...to give LIGHT to them that sit in darkness and in the shadow of death, to guide our feet into the way of peace.*"

[354] Micah 7:18-19.

[355] Cf. Lk. 1:72-75.

PROPHET ZEPHANIAH

The Lord through Zephaniah again warned He would consume all things from off the land, including man and beast; cutting off the remnant of Baal and those who had turned back from the Lord; those who did not seek Him nor inquire of Him. Further, that He did not contemplate the complete removal of all mankind from the earth, but only those individuals who remained disobedient:

> *The great day of the Lord is near... That day is a day of wrath, a day of trouble and distress, a day of wasteness and gloominess, a day of clouds and thick darkness. A day of the trumpet and alarm against the fenced cities, and against the high towers. And I will bring distress upon men, that they shall walk like the blind because they have sinned against the Lord: and their blood shall be poured out as dust, and their flesh as the dung. Neither their silver nor their gold shall be able to deliver them in the day of the Lord's wrath; but the whole land shall be devoured by the fire of His jealousy: for He shall make even a speedy riddance of all them that dwell in the land. (Zeph. 1:14-18)*[356]

The Lord forewarned through Prophet Zephaniah that the Tribulation was to come upon all those who did not do the Lord's Will; but He added:

---

[356] This Proclamation by the Lord had already appeared in Ezek. 7:19, a plain reference to the time of the great Tribulation — the Lord the Son of GOD's Second Coming — when all negative souls are to be removed from the earth in order that the Millennium of the First Resurrection may proceed without Satanic obstructions.

> *Seek ye the Lord, all ye meek of the earth, which have wrought His judgment; seek righteousness, seek meekness: it may be ye shall be hid in the day of the Lord's anger. (Zeph. 2:3)*

He then foretold that a remnant of His spiritually refined people would remain after the Tribulation had fulfilled its purpose:

> *I will also leave in the midst of thee an afflicted and poor people, and they shall trust in the name of the Lord. The remnant of Israel shall not do iniquity, nor speak lies; neither shall a deceitful tongue be found in their mouth: for they shall feed and lie down,[357] and none shall make them afraid. (Zeph. 3:12-13)*

The Lord then foreshadowed a time when He would be among His sheep; meaning when His Second Coming would take place and He would return on a cloud even as He had been raised up into a cloud as Jesus Christ.[358] He had guided, protected, moved and directed the people of Israel from a cloud during their remarkable Exodus out of Egypt.[359]

The Lord closed His Word through Prophet Zephaniah with the promise that His people were to return as sheep in His fold at a critical time on earth:

> *And at that time **will I bring you again**, even in the time that I gather you: for I will make you a*

---

[357] Cf. Ps. 23; Jn. Ch. 10:1-30; and see esp. Ezek. 34:1-24, in which verses the Lord promises to find His sheep, and to set up one shepherd over them to feed them, even His servant David.

[358] Acts 1:9-11.

[359] 1 Cor. 10:1-5.

> *name and a praise among all people of the earth,
> when I turn back your captivity before your eyes,
> saith the Lord. (Zeph. 3:20)*

The Lord's comment that He would bring them again when He would gather them, correlates with His subsequent promise through Prophet Malachi that these were to reincarnate at a later time.[360]

PROPHET HAGGAI

Haggai wrote at the end of the seventy-year exile when the Lord began to prepare His people of Israel for their return to Jerusalem. He noted that although some were saying that it was not yet time for it, He spoke through Prophet Haggai to reassure them that He was with them.[361] He then stirred up the spirit of Zerubbabel, governor of Judah, and that of Joshua as well as the spirit of all the remnant of the people who had made it through the sifting process of the seventy-year exile in order that they might prepare for their return to Jerusalem.[362]

The Lord again spoke through Haggai to the residue of the people — those who had been sifted and screened out from among many others who had fallen

---

[360] Mal. 3:16-18.
[361] Haggai 1:1-3.
[362] Haggai 1:14. The Books of Ezra and Nehemiah carry many details of the circumstances and conditions existent at the time when the remnant returned to Jerusalem. These details are omitted from this work, which is concerned more directly with biblical writings providing linkages which connect the Old Testament with the New Covenant.

victim to Satan and his wiles through the centuries of testing they had endured — that they might continue serving the Lord as they had in former days: in previous incarnations. Life after life they had been incarnating on the earth, and many had fallen away: but those who had continued to have faith, belief and trust in GOD and the Son He chose, and did His Will, continued to go forward through the generations. This was implicit in the Lord's Word through Prophet Haggai:

> *Who is left among you that saw this house (of Israel) in her first glory? And how do ye see it now? Is it not in your eyes in comparison of it as nothing? (Hag. 2:3)*

In the above-quoted verse, the Lord particularly addressed those who had remained true to him as they had passed under the rod of His testing. They had been with Him since the beginning — in the first Glory — having been among the positive sons incarnated when the separation came in the time of Adam and Eve.[363]

---

[363] The separation referred to is detailed in Deut. 32:8-9, where it was inscribed that the Lord's portion is His people, Jacob is the lot of His Inheritance. (Cf. Heb. 2:13-18 which confirms that Christ the Son of GOD was given these particular people to save them. When the Son manifested in flesh as Jesus Christ His initial mission involved only the Jews — Mt. 10:5 — but it was later extended to include Gentiles as well (Jn. 10:16). Also cf. Jn. 15:27, which quotes Jesus as advising His followers that He *"had been with them from the beginning."* He referred to the beginning when He was Adam, and many of *the remnant* had been with Him.

The Lord emphasized to this remnant who were to emerge from exile in Babylon that it was likely that when they compared the initial state of their "*first glory*" to circumstances and conditions as they departed from Babylon on their return to Jerusalem, their latter state would compare to it as nothing, *supra*. As before stated, the exile was designed to sort out the finest of Israel, whose latter state was to be improved. That the people who composed this above-described remnant had been with the Lord when they came out of Egypt was confirmed when He spoke to them through Prophet Haggai, saying:

> *According to the word that I covenanted with you when ye came out of Egypt, so my spirit remains among you: fear ye not. (Hag. 2:5)*

This remnant of Jews was largely composed of souls who had manifested with Adam, or in the Adamic generations, in the beginning. They had remained with Him as He had continued to shepherd His flock from Heaven, as well as on earth during His quite numerous earth appearances in flesh. He regaled them when they fell victim to Satan's negative ways and comforted them with kind words at times when they deserved it, all the while warning them of their need to depart from evil ways and follow Him. The pattern of the Lord's several departures from heaven to manifest in flesh on the earth, in accordance with prophesies,[364] was confirmed by Him when, as Jesus

---

[364] Heb. 2:13-18.

of Nazareth, He revealed that at the same time He walked on the earth His Spirit was in Heaven.[365]

The Lord through Prophet Haggai recounted how He had afflicted Israel because the people had remained unclean. He had shortened the measure of their goods, blasted them with mildew and hail, yet they had refused to turn to Him: the seed was not yet in the barn, so to speak. They were failing to reap the spiritual gains they so desperately needed.[366] The Lord through Prophet Zechariah, whose prophecies are next examined, contains additional exalting comments the Lord made about Zerubbabel. He and High Priest Joshua son of Josedech were called to lead a dedicated spiritualized contingent of the people given to the Lord by GOD[367] who were on their way to becoming the exalted remnant of Israel.[368] Centuries of scourging earth testing had reduced the

---

[365] The spiritual mechanics of this phenomenon were revealed by the Son when He was Jesus of Nazareth. He told followers: *"No man has ascended up to heaven, but he that came down from heaven, even the Son of man which is in heaven."* (Jn. 3:13) In short, at the same time a portion of Christ the Son's Holy Spirit — His soul — was incarnated in flesh on the earth as Jesus of Nazareth, a much greater portion of His Spirit remained in Heaven, from which place He was able to exert His all-powerful influences. Apostle Paul confirmed this principle in his letter to the Ephesians, in which he wrote: *"Now He that ascended, what is it but that He also descended first into the lower parts of the earth? He that descended is the same also that ascended up far above all heavens, that He might fulfill all things."* (Eph. 4:9-10)

[366] Haggai 2:12-19.

[367] Heb. 2:13-18.

[368] Haggai 1:1,14.

numbers of the chosen people who remained of Israel but their trials were not yet finished. As will be seen, they were yet to undergo an even more intense sifting during earth experiences in a time to come, during which they would be baptized with the Holy Ghost and with fire.

PROPHET ZECHARIAH

Through Prophet Zechariah, the Lord continued the gradual process of preparing His children for the Covenant He was making ready for them. At the end of their seventy-year exile in Babylon, the Angel of the Lord appeared to Zechariah with a sobering message:[369]

> *Thus saith the Lord of hosts; turn ye unto me, and I will turn unto you. Be not as your fathers, unto whom the former prophets have cried, saying, Thus saith the Lord of hosts; Turn ye now from your evil ways, and from our evil doings: but they did not hear, nor hearken to me, saith the Lord. But my words and my statutes, which I commanded my servants and prophets, did they not take hold of your fathers? And they returned and said, Like as the Lord of hosts thought to do to us, according to our*

---

[369] Zechariah 1:12-14.

ways, and according to our doings, so hath he dealt with us. (Zech. 1:3-6)[370]

This was another expression of what has come to be known as karmic law. In the case of the people of Israel, each individual — and the nation as a whole — were reaping as they had sown. As the nation's belief and faith in the Lord moved the people to improve their ways, they increasingly received the Lord's assistance.[371] And as each soul strove to follow the Lord, doing good and not evil, that individual's spirituality was increased.[372]

---

[370] The people of Israel had through the generations repeatedly turned away from the Lord, starting even when Moses and Joshua went up to the Holy Mount to receive the Law which became known as the Law of Moses. They influenced Aaron to make a golden calf for them, and then danced and reveled at a time when they should have been repentant, believing and faithful. (This situation still exists today, many dancing and singing loudly and in devilish ways, paying no heed to their spiritual need to seek the Lord and His Spirit able to quicken them into eternity, as Apostle Paul foretold of this time before the Lord's return to take dominion: (2 Tim. 3:1-7.) The Lord knew the fault lay with Satan and his angels, whom He and His Angels confined to the earth plane, where they have continued to afflict and mislead all souls incarnated on the earth (Rev. 12:7-12). But the Lord has mercifully forgiven sins, and once again repeated to Prophet Zechariah His entreaty to all people everywhere, pleading with them to return to Him, their Maker, in order that they might be Saved as part of the remnant of Israel.

[371] Cf. Joshua Ch. 7, which relates that when Israel attacked an inferior force at Ai and was defeated, it turned out to have been caused by Achan's negative act (Josh. 7:1, 10-12, 18-26). Evil has its own negative reward.

[372] 1 Cor. 3:6-7; 2 Cor. 9:10; 1 Thess. 3:11-12; 4:10.

By means of their earth experiences, the Lord was teaching that success or failure depended entirely on the peoples' spirituality. Each gain or loss by one or more individuals evoked a proportionate spiritual gain or loss sustained by the whole people.[373] By their iniquity some were falling away from their spiritual heritage, while others who faithfully and obediently followed their Lord were being quickened into higher levels of consciousness, moving closer to their Lord the Son, and to GOD. They were helping others who, whether or not they were aware of it, were on their way to becoming *"the remnant of Israel."* The rule still holds today: those who do the Lord's Will, offering their hand to help in any way the Lord sees fit, are protected, guided, moved and directed to do that which He will have done. It results in spiritual gains to the soul while it is incarnated in flesh, which apply to the soul's higher self in Heaven — the angel it is there.[374] The New Covenant was designed to make it possible for individual souls to be quickened into eternity, and the Lord patiently, step by step, moved the people toward the day when it would be made available to all souls incarnated on earth.

After the seventy-year exile was fulfilled, when there was a move to gather the priests and prophets to pray to the Lord, it was asked whether the people should weep and fast as they had during their exile in Babylon. The Lord reminded His people that when

---

[373] As would be so eloquently written long afterward: *"No man is an island unto himself: each is a part of the main."*

[374] Mt. 18:18; 2 Cor. 5:10. Jesus taught that those who participate in the resurrection will be as Angels of GOD in heaven (Lk. 20:34-36).

they had before fasted, mourned, eaten and drank, it had not been unto Him: and that when He had urged them to show mercy and compassion for their brethren they had not done so, but had instead refused to hear Him or to hearken to Him: [375]

> Yea, they made their hearts as an adamant stone, lest they should hear the law, and the words which the Lord of hosts had sent in his Spirit by the former prophets: therefore came a great wrath from the Lord of hosts. Therefore it came to pass that as He cried, and they would not hear, so they cried, and I would not hear, saith the Lord of hosts. (Zech. 7:12-13)

For these reasons, the Lord declared through Prophet Zechariah, He had scattered them with a whirlwind among all nations whom they knew not.[376] It was part of His Plan to take effect under His New Covenant, which was designed to provide opportunities for all incarnated souls to find the way He was preparing into heaven. He spoke of his great love for His people, foreseeing a time of peace and plenty *"when He would rejoin them in the midst of Jerusalem,"* and they would be His people and He would be their God in truth and righteousness.[377] In this way He forecasted His coming appearance as Jesus of Nazareth, when He would walk among the children He had long before been given. He promised that *the remnant* of His people would possess all good things, and that Judah and Israel would be saved, provided each would speak the truth to his neighbor and execute the judgment of truth and peace.[378]

---

[375] Zech. 7:3-7.
[376] Zech 7:14.
[377] Zech. 8:1-8.
[378] Zech. 8:7-15.

The remnant of whom He spoke was predestined to be composed of the remainder of the children He had long before been given.[379] At the time He had received them a separation had been made between the lineages of the sons of Adam — when "*the bounds of the people were set according to the number of the children of Israel*" — when GOD proclaimed that the Lord the Son's portion would be His people and Jacob the lot of His inheritance.[380]

The Lord then foretold to Zechariah a crucially important event to come by which all people on the earth would know that the events described by that prophet had come to pass. The Lord had promised His people He would rejoin them in the midst of Jerusalem, *supra*, and that in that day *some* would "*take hold of the skirt of him that is a Jew,*" saying:

> *We will go with you: for we have heard that GOD is with you. (Zech. 8:23)*

This prophecy would be fulfilled many generations later when the Son of GOD, born a Jew as had been foretold, walked the earth as Jesus of Nazareth. It was confirmed by an illuminating sign given through Zechariah which could not be readily misinterpreted:

> *Rejoice greatly, O daughter of Zion; shout, O daughter of Jerusalem: behold, thy King cometh unto thee: he is just, and having salvation;* ***lowly, and riding upon an ass, and upon a colt the foal of an ass.*** *(Zech. 9:9)*

When this prophesied incident took place, all who became aware of it would know that Zechariah's

---

[379] Heb. 2:13-18.
[380] Heb. 2:13-18; Deut. 32:8-9.

prophecy had been fulfilled: that the Lord the Son of GOD had incarnated in flesh on the earth. And that, as foretold, He had appeared in Jerusalem among His people, who would follow Him because they had heard that God was with Him. By this sign, all people of the earth who incarnated after Prophet Zechariah's time — especially those of *the remnant* of Israel who were familiar with the forecasts of the prophets — could be certain when their Lord had manifested in flesh and was among them. As related in the New Testament, the event came to pass precisely as had long before been foretold by the Lord through His Prophet Zechariah.

Mark's version of this extraordinary event[381] relates that Jesus commanded two of His Disciples to go to a certain place, where they would find an unbroken colt tied. They found the colt caught where two ways met, and they released him and brought him to Jesus. Colorful garments were cast upon the colt and Jesus sat upon him. It was a tumultuous jubilant scene, many having strawed the narrow way with their garments and with branches they had torn from the roadside trees. As Jesus imperturbably rode the unbroken beast without it resisting, the clamor was great, the jubilant people bursting with joy knowing they were seeing Zechariah's prophecy unfold before their very eyes. They realized they were at last in the presence of their Lord in the flesh, who had appeared as Prophet Zechariah had long before foretold.

---

[381] Mk. 11:1-10; Mt. 21:1-9; Lk. 19:29:38.

Zechariah was given another sign forecasting an occurrence to take place when the Lord the Son of GOD would manifest as Jesus of Nazareth:

> And they shall look upon me **whom they have pierced**, and they shall mourn for him, as one mourns for his only son, and shall be in bitterness for his firstborn. (Zech. 12:10)

Through Prophet Zechariah the Lord also foretold what would be the result of the Desolation to come upon the earth, the Tribulation which is Armageddon:

> And it shall come to pass that in all the land, saith the Lord, two parts therein shall be cut off and die: but the third shall be left therein. And I will bring the third part through the fire, and will refine them as silver is refined, and will try them as gold is tried: they shall call on my name, and I will hear them: I will say, It is my people: and they shall say, The Lord is my God. (Zech. 13:8-9)

Zechariah thus began to receive information concerning the Second Coming of the Lord when He will return in a cloud as biblically foretold:

> Behold, the day of the Lord cometh, and thy spoil shall be divided in the midst of thee. (Zech. 14:1)

It meant that the people were to be divided by the plumb line the Lord had promised through Prophet Amos, which was specifically designed to separate those who were to continue as the remnant of the Saved of Israel, from those who had not yet as of that time been sufficiently quickened by GOD's Holy Spirit to warrant their being included.[382] The Lord then spelled out more details of what would take place at the time of His Second Coming:

> *For I will gather all nations against Jerusalem to battle; and the city shall be taken, and the houses rifled, and the women ravished; and half of the city shall go forth into captivity, and the residue of the people shall not be cut off from the city. Then shall the Lord go forth, and fight against those nations, as when He fought in the day of battle. (Zech. 14:2-3)*

It became evident from the Lord's next Word to Zechariah that this above prophesy — albeit in a dual sense it could have by one understanding referred to Jerusalem's being crushed by the Roman army about 70 C.E.— principally applied to the Lord's Second Coming:

> *And His feet shall stand in that day upon the mount of Olives, which is before Jerusalem on the east, and the mount of Olives shall cleave in the midst thereof toward the east and toward the west, and there shall be a very great valley; and half of the mountain*

---

[382] Cf. Amos 7:7-8. Prophet Isaiah explicitly wrote of this catastrophic event to come: *"Behold, the day of the Lord cometh, cruel both with wrath and fierce anger, to lay the land desolate: and He shall destroy the sinners thereof out of it. For the stars of heaven and the constellations shall not give their light: the sun shall be darkness in His going forth, and the moon shall no more cause her light to shine. And I will punish the world for their evil, and the wicked for their iniquity; and I will cause the arrogancy of the proud to cease, and will lay low the haughtiness of the terrible."* (Isa. 13:9-11)

> *shall remove toward the north, and half of it toward the south. And ye shall flee to the valley of the mountains; for the valley of the mountains shall reach unto Azal: yea, ye shall flee, like as ye fled from before the earthquake in the days of Uzziah king of Judah: and the Lord my God shall come, and all the saints with thee. (Zech. 14:4-5)*

Those who report having envisioned angels — especially the great Archangels — universally report their colossal size. When the Lord the Son of GOD stands with his feet atop the mount of Olives, a huge valley is to erupt there, and the people will flee as they had in the day of the great earthquake in the time of Uzziah king of Judah. Then, Zechariah foretold, his God would come with all His Saints. The coming of the Lord is so often described in the Bible only comparatively few citations are here footnoted.[383] Of this cataclysmic event, Prophet Isaiah wrote that Israel would at that time be visited by the Lord of hosts with thunder, earthquakes and great noise. He prophesied that the multitude of nations would fight against Ariel,[384] and against mount Zion.[385] Prophet Joel also connected this time to come to the final conflict between the earth and the heavens, which is to precede the Lord's judgment of the heathen.[386] After reiterating that which had been previously given through the prophets — that it shall be a day known to the Lord, etc. — Zechariah prophesied:

---

[383] 1 Sam. 2:1-10; Ps. 37:23-28; 89:5-7; Dan. 7:22-27; 1 Thess. 3:11-13; 2 Thess. Ch. 2; Heb. 12:18-29; Jude 14-25; Rev. 7:14-17; Rev. Ch. 14; Rev. Chh. 15-20.

[384] Ariel is identified in Isa. 1-7 as a city; but Ariel is also referred-to in some ancient writings as a powerful negative associate of the Archangel Satan.

[385] Isa. 29:5-8.

[386] Joel 3:9-17.

> *And the Lord shall be king over all the earth: in that day shall there be one Lord, and His name one. (Zech. 14:9)*

This verse relates to Apostle John's writings[387] in which it is inscribed that those who patiently keep the Lord's Word, He will keep from the hour of temptation which shall try all on the earth. Included is the Lord's notice that He will come swiftly when He returns, and that everyone should live as spiritually as possible in order that nobody will take his crown. He promises all who overcome the temptations of earth that He will make each of them a pillar in the heavenly temple of His GOD, and He makes other promises to them of crucial importance.[388]

---

[387] Rev. 3:8-10, 21.

[388] This bore proof that the speaker of these words was Christ the Son of GOD, because He makes it clear that He will reveal the name of His GOD to those who overcome the vicissitudes of earth and remain as spiritually pure as possible, He will grant positions in the Heavenly hierarchy He is rebuilding with Satan and the negative Archangels removed from all consideration. To those who succeed in overcoming, He promises to reveal the name of the city of His GOD, which He confirms is the New Jerusalem. Of extreme importance is His promise to write His new name upon those who overcome. Apostle Peter in his time taught that there is no salvation in any other name known than Jesus Christ, because no other name had been given under heaven, among men whereby men may be saved (Acts 4:12). From this it is presumable that another name of the Lord the Son may be forthcoming, to be known among those who are His. According to Rev. 19:10-16, the Lord the Son's name in Jesus' time was known only to Himself (Rev. 19:12).

The Lord closed His prophesying through Zechariah with descriptions of the terrible Tribulation to come upon the earth:

> *And it shall come to pass in that day, that a great tumult from the Lord shall be among them; and they shall lay hold every one on the hand of his neighbor, and his hand shall rise up against the hand of his neighbor. (Zech. 14:13)*

Prophet Zechariah's illuminating writings moved mankind a giant step forward toward understanding the thrust of the New Covenant the Lord had announced through Jeremiah.

The prophesies of Prophet Malachi, next considered, projected man still another giant step forward toward understanding how all on earth — including the remnant of Israel — would be propelled forward into the next period of spiritual development. Known as the Age of the Gentiles, and also as the Piscean Age, it would lead directly from the Old Testament into the New Testament in an unexpected way which would surprise both Jews and Gentiles. According to their divers beliefs, each had presumed it would turn out to favor their disparate points of view. Actually, it favored all who would find, follow and obey the Lord of Israel — the Son of GOD.

PROPHET MALACHI

The Lord speaking through Prophet Malachi admonished the Levitical priesthood for having become corrupted, which again highlighted the fallibility of human priests:

> *For the priests' lips should keep knowledge, and they should seek the law at his mouth; for he is the messenger of the Lord of hosts. But ye are departed out of the way; ye have caused many to stumble at the law; ye have corrupted the covenant of Levi, saith the Lord of hosts. (Mal.2: 7-8)*

The Lord then broached the subject of marriage. It is apparent that the children of Israel, because of their gradually acquired and increasing disrespect of the Levitical Priesthood, were being denied the spiritual guidance and assistance required to keep them in a state of holiness. Consequently, they had gone astray and polluted the holy seed essential to the formation of future lineages of Israel's Divine Genealogical Tree. The Lord warned that marriage was to be revered as a sacrosanct union foreordained by GOD since the beginning. This exhortation was based on the principle that when spirit forces took expression on earth at the beginning, man and woman were considered as One — in effect, binary souls. It was with their respective helpmeets that the godly seed were to continue to multiply on the earth, as explained in Part One of this work.

As difficult as it has become for man to understand and accept, spiritual unions actually are designed in heaven, subject to the Lord's guidance and protection on earth. But man is also subjected to the Devil's deceptive negative lies, deceits and temptations. The Bible advises that it is inordinately important that binary souls, when they incarnate together during a particular life cycle, seek to find one another by the guidance of the Lord and His angels; as exemplified in the cases of Abraham and Sarah, Isaac and Rebekah, and Jacob and Rachel:

> *Yet, ye say, Wherefore? Because the Lord hath been witness between thee and the wife of thy youth, against whom thou hast dealt treacherously: yet is she thy companion, and the wife of thy covenant.* **And did not he make one? Yet had he the residue of the spirit. And wherefore one? That he might seek a godly seed.** *Therefore take heed to your spirit, and let none deal treacherously against the wife of thy youth. (Mal. 2:14-15)*

As the Bible reveals, if and when a marriage between the children of Israel produced negative seed, the Lord removed them from occupying any important positions in the Divine Genealogical Tree growing up through the spiritual generations of Jacob — known as Israel. This is especially apparent in the Divine Lineage, destined to birthe Jesus of Nazareth, the Son of GOD incarnate. As noted in previous chapters, when Judah had married the daughter of a strange god, his children were revealed in the Bible to have been of a negative spirit.[389] The Lord Himself saw to the destruction of Judah's first two sons [390] as a warning to His people that overlooking spiritual laws would be less than fruitful. And He cautioned Israel through Prophet Malachi that those who did as Judah had done would be cut off:

> *Judah hath dealt treacherously, and an abomination is committed in Israel and in Jerusalem, for Judah hath profaned the holiness of the Lord*

---

[389] Mal. 2:11.
[390] Gen. 38:7-10.

> *which he loved, and hath married the daughter of a strange god. (Mal. 2:11)*

A principal inference to be drawn from this warning was that those who — like Judah — would incautiously fail to use care in planning and protecting their lineage, not carefully following spiritual rules and laws in selecting a mate, ran the risk of being removed from the Lord's consideration. But He is merciful and forgiving in His execution of the 3 to 4 generation rule, as He revealed when He announced its establishment to and through Moses.[391]

The Lord through Prophet Malachi built a bridge extending between the Old and New Testaments, delineating between the Hebraic Age founded upon the Mosaic Law, and the current Age of the Gentiles which succeeded it. The spiritual roots of Judaism were predestined to subsequently sprout up into the New Covenant which the Lord had promised through Prophet Jeremiah. It turned out not to be the kind of covenant many on earth had anticipated: for example its purpose was loftier than many Jews had anticipated. It was not designed for the comparatively earth-wise purpose of helping Jews overpower and overthrow their Roman conquerors in order that they might be regenerated to continue their religion as it stood under the Law of Moses. Nor was it a Covenant under which the Gentiles were to be empowered over Jews, who had been the Lord's chosen people from the beginning. The Mosaic Law had served its purpose and GOD's plan was to supercede it with a new and different Covenant in which all people on earth who chose to do so were to participate. The writer to the Hebrews described in detail

---

[391] Ex. 20:3-5; 34:7.

the transition from the Lord's Old Covenant to His new one.[392]

Through Prophet Malachi the Lord revealed the status of the remnant of the sons of Jacob in the time when he prophesied. He disclosed what was expected of His children if they were to receive His Holy Spirit by which they could attain to successively higher levels of consciousness, ultimately to reach heaven itself. Elevated positions awaited them in the heavenly hierarchy the Lord was rebuilding to the exclusion of all negative individuals from that sanctified place in the Light.[393] But it was required of them to remain obedient to His Will during their continuing flesh incarnations on earth, whether or not they found His New Covenant spiritually palatable.

At the time when Malachi was inspired to write the Lord's Word, the curtain was starting to be drawn on the Hebraic Age and its Mosaic Law. The Lord briefly recapitulated certain past occurrences, and then promised wonderful things to come for the sons of Jacob: provided they would acquit themselves according to GOD's Will during their earth incarnations in the coming Age. But without an understanding of principles or reincarnation, certain of Malachi's prophesies remain for the most part unfathomable, impervious to a shallow letter understanding because they incorporate abstract spiritual meanings of the kind Apostle Paul later described.[394] The children of Israel, along with all souls incarnating in flesh on the earth, had been

---

[392] Heb. Chapters 5 through 10. Note esp. Heb. 8:13: *"A new Covenant, HE hath made the first old. Now that which decayeth and waxeth old is ready to vanish away."*

[393] Cf. Rev. 21:22-23.

[394] Esp. Malachi Chapter 3. Cf. 1 Cor. 2:9-15; 2 Cor. 3:3-6.

entering and reentering the earth plane striving to learn from their experiences what GOD required of them. By Malachi's time many had passed under the rod of testing and done well — they composed the remnant of the children of Israel — but they were yet to be confronted with another period of testing calculated to stretch the limits of their belief and faith.

Speaking through Prophet Malachi, the Lord the Son of GOD announced:

> *Behold, I will send my messenger, and he shall prepare the way before me: and the Lord whom ye seek, shall suddenly come to his temple, even the messenger of the covenant, whom ye delight in: behold, he shall come, saith the Lord of hosts. But who may abide the day of His coming? And who shall stand when he appears? for he is like a refiner's fire, and like fullers' sope: And He shall sit as a refiner and purifier of silver: and he shall purify the sons of Levi, and purge them as gold and silver, that they may offer unto the Lord an offering in righteousness. (Mal. 3:1-3)*

This came to pass about 400 years later when John the Baptist began his ministry, preaching in the wilderness of Judea, entreating everyone to repent because the kingdom of heaven was at hand:[395]

> *In those days came John the Baptist. . . . For this is he that was spoken of by the Prophet Esais, say-*

---

[395] Cf. Isa. 40:3, which asserts: *"The voice of him that crieth in the wilderness, Prepare ye the way of the Lord, make straight in the desert a highway for our God."* This implied that the Lord the Son was the God of Israel, who was to incarnate in flesh on the earth. The Son of God is understood by some as the part of GOD that incarnates.

> *ing the voice of one crying in the wilderness, prepare ye the way of the Lord, make his paths straight. (Mt. 3:3)*

This prophesy presaged the coming appearance of Jesus of Nazareth at the Jordan River, where He would be baptized by John the Baptist. The Lord through Malachi laid the groundwork for what was to come for those of Israel who had been with Him in previous times, and had striven to serve Him as best they were able, considering that Satan's negative force was continually raking them over the coals. The Lord began by foretelling that the offering of Judah and Jerusalem would be pleasant unto the Lord, as in days gone by, and as "*in former years.*"[396] In the prophetic sense it meant that in the period to come many of those who had before incarnated on the earth — even in the days when the sons of Jacob had walked the earth — would again serve Him in Jerusalem, where it had been prophesied He was to be among them, *supra*.

The Lord the Son — the Lord of Hosts[397] — then foretold that He would come near to those individuals in judgment. That He would be a swift witness against sorcerers, adulterers and false swearers, and against those who oppress those they hire at unfair wages, as well as widows and orphans and those who turn aside the stranger from his right — including those who did not fear Him.[398] It meant that in the time to come, when the Lord the Son would bring in His New Covenant, it would be incumbent upon those who were to

---

[396] Mal. 3:4.

[397] "*Thy Maker is thy husband: the Lord of hosts is his name: and thy redeemer the Holy One of Israel; the God of the whole earth shall He be called.*" (Isa. 54:5)

[398] Mal. 3:5.

find Him to be spiritually true and faithful, or He would in heaven be a witness against them, as Prophet Micah had foretold.[399] The change to the New Covenant would be radical, offering Jews, Gentiles and the heathen alike a direct way to be in touch with GOD by way of the intercession of one eternal heavenly Priest, rather than through human priests. For that reason the Lord's message given through Prophet Malachi was designed to provide fair notice to all on earth of the radical change to come.

The Lord began by elaborating on conditions existent at that time, associating them with what had gone before, and pleading with those of His Chosen people who had gone astray to return to Him:

> *For I am the Lord, I change not:* **therefore ye sons of Jacob** *are not consumed. Even from the days of your fathers (of the twelve tribes of Israel) ye are gone away from mine ordinances, and have not kept them. Return unto me, and I will return unto you, saith the Lord of hosts. But ye said, Wherein shall we return? (Mal. 3:6-7)*

The import of this message was that the sons of Jacob — including their angelic higher selves existent in higher dimensions — had not been consumed: they had not been destroyed despite the stringent conditions of the 3 to 4 generation rule. Under Mosaic Law, the Lord the Son who spoke these words through Prophet Malachi was and is man's redeemer, holding the power of redemption, as had been before confirmed by Prophet Isaiah.[400]

---

[399] Micah 1:2-3.

[400] Isa. 47:4: *"As for our redeemer, the Lord of hosts is his name, the Holy One of Israel."*

The title "*redeemer*" applies to the Son of GOD — the "*God of the whole earth*" — the Son to whom GOD promised to give the whole earth for His Inheritance when He asked HIM for it.[401] The Lord who spoke through Prophet Malachi thus held the power of redemption, and was able to issue His proclamations with the power of the Holy Spirit GOD had given Him without measure. As Maker of the sons of Jacob, He could at His Will relieve them of any stains of sins they had acquired during their earth incarnations in flesh. That He planned to do exactly that became evident in a message He conveyed to them through Prophet Malachi noting that some had asked the Lord wherein would they be able to return. It was evident they did not understand what He meant when He advised them they were to return. He thereupon explained that because they had robbed Him in their tithes and offerings, they were cursed with a curse; for they had robbed the Lord and the whole nation.[402] Despite their having suffered spiritual losses for having done so, the Lord nevertheless offered them His mercy. He had continually promised it to those who would turn themselves around and obey Him — even though they had sinned — when He had long before announced His 3 to 4 generation rule in Moses' time.[403] At the time Malachi prophesied, Jews were still under the Law of Moses and the Lord's word to them was appropriately framed:

> *Bring ye all the tithes into the storehouse, that there may be meat in mine house, and prove me now here-*

---

[401] Isa. 54:5. Cf. Ps. 2:8. The parable found in Mt. 21:33-43 confirms that the Son will inherit the earth.
[402] Mal. 3:7-9.
[403] Ex. 34:7.

> with, saith the Lord of hosts, if I will not open you the windows of heaven, and pour you out a blessing, that there shall not be room enough to receive it. And I will rebuke the devourer for your sakes, and he shall not destroy the fruits of your ground; neither shall your vine cast her fruit before the time in the field, saith the Lord of hosts. (Mal. 3:10-11)[104]

The Lord was again calling on His flock of Israel to repent and return to Him, promising that if they would obey Him that their gains would be remarkable — there would be more than they could store. He reminded them that their words had been stout against Him, but at the same time they asked what it was they had spoken which was so much against Him? He replied that they had said it was vain to serve GOD; they had asked what profit there was for them to keep His ordinances? while at the same time they walked mournfully before Him. They were calling the proud happy; and claiming that those who worked wickedness were being elevated — even saying that those who tempted GOD were to be delivered.[405]

---

[104] These two verses may well have contributed to the gathering of various Essene sects who began to separate themselves from the main body of Jews near the end of the Hebraic Age in order to strictly follow the Mosaic Law. As explained in the Dead Sea Scrolls, they sought help to bring into the world the One they knew was to be their "*Teacher of Righteousness*– the *Shiloh*" of Gen. 49:10. Aware of prophesies, they sensed the time for it was drawing near. This is why in this current time all who strive to obediently follow Christ the Lord the Son of GOD do well before His Second Coming to live spiritual lives, and to pray for the Lord's return to take dominion.

[405] Mal. 3:13-15.

After Prophet Malachi had delivered this Word of the Lord's to the people of Israel, certain ones among them reacted positively:

> *Then they that feared the Lord spake often one to another: and the Lord hearkened, and heard it, and <u>a Book of remembrance</u> was written before Him for them that feared the Lord, and that thought upon His name. (Mal. 3:16)*

This revealed that the names of those who had feared the name of the Lord and who understood and accepted the offer He had made to them through Prophet Malachi, had thought upon His name, and had spoken to one another about His remarkable spiritual disclosures. Their names were inscribed in *"<u>a Book of remembrance</u>"* so they would not be forgotten: they were set aside for special consideration by the Lord at a later time:

> *And they shall be mine, saith the Lord of hosts, in that day when I make up my jewels; and I will spare them, as a man spares his own son that serves him. **Then shall ye return**, and discern between the righteous and the wicked, between him that serves GOD and him that serves him not. (Mal. 3:17-18)*

Thus was answered the question of those who had asked, *"Wherein shall we return?"*[406] It appears from this that not all would return: that the Lord's promise applied to those who feared Him and conversed about it with one another, their interest having been aroused by what He had promised them.[407] Those

---

[406] Mal. 3:7.
[407] Mal. 3:16.

who were loyal to Him, and desired to continue to serve Him were to be His in the day when He composed His *"Jewels"* — when He would manifest on earth and reassemble them a few hundred years after Malachi prophesied.

The Lord also foretold through Malachi that a day would come when the proud and the wicked would burn, leaving them neither root nor branch.[408] But He promised that those who feared His name *"would arise with healing wings"* and that those of *the remnant* would go forth and be protected to *"grow up as calves in a stall"* in the Lord's barn.[409] These were to *"tread down the wicked,"* who, the Lord foretold, would be ashes under the soles of their feet in the day when He would fulfill His promise of Judgment. He then admonished them to remember the law of Moses, which was still in effect — the law which He had commanded unto Moses in Horeb for all Israel, with its statutes and judgments. And He then added an unusual promise:

> *Behold, I will send you Elijah the prophet before the coming of the great and dreadful day of the Lord: and he shall turn the heart of the fathers to the children, and the heart of the children to their fathers, lest I come and smite the earth with a curse. (Mal. 4:5-6)*

Jesus taught that Elijah the prophet had reappeared in flesh in His time as John the Baptist.[410] But that was not the time of *"The great and dreadful day of the*

---

[408] Mal. Ch. 4.
[409] Mal. 4:1-2. Cf. Rev. 7:3-11 which includes the remnant of Israel.
[410] Mt. 11:7-14 and other verses.

Lord," which day has not yet arrived as of the year of this writing. In that dreadful day, yet to come, the Lord will return with His Angels to take dominion over the earth in the cataclysmic war known as Armageddon, as repeatedly foretold through the ages.[411]

Malachi's prophesies marked the line of demarcation between the Old Testament and the New One, which was to be fulfilled by many of those who had been with the Lord the Son of GOD from the beginning of spirit incarnations on the earth. Obviously many had reincarnated in Malachi's time, still inexorably striving to attain to positions in the heavenly hierarchy the Lord was rebuilding. Those who feared the Lord and thought upon His name were to return in accordance with His above-quoted promise. He was gradually sifting His people as wheat, removing from among His children those who refused to do His Will; which was GOD's Will. When He returned He would be accompanied by those who had intrepidly followed Him in times past during repeated incarnate life experiences. Some of these were to reappear in spiritually exalted positions, as will be explained in Part Three of this work.

---

[411] Cf. Ps. 2:6-12; Ps. 110:1,4-6; 1 Sam. 2:1-10; Dan. 8:13; Dan. 12:1-3; Mt. 24:25-33; Mk. 13:14-37; Rev. 16:14-16.

—CHAPTER SIX—

THE NEW COVENANT: PAVING THE WAY TO HIGHER DIMENSIONS

When our parental forerunners, Adam and Eve, fell victim to earthly desires the Tree of Life — the ethereal imprint of the Holy Spirit — was removed from the earth plane.[412] Consequently, they and those who had accompanied them in their earth adventure, as well as their descendants, became confined in this comparatively dense plane, made accountable to 3rd dimensional laws. It rendered them unable to effectively fulfill their missions and return to their heavenly estate. The Lord GOD foresaw how difficult it would be for Adam's descendants to extricate themselves from cycles of reincarnation because their flesh desires were all but insurmountable. In order to help them reach a quickened state of holiness by which they could again return to higher realms of Light — which were undergoing reconstruction as a result of the fall — He successively established with them two covenants. First, the so-called Old Covenant instituted by Moses, which in time was followed by the New Covenant subsequently brought in by the Son of GOD when He afterward incarnated as Jesus Christ of Nazareth.

---

[412] Gen. 2:9, 3:22-24.

THE OLD COVENANT

> *The Holy Ghost. . . . the way into the holiest of all was not yet made manifest, while the first tabernacle was yet standing. (Heb. 9:8)*

It wasn't until the close of the idolatrous Egyptian Age that GOD established His Covenant with the children of Israel through Moses. Its main part consisted of ten commandments originally written on two tablets of stone, and including other applicable statutes and judgements.[413] Most importantly, the Mosaic Law preempted man's worship of other gods by focusing his belief on the one preeminent GOD, and further served to establish a standard by which sin could be imputed and measured. By adhering to the terms of the Old Covenant, the descendants of Adam and Eve, the Children of Israel, would be protected by Divine Providence, and assured an earthly inheritance,[414] to which celestial ramifications would also attach. But as time progressed the written Mosaic laws and stringent temple ordinances soon became stumbling blocks for the chosen people because of a corrupted priesthood which led them astray. False prophets eventually began to strike out on their own, inadvertently, or at times intentionally, altering the meaning of the law for self-serving purposes. Because the Lord did not communicate with them, their often erroneous ministrations brought about divisions and variances which ultimately led to a general state of spiritual apostasy. Because of this schism, a time came when the Old Covenant had decayed and waxed old.[415] At a certain point in this spiritual decline, the Lord had declared through

---

[413] Deut. 4:13-14.

[414] The earthly promised land, Canaan.

[415] Heb. 8:13.

Prophet Jeremiah that He would bring in a New Covenant to replace the first one:

> Behold the days come, saith the Lord, that **I will make a new covenant** with the house of Israel. . . . But this shall be the covenant that I will make with the house of Israel: After those days, saith the Lord, **I will put my law in their inward parts and write it in their hearts;** and I will be their GOD; and they shall be my people. And they shall teach no more every man his neighbor, and every man his brother, saying, Know the Lord: for they shall all know me, from the least of them unto the greatest of them, saith the Lord; for I will forgive their iniquity, and I will remember their sin no more. (Jer. 31:31-34)

THE NEW COVENANT

Ages later, Jeremiah's prophesy found expression again in the New Testament:

> But now hath he (Christ) obtained a more excellent ministry, by how much also he is the mediator of a better covenant, which was established upon better promises. For if that first covenant had been faultless, then should no place have been sought for a second. For finding fault with them, he saith, Behold the days come, saith the Lord, when **I will make a new covenant** with the house of Israel and with the house of Judah.[416] Not according to

---

[416] Israel defined as all those who abide in faith in Jesus Christ regardless of race and culture — every individual who obeys Him has the opportunity to receive the promised fruits of His New Covenant (Gal. 3:26-28).

> *the covenant that I made with their fathers in the day when I took them by the hand to lead them out of the land of Egypt: because they continued not in my covenant, and I regarded them not, saith the Lord. (Heb. 8:6-9)*

To this was subsequently added:

> *Whereof the Holy Ghost also is a witness to us: for after that he had said before, This is the covenant that I will make with them after those days, saith the Lord, <u>I will put my laws into their hearts, and in their minds will I write them</u>. (Heb. 10:15-16)*

Jesus, our high heavenly Melchizedekian Priest, expiated the Adamic sin by His sacrificial offering — shedding of His blood on the Cross — thereby paying the debt in the same realm of existence in which the original offence had been incurred.[417] With the brutal piercing of His physical body, the living water of His Holy Spirit was released and allowed to flow into a dimension where carnality still prevailed.[418] Most significantly, because the FATHER and Son are at-One, the piercing sacrifice allowed souls still existent in the lower earth dimension to attune to the Son's Holy Spirit, and by His Spirit to attune to GOD the FATHER. This overtly contrasted against the Old Covenant in that the children of Israel, until the Crucifixion, had been dependent upon human priests to intercede to GOD on their behalf. With the emergence of the New Covenant the old fell away, heralding a new era of spiritual enlightenment — a period in which Christ Himself would manifest to the people GOD had given Him by quickening them into eternal life:

---

[417] Rom. 5:12-21.
[418] 1 Jn. 5:6-7; 1 Jn. 3:31-36.

> *How much more shall the blood of Christ who through the eternal Spirit offered himself without spot to God, purge your conscience from dead works to serve the living God? And for this cause he is the mediator of the new testament that by means of death, for the redemption of the transgressions that were under the first testament, they which are called might receive the promise of eternal inheritance. (Heb. 9-14-15)*

In accordance with the terms of the New Covenant, GOD's laws were subsequently made to manifest in man's mind and heart by the guidance of the Celestial Teacher, the Holy Ghost, the Messenger of GOD's Holy Spirit,[419] made available as a gift to mankind by the empowered Christ through the Atonement. The Holy Ghost bridges the gulf between lower and higher dimensions for us, in order that we may maintain spiritual contact. As GOD's Messenger, He assists man with his spiritual escalation, for the purpose of ultimately leading him into a state of attunement with GOD. Though the FATHER, Son, and the Holy Ghost are three separate powers of the GOD-head, they are completely attuned as One:[420] There is no disagreement between them because they all share the same Spirit of GOD the FATHER "... *who is above all, through all, and in us all:*"[421]

> *For there are three that bear record in heaven, the Father, The Word, and the Holy Ghost; and these three are one. (1 Jn. 5:7)*

---

[419] Celestial Teacher: Holy Spirit assigned to guide man into all truths. Christ restored the Holy Ghost to mankind: Acts. 2:33; Jn. 14:16-26; Jn. 15:26-27; Jn. 16:12-15.

[420] 1 Jn. 5:7.

[421] Eph. 4:6.

> *Therefore (Jesus Christ) being by the right hand of God exalted, and having received of the father the promise of the Holy Ghost . . . (Acts. 2:33)*

That GOD would write HIS laws *"in the minds and in the hearts"* of mankind, as foretold through Prophet Jeremiah, through this Celestial Messenger was divulged by Jesus during the course of the Last Supper. Knowing that His remaining time on earth with His Apostles was short, the Master explained that He would not leave them comfortless, but would send One who would continue to teach them *"all things and bring all things to their remembrance":*

> *Believest thou not that I am in the Father, and the Father in me?. . . . And I will pray the Father, and he shall give you another Comforter, that he may abide with you for ever, Even the Spirit of truth; whom the world cannot receive because it seeth him not, neither knoweth him: but ye know him; for he dwelleth with you, and shall be in you. I will not leave you comfortless: I will come to you. . . . At that day, ye shall know that I am in my Father, and ye in me, and I in you. . . . But <u>the Comforter, which is the Holy Ghost, whom the Father will send in my name, he shall teach you all things, and bring all things to your remembrance</u>, whatsoever I have said unto you. (Jn. 14:10-26)*

How Jesus would remain at-One with His Apostles — and with all those incarnated souls who would set about following Him after He had departed from the earth — is a matter of spirit merging into spirit, not an easy concept to grasp. Nevertheless, He made it abundantly clear that it was <u>possible for souls to</u>

remain at-One with Him and reap celestial knowledge through the synergistic operations of the Holy Triune. This meant that the children of Israel were no longer bound to earthly doctrines as was seen in the Old Covenant law of Moses, nor would they need to be subjected to the fallibility of earth teachers for their spiritual guidance and direction:

> *Nevertheless, I tell you the truth: It is expedient for you that I go away: for if I go not away, the Comforter will not come unto you; but if I depart, I will send him unto you. . . . Howbeit when he, the Spirit of truth, is come, he will guide you into all truth: for he shall not speak of himself; but whatsoever he shall hear, that shall he speak; and he will shew you things to come. He shall glorify me: for he shall receive of mine, and shall shew it unto you. A little while, and ye shall not see me: and again, a little while, and ye shall see me, because I go to the Father. (Jn. 16:7-16)*

TERMS OF THE NEW COVENANT

Unlike the mechanistic written laws of Moses, and the temple rituals of the Old Covenant, Christ's Covenant is rooted in love. Unconditional Love is the lever that lifts the veil from our clouded eyes, opening the door to an incipient understanding of the reach of the New Covenant, which still acknowledges, among other spirit-guided laws, GOD's Ten Commandments.[422] Instilling love as the root of our desires and thoughts is the simplest and most effective way to discipline and stabilize a fickle mind that too easily reacts to distracting external material stimuli.

---

[422] Ex. 34:28; Ex. 20:1-17; Mt. 22:37-40; 1 Jn. 2:3-7

It is easy to see why GOD instructed that a carnal mind is enmity against HIM. Such a mind is unable to contemplate the natural state of the spirit: it prefers to remain attached to the temporal pleasures of the earth. Conversely, those who abide in the Christ Spirit recognize unconditional love as the universal law through which GOD's Holy Spirit manifests on earth: such souls no longer rely on religious laws or ritualistic dogmas designed by man to attain to salvation. Instead they have the potential of being governed by consciences attuned to GOD and Christ and are thus able to draw the Holy Ghost.

> *The Spirit itself beareth witness with our spirit, that we are the children of God: (Rom. 8:16)*

> *I SAY the truth in Christ, I lie not, my conscience also bearing me witness in the Holy Ghost. . . . (Rom. (9:1)*

> *But now we are delivered from the law, that being dead, wherein we were held: that we should serve in newness of spirit, and not in the oldness of the letter. (Rom 7:6)*

By abiding in the Spirit of the Son of GOD, obeying His commandments, and following His doctrine of Love, anyone can become a beneficiary of the New Covenant and attain to eternal life in the twelve heavenly levels of the New Jerusalem.[423] It is also crucially important to let go of negative habits; repent all past misdeeds, maintain unbreakable faith, feed the soul with good works,[424] prayers, meditations, devotionals and align the will with GOD's Will:

> *Master, which is the great commandment of the law? Jesus said unto him, THOU SHALT LOVE THE LORD THY GOD WITH ALL THY HEART, AND WITH ALL THY SOUL, AND WITH ALL THY MIND. This is the first and great commandment. And the second is like unto it, THOU SHALT LOVE THY NEIGHBOUR AS THYSELF. On these two commandments hang all the law and the prophets. (Mt. 22:36-40)*

> *If ye love me, keep my commandments, And I will pray the Father and he shall give you another Comforter, that he may abide with you for ever. Even the Spirit of truth, whom the world cannot receive, because it seeth him not, neither knoweth him, but ye know him, for he dwelleth with you and shall be in you. But the Comforter, which is the Holy Ghost, whom the Father will send in my name he shall teach you all things, and bring all things to your remembrance, whatsoever, I have said unto you. (Jn. 14: 15-26)*

> *And this is his commandment, That we should believe on the name of his Son Jesus Christ, and love one another as he gave us commandment. And he that keepeth his commandments, dwelleth in him, and he in him. And hereby we know that he abideth in us, by the Spirit which he hath given us. (1 Jn. 3:23-24)*

Years after the Lord had left this world, Apostle Paul expounded on Jesus' commandments when He explained that <u>unconditional love releases one from the bonds of karmic laws</u>:

> *Owe no man any thing, but to love one another: for he that loveth another hath fulfilled the law. (Rom. 13:8)*

> *Love worketh no ill to his neighbour: therefore love is the fulfilling of the law. (Rom. 13:10)*

THE PURGING FIRE OF THE HOLY GHOST

When we earnestly seek to return to GOD, while honoring Christ's commandments, He reciprocates by sending the Holy Ghost, who in turn primes the soul by first purging and testing it with fire. Depending on one's state of spirituality, it can be a protracted process requiring radical and often painful changes. Anyone who today takes up his cross and follows Jesus Christ into higher states of consciousness commensurate with higher dimensions of existence, will not find the going easy, because every soul worthy of the Lord's Grace undergoes chastening.[425] Depending upon the character of a soul's previous and current life experiences, an extremely intense buffeting may take place as the Lord's Spirit is infused into the whole being at the spiritual, mental and physical levels.

> *Then Peter said unto them, Repent, and be baptized every one of you in the name of Jesus Christ for the remission of sins and ye shall receive the gift of the Holy Ghost. For the promise is unto you, and to your children, and to all that are afar off, even as many as the Lord our God shall call. (Acts. 2:38-39)*

---

[423] Rev. 21:10-27.
[424] 2 Cor. 5:10; Jas. 2:26.
[425] Heb. 12:5-13.

> ... *but he that cometh after me (John the Baptist) is mightier than I, ... he shall baptize you with the Holy Ghost and with fire: Whose fan is in his hand, and he will thoroughly purge his floor, and gather his wheat into the garner, but he will burn up the chaff with unquenchable fire. (Mt. 3:11-12)*
>
> *And when he (the Comforter) is come, he will reprove the world of sin, and of righteousness, and of judgement. (Jn. 16:8)*
>
> *For whom the Lord loveth he chasteneth, and scourgeth every son whom he receiveth. If you endure chastening, GOD dealeth with you as with sons; for what son is he whom the father chasteneth not?. . . . Furthermore we have had fathers of our flesh which corrected us, and we gave them reverence: shall we not much rather be in subjection unto the Father of spirits, and live? For they verily for a few days chasteneth us after their own pleasure: but he for our profit. Now no chastening for the present seemeth to be joyous, but grievous: nevertheless afterward it yieldeth the peaceable fruit of righteousness unto them which are exercised thereby. (Heb. 12:6-11)*

A good housekeeper does not effectively clean house by simply sweeping debris under the carpet. In like manner, each soul is burdened with the responsibility of cleaning the negative debris from his own spiritual house, his soul. Then, as Jesus' parable instructs, once swept out, it must be kept clean;[426] otherwise one risks reactivating karmic laws.[427] Many have been

---

[426] Mt. 12:43-45; Lk. 11:24-26.

[427] Lk. 9:62; Heb. 6:4-8; Heb. 10:26; 2 Pet. 2:22-23.

unable to withstand the purging fires of the Holy Ghost and have regrettably fallen back into old patterns. On the other hand, those who have persevered, having had their senses exercised, instinctually recognize the Holy Ghost's prompting and are better prepared to discern and recognize His voice in everyday manifestations.

THE MYSTICAL CHURCH BODY OF CHRIST

In former times, while the Mosaic Law was in effect, the Holy Ghost was not yet made manifest; for this reason the children of Israel relied on spiritually-quickened priests and prophets for spiritual knowledge, direction and redemption:

> *Then verily, the first covenant had also ordinances of divine service, and a worldly sanctuary. . . . Now when these things were thus ordained, the priests went always into the first tabernacle, accomplishing the service of God. But into the second went the high priest alone once every year, not without blood, which he offered for himself, and for the errors of the people: The Holy Ghost this signifying, that the way into the holiest of all was not yet made manifest, while as the first tabernacle was yet standing: But Christ being come an high priest of good things to come, by a greater and more perfect tabernacle, not made with hands, that is to say, not of this building. Neither by the blood of goats and calves but by his own blood he entered it once into the holy place, having obtained eternal redemption for us. (Heb. 9:1-2)*

But a long-term plan was in the works. The Lord, speaking through Prophet Isaiah, promised that a Redeemer would come for those who turned away from the temptations of the world. This revelation forecasted the coming of Jesus Christ and His New Covenant, which would permanently relieve earth priests and prophets of their duties for those who would accept it:[428]

> *And the Redeemer shall come to Zion, and unto them that turn from transgression in Jacob, saith the Lord. As for me, this is my covenant with them, saith the Lord; My spirit that is upon thee, and my words which I have put in thy mouth, shall not depart out of thy mouth, nor out of the mouth of thy seed, nor out of the mouth of thy seed's seed, saith the Lord, from henceforth and forever. (Isa. 59:16.20-21)*

This correlates with the New Covenant, under which terms every man can potentially become a member of Christ's Spirit-Church, able to access truth by communing in Spirit with the Holy Triune, through the Intercession of Christ, Head of the true Church:[429]

> *For **the law maketh men high priests which have infirmity**; but the word of the oath, which was since the law, maketh the Son, who is consecrated for evermore. (Heb. 7:28)*

> *Now of the things which we have spoken this is the sum: We have such an high priest, who is set on the right hand of the throne of the Majesty in the heavens; a minister of the sanctuary, and of **the true tabernacle which the Lord pitched, and***

---

[428] Mt. 23:8-11; Heb. 4:15-16; 5:1-5; 8:1-2; 9:7-8,11.
[429] Heb. 7:25; Eph. 5:23.

> **not man.** . . . . *But now hath he obtained a more excellent ministry, by how much also he is the mediator of a better covenant, which was established upon better promises. (Heb. 8:1-2)*

For those who will accept it, since the Lord the Son's Atonement on the Cross, human priests and prophets have been replaced by one unblemished, eternal, GOD-ordained Heavenly Priest and Intercessor after the order of Melchizedek — that is, Jesus Christ.[430] Prophet Daniel learned from the Archangel Gabriel that at the time of The Tribulation, which coincides with the return of the Lord, the power of the "*holy people*" will be abolished.[431] Some understand one reason for this to be that too many organized religions have become contaminated with self-serving earthly doctrines and dogmas, and have therefore fallen short of teaching the true principles of Christ's New Covenant, thereby leading His flock astray. The teachings of even well-meaning so-called "*holy people*" — except if they are rooted in the Spirit of Truth — can indeed be misleading, sometimes manipulative and at worst destructive:

> *. . . This people honoureth me with their lips, but their heart is far from me. Howebeit in vain do they worship me, teaching for doctrines the commandments of men.* **For laying aside the commandment of God, ye hold the tradition of men,** *as the washing of pots and cups; and many other such like things ye do. (Mk. 7:6-7)*

> *. . . . and when he shall have accomplished to* **scatter the power of the holy people,** *all these things shall be finished. (Dan. 12:7)*

---

[430] Heb. 4:14-16 and Heb. Chapters 6, 7, 8.
[431] Dan. 12:7.

Under Christ's New Covenant, souls are quickened into a spiritual state enabling them to effectively interact with the Holy Triune and other ministering angels,[432] having access by the Holy Spirit.[433] This is exemplified in the Book of Job, which leaves no doubt but that it is through the Spirit medium that we are to commune with, and obtain instructions from, GOD:

> ***In a dream, in a vision of the night, when deep sleep falleth upon men, in slumberings upon the bed; Then he openeth the ears of men, and sealeth their instruction.*** *That he may withdraw man from his purpose and hide pride from man. He keepeth back his soul from the pit, and his life from perishing by the sword. (Job. 33:15-18)*

Though the Spirit is the ethereal conduit through which we are able to commune with God, cautious discernment must always be exercised to avoid negatively-inspired diversions, distractions, and even delusions. Psychics who abuse their gifts for vain reasons, or financial gain or self aggrandizement, may incur serious spiritual losses. Apostle James taught that those who help others seek GOD's truth, appreciably help not only those who have lost their way, but themselves as well.[434] Psychics should keep this

---

[432] As noted in Ecclesiastes, the winged bird which communes between higher and lower realms is synonymous with an angel (Ecc. 10:20). Cf Heb. 1:14.

[433] Apostle Paul explained in 2 Cor. 3:1-6 that 'tables of stones' (Mosaic Laws and ordinances) would be replaced with the Spirit of the living GOD written in fleshy tables of the heart.

[434] Cf. Jas. 5:20.

core truth in mind and put it into application, rather than superficially speak of mere earthly events and occurrences, which can confuse and mislead others. Although we have the potential of effectively channeling the Holy Ghost by means of direct spirit receptions such as prophetic dreams, visions, strong intuitions, etc., it can be injurious or even fatal to proceed without the utmost caution. Unseen Satanic spirit forces present in the lower dimensional earth plane manifest in the mind tending to draw individuals to commit acts which bind them to karmic laws.[435] By this means, Satan keeps man under his influences and control.

The mystical operations of the Holy Spirit at work in Christ's church are exemplified in Jesus' discourse with His Apostles when He asked: "*Whom do men say that I the Son of man am ?*" To which Peter replied: "*..thou art the Christ, the son of the living God.*"[436] Peter's response described Jesus as GOD's anointed heavenly Son, the Messiah, who despite His majestic heavenly origins, manifested in a flesh body. Jesus, impressed by Peter's response, blessed him, and further explained that "*flesh and blood*" could not have revealed this truth: only GOD. And because GOD is a Spirit,[437] it was through the Holy Spirit — the Holy Ghost — that Peter had received this revelation. Peter's reply exemplified how today one can potentially access knowledge through the Holy Ghost: in fact, it was on this basis that the true church was to

---

[435] For this reason, Apostle John wrote that for anyone to love the earth is spiritually fatal (1 Jn. 2:14-17). One reason is that such desires attract souls to repeatedly reincarnate in temporal flesh. Cf. Eph. 6:12.
[436] Mt: 16:15-16.
[437] Jn. 4:24.

operate. After having blessed Peter, the Master declared that He would build His church on "*this Rock*":

> *For I say unto thee, that thou art Peter, and **upon this rock I will build my church;** and the gates of hell shall not prevail upon it. And I will give to thee the keys of the kingdom of heaven. . . . (Mat. 16:18-19)*

The giving of the keys to Peter was not only synonymous with heavenly knowledge, it also alluded to the fact that he, as well as eleven other leading souls, would each be given a key to one of the heavenly gates leading into twelve higher dimensions, as will be explained. Most significantly, the *"rock"* noted in the above-cited verses did not refer to Peter, nor to religious earthly structures, but instead symbolically referred to Christ's quickening Spirit.[438] Christ was the Rock upon whom the Church was destined to be built, the same heavenly Rock that followed Israel during the Exodus:

> *And did all drink the same spiritual drink for they drank of that spiritual Rock that followed them and **that Rock was Christ**. (1 Cor. 10:4)*

In his epistle, Peter later identified Christ as a symbolic rock: the *"living stone"* who forms the cornerstone of GOD's heavenly edifice. By analogy, he taught that the true temple is Christ's Spirit body, and all those who compose this spiritual edifice are comparable to *"lively stones"* who find truth and life in the same Spirit:

> *To whom coming, as unto a living stone, disallowed indeed of men but chosen of God and pre-*

---

[438] Jn. 5:21.

> *cious. Ye also as lively stones are built up a spiritual house an holy priesthood to offer up spiritual sacrifices acceptable to God by Jesus Christ. Wherefore also is contained in the scriptures. (1 Pet. 2:5)*

> *For through him, we both have access by one Spirit unto the Father. Now therefore ye are no more strangers and foreigners, but fellow citizens with the saints, and of the household of God: And are built upon the foundation of the Apostles and prophets, **Jesus Christ himself being the chief corner stone.** In whom all the building fitly framed together groweth unto an holy temple in the Lord. In whom ye also are builded together for an habitation of God through the Spirit. (Eph. 2:18-22)*

> *Know ye not that you are the temple of God, and that the Spirit of God dwelleth in you? (1 Cor. 3:16)*

> *What? Know ye not that your body is the temple of the Holy Ghost which is in you, which ye have of God, and ye are not your own. (1 Cor. 6:19)*

Some Christian denominations have failed to recognize that the true church is within each individual, and is governed by the Spirit of GOD given to the Son without measure. Instead of upholding and reinforcing this truth, they have usurped Christ's authority and constructed a hierarchy of religious powers to direct, and even to make futile attempts to intercede to GOD on behalf of their congregations. The Bible leaves no doubt that because of man's fallibility, earth priests have been replaced with one heavenly Priest, Jesus Christ, for those who bring themselves under the terms of His New Covenant.[439] Jesus confirmed this principle when he

---

[439] Heb. 4:14-16 and Heb. Chapters 5, 6, 7, 8.

referred to the indulgences and corruption of temple officials to a multitude who had gathered around Him. He further instructed his followers not to call any man on earth "*Father*" because they had only one Father, who is in heaven. Nor were they to call any man "*rabbi*" or "*Master*," because they have only one Master, Christ the Son of GOD.[440] As the New Testament instructs, it is Christ who sends the Holy Ghost, and by His Spirit we can effectively come together as One cohesive family in His Spirit Church Body to share spiritual gifts for the benefit of all. Because some Christ-illuminated individuals have acquired valid spiritual truth through the Spirit,[441] they are enabled to teach those less spiritually advanced. Unfortunately, because of religious hierarchies and rules, many have been repressed from expressing the fruit of the Spirit:

> *How is it then brethren? When ye come together, every one of you hath a psalm, hath a doctrine, hath a tongue, hath a revelation, hath an interpretation. Let all things be done unto edifying. . . . For ye may all prophesy one by one, that all may learn, and all may be comforted. (1 Cor. 14:26-31)*

> *Now there are diversities of gifts, but the same Spirit. And there are differences of administrations but the same Lord. Now there are diversities of operations, but it is the same God which worketh all in all. But the manifestation of the Spirit is given to every man to profit withal. For to one is given by the Spirit the word of wisdom; to another the word of knowledge by the same Spirit, to another faith the same Spirit; to another the gifts of healing by the same Spirit; to another the working of miracles; to another proph-*

---

[440] Mt. 23:1-10.
[441] Gal. 1:11-12.

> *ecy; to another discerning of spirits; to another divers kinds of tongues; to another the interpretation of tongues. (1 Cor. 12:6-10)*

Under the New Covenant, soul accountability has been transferred from obedience to the Law of Moses to the spiritual authority of the Holy Trinity. Unlike Jesus Christ the Son of GOD who was the First to attain to perfection in the earth dimension, all the rest of us have fallen somewhat short of the glory of GOD, in some cases, far short. Consequently we each find ourselves existent in commensurately different spiritual states from those around us. Because of our comparatively depleted condition we are only able to communicate with GOD the FATHER by the intercession of Christ, GOD's eternal heavenly Priest, because the vibrations of the respective energies are so markedly incompatible. This gap, which was infinitely wider under the Mosaic Law, was bridged by Jesus Christ's sacrificial Atonement on the Cross, by which He gifted mankind with the Holy Ghost, the Celestial Messenger who relays information between man and GOD by the Intercession of Christ.[442] Without this life-giving Holy Spirit, man would have remained subjected indefinitely to manmade doctrines, temple rituals and written laws:

> *But now we are delivered from the law, that being dead, wherein we were held: that we should serve in newness of spirit, and not in the oldness of the letter. (Rom. 7:6)*

> *For **as many who are led by the Spirit of God they are the sons of God**. (Rom. 8:14)*

---

[442] 1 Tim. 2:1-6; Heb. 7:25; 9:15; 10:11-14.

GOD is a Spirit,[443] and Jesus revealed that GOD the FATHER's Holy Spirit dwells in Him, and that if we abide in Him, the Spirit of the FATHER, the Son and the Holy Ghost will abide in us as well. <u>Through the synergistic operations of the Holy Trinity, we become receptive to higher states of consciousness</u>, allowing us to <u>overcome the constricting effects of earth's 3rd dimensional laws</u>. This was illustrated by Jesus, who frequently overcame physical laws by His miraculous works, phenomenally healing long-term afflictions of all kinds: even in at least one case reviving into life a man who had undergone flesh death.[444] It is noteworthy that <u>Jesus never took personal credit for the wondrous works He accomplished but rather credited His heavenly FATHER who worked in and through Him</u>. It emphasized that whatever a man is able to accomplish, it is actually attributable to the workings of the much more powerful Spirit forces of GOD, Christ the Son, the Holy Ghost and the great Archangels and angels of the Light who minister to each according to the level of his quickened spiritual state. Man can attain to higher states of consciousness and accomplish excellent works for as long as He obeys the Lord's commandments while attuning to the spirit forces of the Holy Triune. However, this is not for the faint of heart, *"For unto whomsoever much is given, of him shall be much required."*[445]

> *Believest thou not that I am in the Father, and the Father in me? The words that I speak unto you I speak not of myself: but the Father that dwelleth in me, he doeth the works. . . . Verily, verily I say unto you, He that believeth on me the works that I do*

---

[443] Jn. 4:24.
[444] Jn. 11:1-44; 12:1-17.
[445] Lk. 12:48.

> *shall he do also; <u>and greater works than these shall he do</u>; because I go unto my Father. (Jn. 14:12)*

THE 144,000 FORERUNNERS

> *These are they which were not defiled with women: for they are they which follow the Lamb whithersoever he goeth. . . . (Rev. 14:4)*

About two thousand years after Abraham's time and about fifteen hundred years after the Mosaic Law took effect, the Old Covenant came to an end. It had served its purpose for its epoch, having afforded the children of Israel a spiritual developmental period during which they had the potential of attaining to successively higher levels of consciousness. Certain of those who made spiritual gains during the Hebraic Age continued to reincarnate in the period that succeeded it when the Son of GOD[446] manifested in flesh on earth as Jesus of Nazareth.

Having passed through stringent earth testing and development, these firstfruits who descended with the Lord in the garden of Eden, will reenter the earth plane as highly-spiritualized souls able to respond to the teachings of the Holy Ghost, enabling them to assist in implementing GOD's Master Plan in the earth plane. Though they constitute the remnant of the twelve tribes of Israel, they will no longer remain attached to the Jewish belief nor to the Mosaic Law:

> *Saying, Hurt not the earth, neither the sea, nor the trees, till we have sealed the servants of our God in their foreheads. And I heard the number of them*

---

[446] Ps. 2:6-12; 110:1, 4-6.

> *which were sealed: and there were sealed an hundred and forty and four thousand of all the tribes of the children of Israel. (Rev. 7:3-4)*
>
> ***And they sung as it were a new song*** *before the throne and before the four beasts and the elders; and no man could learn that song but the hundred and forty and four thousand which were redeemed from the earth. . . . These are they which follow the Lamb whithersoever he goeth.* ***These were redeemed from among men, being the firstfruits unto God and the Lamb*** *. . . (Rev. 14:3-4)*

Because the 144,000 elect successfully passed under the rod of the Holy Ghost's testing fire,[447] they will have become so intensely quickened as to defy laws associated with reincarnative cycles of life and death, and will not be subjected to the second death predestined to follow the Millennium of the First Resurrection.[448] Being no longer subjected to human mortality, they will be able to materialize in flesh bodies at will without having to undergo earthly conceptions, which ages ago resulted from the Adamic transgression:

> *Blessed and holy is he that hath part in the first resurrection: on such the second death hath no power, but they shall be priests of God and of Christ, and shall reign with him a thousand years. (Rev. 20:6)*

As highly evolved, spiritually-seasoned souls, they will have met the criteria to form part of the heavenly army destined to battle against the forces of darkness and to remove them from the earth plane, where they were long ago confined by Michael.[449] The

---

[447] Mt. 3:11-12.

[448] Rev. 20:6.

[449] Rev. 12:7-12.

cleansing action of these elect emissaries will make it possible for the Millennium of the First Resurrection to proceed without negative obstructions.

During the 2000 years since Jesus brought in His New Covenant, countless others have made their robes white and have effectively passed through the purification process. However, they are not categorized in the same rank as the 144,000 because they have not yet attained to as high a spiritual status. It appears, however, that they have another thousand years to escalate into higher heavenly levels by assisting the 144,000 fulfill their roles, as will be explained. A third group — those souls who will not have attained to an acceptable elevated state of consciousness — will undergo further development and testing during the coming thousand years of reincarnative cycles in order to become adequately perfected to overcome the desires and temptations that have for so long kept them bound to the earth plane.[450] It is fitting of GOD's divine design that the 144,000 will compose a heavenly priesthood who, with the assistance of those clothed in white robes, will assist the third group of souls still "*dead*" in the spirit achieve their goal.

When the population again begins to multiply on the earth after the return of Christ, those souls who will have made their robes white during the tribulation period,[451] will be drawn into the earth plane, each in accordance with the level of spirituality attained. Accordingly, a strong root race of souls will

---

[450] Scriptures refer to this third group as still being "dead" for another 1,000 years — they have not awakened to life in the spirit in accordance with the terms of the new Covenant (Rev. 20:5).

[451] Rev. 7:9-17.

be seeded at the outset, with lesser spiritualized entities entering at a later time; the intention being to allow developing souls an opportunity to be quickened by the Christ Spirit into increasingly higher levels of consciousness prerequisite to their being able to attain to higher levels in the eternal heavenly New Jerusalem.[452] Thus when Satan is released at the end of the period of the First Resurrection, those who will be subjected to his negative ways will be better prepared to overcome his last period of testing in the earth plane before final judgment — after which comes the second and final death.[453]

---

[452] Many of those who made their robes white during the Hebraic Age, thereby becoming part of the *remnant* of Israel, have since reincarnated on earth, and been converted to serve the Lord under Christ's New Covenant.

[453] Rev. 20:6-15.

PART THREE

—CHAPTER ONE—
THE SONS OF JACOB RETURN

TWELVE GREAT ARCHANGELS: FRUIT YIELDING TREES

It is understood that in the beginning angelic beings incarnated with Adam. Twelve of these heavenly entities later reappeared as the twelve sons of Jacob. In light of Rev. 21:12-14, it may be concluded that twelve of these heavenly representatives, in some cases the same entities, were drawn from each of the tribes, and reappeared as the Apostles of Jesus. This is subtly revealed in symbols incorporated in Genesis where it is written that GOD created fruit-yielding trees to serve as *"food"* for man but cautioned against partaking of food from the Tree of Knowledge of Good and Evil which had the power of death.[454]

> And out of the ground made the Lord God to grow every tree that is pleasant to the sight, and good for food: the tree of life also in the midst of the garden and the tree of knowledge of good and evil. . . . And the Lord God commanded the man, saying, Of every tree of the garden thou mayest freely eat: But of the tree of the knowledge of good and evil, thou shalt

---
[454] Cycles of life and death in the earth plane through the reincarnative process.

> *not eat of it: for in the day that thou eatest thereof thou shalt die. (Gen. 2:9-17)*

At first glance, the above verses appear to refer to the physical ingestion of food. That the term *"fruit yielding trees"* applied to spiritual food was brought to light in the New Testament when Jesus metaphorically explained to a group of doubting Pharisees that He was the vine, and that it was by His Spirit that those who were His — His spirit-branches — were enabled to produce good spiritual fruit.[455] In part, these parables subtly reveal that the twelve angelic leaders of the twelve tribes of Israel — along with their respective twelve thousand kindred souls, also known as the firstfruits — [456] were the initial planting of *"fruit-yielding trees"* in the Garden of Eden. Before the Fall, these Adamic forerunners radiated twelve different levels, or frequencies and wavelengths of spirit forces, each of which were activated by the Tree of Life — the brilliant, quickening Light imprint of GOD's Holy Spirit. Because they were rooted in the Eternal Spirit of their Maker, the Son,[457] all that emanated from them before the fall was formalized in beauty and harmony. However, when their Progenitors and Leaders, Adam and Eve, fell victim to the wiles of Satanic influences, the Tree of Life was removed from all Adamic forerunners. As a result, they lost the heavenly essence that allowed them to yield highly-spiritualized fruit and became increasingly more vulnerable to Satanic influences. Like their progenitors, Adam and Eve, they were thereafter required to undergo numerous cycles of life and death in the earth plane until they could once again be quickened by GOD's Holy Spirit.

---

[455] Jn. Ch. 15.

[456] Rev. 14:4.

[457] Ps. 33:6; 1 Cor. 8:6; Eph. 3:9-10; Heb. 1:1-2.

Their mission hampered by powerful Satanic forces, the twelve Archangelic leaders and their respective tribes nevertheless embarked upon a continuous effort to attain to the unique spirit essence they had lost in the Garden. It was a struggle that took place through centuries, but could not be effectively accomplished until after the Holy Spirit was restored through the Atonement by Jesus Christ while in a perfected state.[458] Having subsequently reached a spiritually-evolved condition by the guidance of the Holy Spirit, they have attained to the Christ consciousness, with the result that, at the time of the Lord's Second Coming, they and those who have overcome the earth will be favorably positioned to undertake the same mission which had been foiled by Satan and his angels in the beginning — that of spiritualizing the earth with lineages of GOD's Light.

Considering these matters in an esoteric light, the twelve levels of the heavenly New Jerusalem represent the twelve influences of the zodiacal signs and are synonymous with Jacob's twelve sons and their respective tribes. The twelve levels of the New Jerusalem/twelve divisions of the Zodiac are presently under reconstruction by the Holy Trinity, the twelve archangelic leaders and 144,000 forerunners. Because that which manifests in the material plane reflects that which correlates with its corresponding spiritual dimension, the heavenly remodeling will reflect a new ethereal/terrestrial body and a new

---

[458] In the beginning was the Word, and the Word was with God, and the Word was God. *"The same was in the beginning with God...... **In him was Life; and the life was the light of men.**"* (Jn. 1:4) *"**I am** the way, the truth and **the life....**"* (Jn. 14:6). *"....I (Jesus Christ) will give to eat of the **Tree of Life**"....(Rev. 2:7).*

earth. At the time of the first universal resurrection, the 144,000 will form part of a heavenly priesthood[459] under Christ, and assist in establishing and guiding the new root race and their descendants. The twelve archangelic leaders, the 144,000 kindred souls, and the multitude of others who have made their robes white will, through various incarnations, have succeeded in planting and cultivating a variety of spiritual fruit whose origins are rooted in twelve different ethereal sources.[460] At the time of fulfillment, this harvest will be consumed by the nations of the world, as biblically explained by the metaphoric life-giving essence of their leaves:

> *In the midst of the street of it, and on either side of the river, was there **the tree of life which bare twelve manner of fruits and yielded her fruit every month: and the leaves of the tree were for the healing of the nations**. And there shall be no more curse: but the throne of God and of the Lamb shall be in it; **and his servants shall serve him: And they shall see his face: and his name shall be in their foreheads**. (Rev. 22:2-4)*

TWELVE SONS: TWELVE APOSTLES

The Lord speaking through Prophet Malachi declared that a Book of remembrance had been written about all the children of Israel who had feared the Lord. The scriptures leave no doubt but that they

---

[459] Rev. 20:6

[460] All things gained or lost on earth are gained or lost in heaven (Mt. 18:18), which is why earth incarnations are of such importance; it will be a major consideration in the Final Judgement (2 Cor. 5:10).

would be the jewels who would *"later return"*[461] to discern between the righteous and the wicked:

> *For I am the Lord, I change not; therefore **ye sons of Jacob are not consumed**. . . . Then they that feared the Lord spake often one to another; and the Lord hearkened, and heard it, and **a Book of remembrance was written** before him for them that feared the Lord, and that thought upon his name. And they shall be mine, saith the Lord of hosts, in that day when I make up my jewels; and I will spare them, as a man spareth his own son that serveth him. **Then shall ye return and discern between the righteous and the wicked**, between him that serveth God and him that serveth him not. (Mal. 3:6, 16-18)*

That these GOD-fearing souls had lived previous lives in order to "*return*" and fulfill these important roles can only be explained through the process of reincarnation. The Son of GOD, the Lord of the Old and New Testaments,[462] had striven through the centuries after His fall as Adam to revivify and reconstitute those who had also fallen prey to Satanic influences. There remains much yet to be revealed about how this took place, but a substantial part of the picture may be reconstructed by assembling and correlating scriptural pieces of this spiritual puzzle. For example, in the above noted verse, the Lord speaking through Malachi prophesied that many who formed Israel's lineages would return to discern between the righteous and the wicked. That Jacob's twelve sons or in some cases other representatives in their respective tribes, would return

---

[461] Heb. 2:13.
[462] Ps. 2:6-9.

as Jesus' Apostles to assist in this grand design is found interspersed in scriptures. This is exemplified in the Gospel of Matthew and Luke in which Jesus tells His Apostles the preeminent roles they would play in judging the twelve tribes of Israel, thereby linking them with those who had been prophesied would return to discern between the righteous and the wicked:

> *And Jesus said unto them, Verily I say unto you, That ye which have followed me, in the regeneration when the Son of man shall sit in the throne of his glory,* **ye also shall sit upon twelve thrones, judging the twelve tribes of Israel.** *(Mt. 19:28)*

> **And I appoint unto you a kingdom**, *as my Father hath appointed unto me; That ye may eat and drink at my table, in my kingdom, and* **sit on thrones judging the twelve tribes of Israel.** *(Lk. 22:29-30)*

From Apostle Paul we learn that the 144,000 and those who have made their robes white, will also be adjudicators under the leadership of these twelve great Archangels, which fits within the divine architectural plan of the restructuring of the New Jerusalem:

> *Do ye not know that the saints shall judge the world? . . . . Know ye not that we shall judge angels? (1 Cor. 6:2-3)*

It is in Jesus' illuminating dialog with His Apostles during the Last Supper that another important clue is disclosed linking them to the metaphorical twelve fruit-yielding trees in the Garden. On the evening of the Passover, the Master told His Apostles that it would be the Holy Ghost who would bring all knowledge to their "*remembrance.*"[463] During the course of this discussion, He tells them that their spirit would bear witness with the Holy Ghost, also known as the Spirit of Truth and other comforter,[464] empowered to reveal to them that they had been with Jesus since the beginning:

> *But when the Comforter is come, whom I will send unto you from the Father, even the Spirit of truth, which proceedeth from the Father, he shall testify of me: And ye also shall bear witness,* **because ye have been with me from the beginning**.[465] *(Jn. 15:26-27)*

In order to understand the word "*beginning*" in the context as above intended, we turn to the first chapters in the Book of Genesis which explain how evolution and creation systemically came into existence. On a different level of interpretation, the spirit meaning of Genesis' written symbols, as exemplified in the creation and manifestation of the "*trees*," is also

---

[463] The Holy Ghost is appointed to bring all knowledge to the Apostle's remembrance (Jn. 14:26); cross-references with Mal. 3:6-18 which teach that a Book of "*remembrance*" was written of those who would return.

[464] Jn. 14:16-18, 26; 16:7, 12-15.

[465] When Jesus told a group of doubting Jews that He was the One who was from the "*beginning*" — the Lord of the Old Testament sent by the FATHER — the perplexed Jews were unable to understand that it was the FATHER who had sent Him (Jn. 8:25-27). The beginning could not have referred to the time Jesus began His ministry because He did not select His Apostles until some time after that. In Matthew Chapters 3 and 4, Jesus was alone when he met John the Baptist at the Jordan in Nazareth; went into the wilderness for 40 days by Himself and traveled alone to Galilee before selecting His Apostles.

analogous to man. When the Adamic forerunners incarnated in the earth plane to restore order in the beginning, they descended as souls taking expression in flesh bodies which had sufficiently evolved to accommodate higher states of consciousness. In accordance with their mission, these *"trees"* — holographic replicas of the Tree of Life[466] — had the ability to yield seeds after their own kind by projecting their particular spirit essence into their offspring.[467]

> *And God said, Let the earth bring forth grass, the herb yielding seed, and the fruit **tree yielding fruit after his kind, whose seed is in itself**, upon the earth: and it was so. (Gen. 1:11)*

The symbolic meaning of a tree as it relates to man is explained in numerous biblical verses. Two of the most revealing disclosures of its metaphoric meanings are found in Jesus' parable of the cultivated mustard seed and in the Book of Psalms, which patently associates man with a tree:

> *Blessed is the man that walketh not in the counsel of the ungodly. . . . he shall be like a tree planted by the rivers of water. . . . (Psalm 1:1-3)*

> *The Kingdom of Heaven is like to a grain of mustard seed, which a man took, and sowed in his field. Which indeed is the least of all seeds: but when it is grown, it is the greatest among herbs, and*

---

[466] Refer to Diagrams 1 to 4 in Chapter: "Transposition of Spirit Energy Into Physical Bodies."

[467] The "*seed*" of the fruit yielding trees in the Garden (Gen. 1:29) are synonymous with the children of the Kingdom of GOD (Mt. 13:38).

> *becometh a tree. . . . The field is the world; the good seed are the children of the kingdom. . . . (Mt. 13:31-38)*

That the "*trees*" in the garden underwent multiple life experiences from the beginning to overcome carnal influences which keep the soul earthbound, is confirmed in the Book of Ezekiel. The Lord speaking through that prophet left no doubt but that one garden tree, along with its seed, had returned ages later as a negative Egyptian Pharoah with his kingdom. Unless explained through the process of reincarnation, how else could Pharoah have existed in the Garden at the beginning?

> *Son of man, speak unto Pharaoh king of Egypt, and to his multitude; Whom art thou like in thy greatness? Behold the Assyrian was a cedar in Lebanon with fair branches, and with a shadowing shroud and of an high stature; and his top was among the thick boughs. The waters made him great, the deep set him up on high with her rivers running round about his plants, and sent out her littler rivers unto all the trees of the field. Therefore his height was exalted above all the trees of the field, and his boughs were multiplied, and his branches became long because of the multitude of waters, when he shot forth. All the fowls of heaven made their nests in his boughs, and under his branches did all the beasts of the field bring forth their young, and under his shadow dwelt all great nations. Thus was he fair in his greatness, in the length of his branches: for his root was by the great waters.* **The cedars in the garden of God could not hide him: the fir trees were not like his boughs,**

and the chestnut trees were not like his branches; nor any tree in the garden of God was like unto him in his beauty. I have made him fair by the multitude of his branches: so that all the trees of Eden, that were in the garden of God envied him. Therefore thus saith the Lord God; Because thou hast lifted up thyself in height, and he hath shot up his top among the thick boughs, and his heart is lifted up in his height: I have therefore delivered him into the hand of the mighty one of the heathen: he shall surely deal with him: I have driven him out for his wickedness. And strangers, the terrible of the nations have cut him off, and have left him: upon the mountains and in all the valleys his branches are fallen, and his boughs are broken by all the rivers of the land: and all the people of the earth are gone down from his shadow and have left him. Upon his ruin shall all the fowls of the heaven remain, and all the beasts of the field shall be upon his branches: To the end of that none of all the trees by the waters exalt themselves for their height, neither shoot up their top among the thick boughs, neither their trees stand up in their height, all that drink water for they are all delivered unto death to the nether parts of the earth in the midst of the children of men, with them that go down to the pit. Thus saith the Lord God: In the day when he went down to the grave I caused a mourning: I covered the deep for him, and I restrained the flood thereof, and the great waters were stayed: and I caused Lebanon to mourn for him, and all the trees of the field fainted for him. I made the nations to shake at the sound of his fall, when I cast him down to hell with them that descend into the pit: **and all the trees of**

> ***Eden, the choice and best of Lebanon all that drink water, shall be comforted in the nether parts of the earth.*** *They also went down to hell with him unto them that be slain with the sword; and they that were his arm, that dwelt under his shadow in the midst of the heathen.* ***To whom art thou thus like in glory and in greatness among the trees of Eden? Yet shall thou be brought down with the trees of Eden unto the nether parts of the earth:*** *thou shalt lie in the midst of the uncircumcised with them that be slain by the sword.* ***This is Pharoah and all his multitude***, said the Lord God. (Eze. 31:2-18)

Because the first Parents were beguiled into misusing the divine creative forces, all the trees in the garden and their offspring became encased in lower-vibrational human flesh bodies, and were compelled to undergo multiple life experiences in an effort to overcome karmic laws and return to a state of Oneness with GOD the FATHER. After the fall Adam regained GOD's Holy Spirit during his incarnation as Enoch. He then returned as Melchizedek to set up the Divine Lineage into which He Himself would eventually long afterward be born as Jesus of Nazareth to restore His Life-giving spirit to all who would obey Him and abide by the terms of His New Covenant. In accordance with His master plan, some souls who had incarnated at the beginning with Him as the first Adam — the Son of GOD incarnate — also returned later to fulfill important roles. That the sons of Jacob, along with two grandsons, would return to help establish a twelve-branched, Divine Genealogical Tree is seen as it unfolds in scriptures.

THE DIVINE GENEALOGICAL TREE

The roots of the Divine Genealogical Tree were first seeded by Adam and subsequently manifested in future generations which, by way of Enoch, led to Abraham. As noted previously, the soul in Adam returned as Melchizedek to guide and move Abraham and Sarah establish future lineages under the 3 to 4 generation rule. The positive effects were reaped by Jacob, a third generation descendant in Abraham's lineage. As a favored prince of GOD,[468] he assisted the Lord in establishing the twelve branches of Israel's Divine Genealogical Tree by drawing into materiality twelve celestial sons, each destined to fulfill an important position in the restructuring of the heavenly hierarchy.

The Lord renamed Jacob to Israel; a name that would eventually become synonymous with all those souls who, regardless of nationality,[469] will have overcome negative influences associated with the carnality of this 3rd dimensional world, *supra*. At the time of the first universal resurrection, they will inherit positions among the twelve branches of the Adamic tree reflective of twelve heavenly levels:[470]

> *When the Most High divided the nations their inheritance, when he separated the sons of Adam, he set the bounds of the people according to the number of the children of Israel. For the Lord's*

---

[468] Gen. 32:28

[469] Gal. 3:28-29

[470] Rev. 2:17 teaches that a new name will be given to those who overcome. Exemplified in Abram and Sarai whose names were changed to Abraham and Sarah; in Peter to Cephas; in Saul of Tarsus to Paul; etc.

> *portion is his people; **Jacob is the lot of his inheritance**. (Deut. 32:8-9)*

When the Lord returns to take dominion of the earth, He will at that time receive as His portion those souls who, having attuned to His Spirit, will have reached an elevated state of spiritual perfection. These foundation stones upon which the Lord's heritage is constructed is synonymous with the 144,000, the remnant of Israel: those who flowed from the Hebraic Age[471] into the current age of the Gentiles as different races in different countries. The inheritance will also include those who will have attained to a quickened spiritual state, and will be judged worthy to compose the restructured twelve levels of the heavenly New Jerusalem.[472] What is seen as a reshuffling of the genealogy of Jacob's twelve sons effectuated changes in the Adamic ancestral inheritance, and also mirrored changes taking place in twelve higher dimensions of existence. The earthly reflection of the New Jerusalem is seen in John's vision as described in the Book of the Revelation. While in a trance state, John allegorically describes twelve angels, each standing at one of the twelve gates leading into higher dimensions. Their soul incarnations are mirrored in the twelve sons of Jacob and the twelve Apostles who incarnated in the twelve lower foundations of the earth plane — the twelve tribes of Israel:

> *And he . . . shewed me that great city, the holy Jerusalem, descending out of heavens from GOD. And had a wall great and high, and had twelve gates, and **at the gates twelve angels** and names written thereon, **which are the names of the twelve***

---

[471] Deut. 32:8-9.
[472] Rev. 21:14-23.

> *tribes of the children of Israel: . . . And the wall of the city had **twelve foundations, and in them the names of the twelve Apostles** of the Lamb. (Rev. 21:10-14)*
>
> *Now therefore **ye are** no more strangers and foreigners, but fellowcitizens with the saints, and **of the household of God: And are built upon the foundation of the Apostles and prophets, Jesus Christ himself being the chief corner stone.** In whom all the building fitly framed together groweth unto an holy temple in the Lord. In whom ye also are builded together for an habitation of God through the Spirit. (Eph. 2:19-22)*

Though in part theoretical, the following chapters describe how certain of the sons of Jacob apparently returned to continue to strive to attain to elevated positions in the heavenly hierarchy as the heads of their respective tribes.

—CHAPTER TWO—

JOSEPH A SOUL INCARNATION OF JESUS OF NAZARETH

THE BRIGHT MORNING STAR

Prophet Balaam prophesied that a "*Star*" would come out of Jacob, who would become the GOD-quickened heavenly Scepter predestined to ultimately rise out of Israel. Balaam wrote that he would see him but not then, because in his time the *Star* had not been born:

> *I shall see him but not now: I shall behold him, but not nigh:* **there shall come a star out of Jacob,** *and a Sceptre shall rise out of Israel . . . (Num. 24:17)*

The *Star* prophesied to come out of Jacob was Joseph, whose higher self in Heaven is the Lord the Son of GOD, whose exalted soul would subsequently incarnate as Jesus of Nazareth in fulfillment of another dream of Balaam's:

> *Out of Jacob shall come he that shall have dominion . . . (Num. 24:19)*

From the beginning, this *Star* was predestined to reign over the Twelve tribes of Israel:

> *I (Jesus) have sent mine angel to testify unto you these things in the churches:* ***I am the root and the offspring of David, and the bright and morning star****. (Rev. 22:16)*

> *For Judah prevailed above his brethren, and of him came the chief ruler;* ***but the birthright was Joseph's****. (1 Chron. 5:1-2)*

It was foretold through Prophet Micah that the one who was to one day rule Israel — the heavenly Israel — would be born on earth in Bethlehem, in Judah; which turned out to be Jesus' birthplace. Micah's prophecy also foreshadowed that a remnant of the tribes of Israel would return in Jesus' time [473] — an event that was heavenly guided by the Son GOD had formed in the beginning.[474] Those children of Israel who had persevered through the generations in faith and belief in their Lord, and who had obeyed the Will of the Son of GOD, were the same souls Prophet Malachi had also foretold were to return,[475] and they did return in flesh bodies of men of Jewish descent, at the time of Jesus of Nazareth's earth incarnation.

JACOB'S PREDICTION

That some of the "*trees*" in the garden would later manifest as the sons of Jacob, and still later as Jesus'

---

[473] Micah 5:2-3.
[474] Ps. 2:6-12.
[475] Mal. 3:16-18.

Apostles, is subtly revealed in Jacob's prediction to Joseph, and in his blessings to some of his twelve sons. Before the age-stricken Jacob blessed them, he provided Joseph with a startling prediction carrying important future ramifications:

> *And Israel (Jacob) said unto Joseph, Behold, I die: but GOD shall be with you, and **bring you again unto the land of your fathers**. (Gen. 48:21)*

This was a dual prophecy, applicable in both the material and spiritual sense. Materially, it foretold that Joseph's bones would be brought out of Egypt at the start of the Exodus, carried into Canaan, and buried there in accordance with Joseph's deathbed request.[476] As subsequently inscribed in the Book of Joshua, Joseph's dying wish was carried out:

> ***And the bones of Joseph, which the children of Israel brought up out of Egypt, buried they in Shechem, in a parcel of ground which Jacob bought** of the sons of Hamor the father of Shechem for an hundred pieces of silver: and it became the inheritance of the children of Joseph. (Josh. 24:32)*

But Jacob's fore-vision, that GOD would bring Joseph again unto the land of his fathers, carried an even more significant spiritual meaning. It did not simply duplicate the prophesy that his skeletal remains would be returned to the land of his fathers: it foretold that GOD would bring the soul of Joseph again unto the land of his fathers. It would not take place during his earth experience as Joseph; but rather foreshadowed that his spirit would again incarnate

---
[476] Gen. 50:25.

on earth — which he did as Joshua son of Nun[477] — after which experience he returned in other incarnations before appearing as Jesus.

JOSEPH'S BLESSING

Jacob's insightful blessings would subsequently come to pass as he had presaged when he told his sons what would befall them at the end of the Hebraic Age; which coincided with the earth appearance of Jesus Christ of Nazareth. Jacob's blessing of Joseph symbolically foreshadowed that the soul in his son was predestined to restore life to Israel's twelve-branched Divine Genealogical Tree:

> *Gather yourselves together, that I may tell you **that which shall befall you in the last days**. (Gen. 49:1)*

> *Joseph is a fruitful bough, even a fruitful bough by a well; whose branches run over the wall. The archers have sorely grieved him, and shot at him, and hated him: But his bow abode in strength, and the arms of his hands were made strong by the hands of the mighty GOD of Jacob; **(from thence is the shepherd, the stone of Israel:)** Even by the GOD of thy father, who shall help thee; and by the almighty, who shall bless thee with blessings of heaven above, blessings of the deep that lieth under, blessings of the breasts and of the womb: the blessings of thy father have prevailed above the blessings of my progenitors unto the utmost bound of the everlasting hills: they shall be on the head of Joseph, and on the crown of the head of him that was separate from his brethren. (Gen. 49:22-26)*

---

[477] Ex. 33:9-12.

When Jacob blessed Joseph as *"a fruitful bough, even a fruitful bough by a well, whose branches run over the wall,"* the spiritual import was that he, as the divine branch, would extend over the wall that divides heaven from earth.[478] It was his spirit which would become the intermediary between GOD and man: the Spirit able to give Life to the other branches growing out of Israel's Divine Genealogical Tree.

In his blessing Jacob explained that Joseph's spiritual strength was attributable to GOD's quickening spirit power, and he then added one of the most striking of all the Bible's illuminating revelations. After commenting that Joseph's bow was held by his hands, which were strengthened by his mighty GOD, Jacob added:

> *. . . From **thence is the shepherd**, the **stone of Israel**. . . . (Gen. 49:24)*

In this way the Bible discloses that Joseph was a flesh manifestation of the *"shepherd of Israel"*; the *"stone"* or **Rock** [479] who guided and protected Moses and the children of Israel during the Exodus. The remarkable Prophetess Hannah was aware that the Son of GOD was the Rock:

> *There is none holy as the Lord: for there is none beside thee: neither is there any **rock** like our GOD. Talk no more so exceedingly proudly; let not arrogancy come out of your mouth, for the Lord is a GOD of knowledge, and by Him actions are weighed. The Lord killeth and maketh alive: he bringeth down to the grave, and bringeth up. The*

---

[478] Mt. 27:51; Mk. 15:38; Lk. 23:45; Heb. 6:19-20.
[479] 1 Cor. 10:4.

> *adversaries of the Lord shall be broken to pieces; out of heaven shall he thunder upon them (Cf. Ps. 2:6-9); the Lord shall judge the ends of the earth (Cf. Jn. 5:21-23; 2 Cor. 5:10); and He shall give strength unto His king, and exalt the horn of His anointed. (1 Sam. 2:1-10)*

King David was also aware of the identity of the Rock of Israel. He knew it was not GOD the FATHER, because he spoke of *two* Lords, one empowered above the other. He wrote that it was the second of these two Lords who was *his* Lord, and who was a priest forever after the order of Melchizedek, who was to one day strike through kings in the day of His wrath, judging among the heathen, filling many places with dead bodies and wounding the heads over many countries.[480] This referred to the great and terrible day of the Lord; Armageddon, the devastating destruction biblically prophesied to come. David is quoted in the Bible as having identified a second Lord as the Rock of Israel; thereby effectively linking Him with Joseph, the Stone of Israel.

> *Now these be the last words of David. David the son of Jesse said, and the man who was raised up on high, the **anointed of the God of Jacob**, and the sweet psalmist of Israel, said, The Spirit of the Lord spake by me, and His Word was in my tongue. The God of Israel said, the **Rock of Israel spake to me**, He that ruleth over men must be just, ruling in the fear of GOD. (2 Sam. 23:1-3)*

When it was written that the God of Israel, the Rock of Israel, spoke to David; telling him that he who rules over men must be just and rule in the fear of GOD, it

---

[480] Heb. 7:1-3; Ps. 110:1,4-6.

meant that the Son of GOD — understood to be the Rock of Israel as the above verses confirm — had spoken to David to advise him of the maxim that all who are empowered by GOD must rule justly and in fear of HIM. The Bible leaves no doubt but that David was to be granted an exalted heavenly position.

TWO PROPHETIC DREAMS

When Joseph son of Jacob — known as the Master of dreams — was in his teens, he began to manifest signs marking him as a soul with extraordinary spiritual gifts. His father, aware of his son's unusual spirituality, made him a coat of many colors. Colors reflect vibrations, and in Joseph's case it indicated that Jacob knew that Joseph had by that earth experience already spiritually advanced through many vibrational levels. As a child he experienced two remarkable dreams allegorically foreshadowing that his eleven brothers, as well as his mother and father, were to one day make obeisance to him:

> *We were binding sheaves in the field, and, lo, my sheaf arose, and also stood upright; and behold, your sheaves stood round about, and made obeisance to my sheaf. (Gen. 37:7)*

This dream of Joseph's would later coincide with Abraham's prophetic dream, which had previously foretold that his seed were to be strangers in a land that was not theirs, afflicted as servants for four hundred years, but predestined to emerge with great substance.[481] Abraham's prophesy came to pass when the children of Israel were exiled and afflicted for

---
[481] Gen. 15:12-14

four hundred years as strangers in Egypt. There they multiplied from their original seed, and grew into a nation unto the Lord. Divine Providence brought about Joseph's being raised above his brothers by the Pharoah, who made him ruler over all of Egypt, in which position he saved Abraham's seed from a famine predestined to come upon the land. The meaning of the dream of the sheaf foretold to rise above his brothers' sheaves presaged that he was one day to save the children of Israel from the ravages of the famine. The dream reflected as well Joseph's pre-eminent rule over his brothers when he later undertook the transfer of the people from Canaan into bondage in Egypt, as Abraham's dream, *supra*, had predicted was to transpire.

Joseph's second dream:

> *And he dreamed yet another dream, and told it his brethren and said, Behold, I have dreamed a dream more; and behold the sun and the moon and the eleven stars made obeisance to me. (Gen. 37:9)*

Joseph's second dream overlapped Abraham's first prophetic dream but instead of earthly events it referred to higher dimensional occurrences. Joseph's empowerment by the Pharaoh is understood to be analogous with the son's empowerment over the twelve levels of the heavenly hierarchy. The stars in his dream were understood by Jacob to represent Joseph's brothers and the sun and moon symbolized his mother and father.[482]

Joseph's eleven brothers — not fully aware of the spiritual import of his dream but fearing the worst

---

[482] Gen. 37:10-11.

— grew increasingly restive and jealous of him. They considered him a nuisance and the prospect that he might one day reign over them did not set well at all. Desiring to relieve themselves of his worrisome ways, they plotted to cast him in a pit and leave him there to die. Judah, concerned about the shedding of his brother's innocent blood, persuaded his brothers to sell Joseph to a band of Midianite merchantmen rather than leave him to his fate in the pit. Then began Joseph's journey to Egypt and into slavery. It was in Egypt that Joseph was sold to Potiphar, an officer of Pharaoh's, a captain of the guard in the army, where he was given charge of his house. Potiphar's wife on a few occasions impressed upon Joseph her desire to be intimate with him, but he refused to reciprocate. During one of her amorous seductive efforts, she grasped and ripped off his garment as he attempted to flee from the scene. It is written that hell hath no fury like a woman scorned, and Potiphar's wife, her upset salted with a generous portion of vengeance, appeased her anger by deceitfully accusing Joseph of attempting to forcefully seduce her. In support of her false accusation she flaunted Joseph's torn garment as evidence of an attack and on her word Joseph was imprisoned.

During his incarceration, Joseph's spiritual abilities continued to manifest. He interpreted the dreams of Pharaoh's chief butler and baker, who were serving time for having offended the king. Joseph explained to them that their dreams had predicted that the chief butler would be restored to his position, but that the chief baker would be hanged on a tree. The interpretation proved to be accurate when the chief butler was returned to his position, and the chief baker was duly hanged. Joseph always remained true to his total belief in the Lord, whose Spirit was always with him. When it was time, the Lord strategically placed him in a position of supreme authority and leadership: not only over all Egypt, in an earthly sense but ultimately over the tribes of Israel, as his dreams had foretold.

Two years after Joseph had interpreted the dreams of the chief butler and baker, the Pharaoh experienced two perplexing dreams which his wise men were unable to interpret. The chief butler recalled that Joseph was skilled at interpreting dreams, and informed the king, who ordered that Joseph be brought before him. When he told Joseph that it had come to his attention that he might be able to interpret his puzzling dream, he replied that GOD alone could do it.[483]

Joseph interpreted Pharaoh's dreams to mean that seven years of famine were predestined to come upon the whole land but that these lean years would be followed by seven years of plenty. Pharaoh accepted Joseph's interpretation and appointed him ruler over all the land of Egypt, second in power only to himself:

> *Thou shalt be over my house, and according unto thy word will my people be ruled: **only in the throne will I be greater than thou**. And Pharaoh said unto Joseph, I have set thee over all the land of Egypt. And Pharaoh took off his ring from his hand,*[484]

---

[483] Gen. 41:16. Cf. Jn. 14:10, which notes similarities of expression used by Jesus when He credited GOD His Father for the miraculous works He accomplished.

[484] Ex. 39:6; Dan. 6:17; Hag. 2:23; convey the efficacy of the signet ring as an expression of permanency in decision making, even in spiritual matters.

> *and arranged him in vestures of fine linen, and put a gold chain about his neck. (Gen. 41:40-42)*

Armed with the foreknowledge of an oncoming famine, Joseph set about gathering food *"as the sand of the sea"* storing it in every available space.[485] When the famine came, the Egyptians under Joseph's rule were able to survive and his eminence was increased to the point that the people accepted him as their Lord.[486] The widespread famine desolated the land of Canaan where Joseph's family dwelled, inducing his brothers to journey to Egypt to buy grain. It was there they met up again with Joseph, the brother they had once cast into a pit to die. When Joseph revealed his identity his brothers feared for their lives, realizing they had sold him into slavery in Canaan. But Joseph, possessing exceptional spiritual insight, overlooked their limited understanding and assured them that all was well; that the predestined situation had been part of GOD's Master Plan to save them from the famine:

> *Now therefore be not grieved, nor angry with yourselves, that ye sold me hither:* ***for GOD did send me before you to preserve life***. *(Gen. 45:5)*

In the prophetic sense, Joseph's Egyptian experience reflected His elevated spiritual status. By analogy, in the same way that Joseph was ranked in power in the materiality of earth under the Pharaoh, He later, as man's Savior Jesus Christ, was empowered in heaven below only GOD the FATHER. Prior to his elevation as ruler over all Egypt Joseph underwent stringent testing, through all of which he remained faithful to GOD. The soul which had been in Joseph, long af-

---

[485] Gen. 41:47-49.
[486] Gen. 47:25.

terward incarnated as Jesus of Nazareth and underwent even more stringent testing designed to ascertain His absolute obedience to GOD's Will. Having proven it beyond the shadow of any doubt, He was empowered with the FATHER's Holy Spirit to save those who obediently follow Him. This had been foreshadowed when, as Joseph, he had been empowered under the Pharoah, and was recognized by the Egyptian people as their lord because He had saved them from the effects of the famine.[487]

MANNA FROM HEAVEN

The sheaves of grain Joseph saw himself binding in his dream, *supra*, represented the enormous quantity of grain to be stored during the famine and baked into bread under his leadership. It was symbolic of the spiritual manna He later, as Jesus Christ, would send from higher dimensions to sustain His people as he had, as Joseph, provided material bread for his people in Egypt:

> *For the bread of God is He which cometh down from heaven, and giveth life unto the world. I am the bread of life: he that cometh to me shall never hunger; and he that believeth in me shall never thirst. (Jn. 6:33-35)*

> *I am that bread of life. Your fathers did eat manna in the wilderness, and are dead. This is the bread **which cometh down from heaven**, that a man may eat thereof and not die. **I am the living bread** which came down from heaven: if any man eat of this bread, he shall live for ever: and the bread I*

---

[487] Gen. 47:25.

> *will give is my flesh, which I will give for the life of the world. (Jn. 6:48-51)*

This is the basis of the sacramental Eucharist ritual fulfilled in remembrance of their Lord by those who know Him to be the Son of GOD who gave His life on the Cross. The bread in the Eucharist symbolizes the flesh body of Jesus Christ given in sacrifice. The wine represents His blood given for the New Testament [488] — the New Covenant He brought in by His agonizing atoning sacrifice on the Cross.[489] Because Christ has the FATHER's Spirit without measure, when we contritely fulfill the Eucharist we activate the quickening Spirit which flowed in Jesus' blood and draw it into our own spiritual, mental and physical constitutions. The Eucharist is spiritual food which quickens the individual soul that it may become at-One with the FATHER and the Son.[490] It is noteworthy that the New Testament does not prescribe the need for an earthly intercessor to administer the Holy Eucharist. The truth of the matter is that no man is perfect enough to perform this ritual on behalf of others at its highest spiritual level. Since GOD made Jesus Christ man's Eternal Heavenly Intercessor — as explained in the Book of Hebrews [491] — those who are His no longer need any human intercessor, because Christ the Son, who perfected Himself in

---

[488] Mt. 26:28; Mk. 14:24; Lk. 22:20; 1 Cor. 11:25.

[489] Significantly, when the Son of GOD had before manifested as Melchizedek, GOD's eternal high Priest, He had blessed Abraham with bread and wine, a sign foreshadowing His later appearance as Jesus.

[490] Jn. 3:34-36; Jn. 6:63; Jn. 14:10-12.

the earth plane, was made the eternal heavenly high Priest empowered to intercede on behalf of all who are His.[492] Those who personally call upon Him to sanctify the bread and the wine, as He did in person for those who attended the Last Supper, fulfill the Eucharist in its purest spiritual sense. It was Jesus who blessed the original Eucharist and He as the risen Christ still blesses it for those who are truly His followers.

Among the many other biblical signs and indications that Jesus of Nazareth had previously lived as Joseph is seen when his brothers arrived on their second trip to Egypt to purchase grain. Joseph ceremoniously served them bread and seated them around the table in a particular order according to their birthright:

> *And they sat before him, the firstborn according to his birthright, and the youngest according to his youth: and the men marveled at one another. (Gen. 43:33)*

Considered in its natural earthly sense, this verse describes a ritual understood by the spiritually-sensitive Joseph to have an important relevant significance. In its spiritual sense, it may have much more importantly presaged the order in which He would long afterward seat His Apostles and break bread with them at the Last Supper.

The end of the Hebraic Age marked 1500 years after Moses brought to mankind GOD's basic preliminary law to the spiritually enlightened Hebrews. What has puzzled many contemporary day Christians, be-

---

[491] Heb. Chapters 5,6,7,8,9,10; in particular Heb. 7:25.
[492] Heb. 7:25; Tim. 2:1-6; Heb. 9:15-24; Heb. 10:11-14.

cause principles of reincarnation have been long hidden from their consideration, is the fact that many souls who incarnated during the Hebraic Age have since returned as Christians during their subsequent earth appearances. As each soul has gained a better envisionment of the heavenly Light and striven to perfect itself by leaving behind earthly desires,[493] it gradually escalated higher on the rungs of Jacob's metaphorical ladder leading to higher dimensions.

The spiritual trail that leads from Genesis to the Revelation is not a seamless pathway. It was interspersed with periodic interruptive pauses as the Lord the Son of GOD has guided, moved and directed man toward salvation through the spiritual minefield of Satan's constant obstructions. The Son by His Holy Spirit given to Him by GOD has brought about man's transcendence from his fallen spiritual condition into successively higher levels of knowledge and understanding, moving those who would be His into increasingly higher states of consciousness in a spiral ever upward toward transformation and translation. It is the pathway leading into the highest of all dimensions of existence available to the souls in man, the place Christ the Son has made available for all who are His. Once we find The Way and begin to follow it, to turn back is to commit serious error, because it may be a long time before another opportunity is provided.[494] Many of those who have followed the Son from the time He was Adam — especially those who were with Him on earth when He was Joseph son of Jacob and later returned as foretold by

---

[493] 1 Jn. 2:15-17.

Prophet Malachi — have been quickened and elevated by GOD's Holy Spirit. The Bible discloses that they have attained to high positions in the heavenly hierarchy being reconstructed by Christ the Son.

As Prophet Balaam had foreseen: Joseph was the *Star* who came out of Jacob, who later appeared as Jesus Christ, whom GOD will raise up to take dominion when He returns at His Second Coming — the time of Armageddon, *"the great and terrible day of the Lord"* — and redemption, the start of the Millennium of the First Resurrection.[495]

---

[494] Jesus taught this principle, instructing his followers: *"No man, having put his hand to the plow, and looking back, is fit for the kingdom of GOD"* (Lk. 9:62). When on one occasion He taught them certain spiritual truths which were beyond their ability to accept at that time, many of them turned back and no longer walked with Him (Jn. 6:64-69). It was when the children of Israel had embarked upon their remarkable Exodus that they soon became dismayed by the stressful conditions to which they were subjected, and disobediently *"in their hearts turned back again into Egypt"* (Acts 7:39). (Heb. 6:4-8; Heb. 10:26; Heb. 10:38-39; 2 Pet. 2:22-23; Rev. 3:10-12,21).

[495] Rev. 20:1-6.

—CHAPTER THREE—

REUBEN
A SOUL INCARNATION OF
APOSTLE PETER?

JESUS SELECTS HIS APOSTLES

The Bible records that soon after Jesus commenced his Ministry, he began to find and call His Apostles from among His other followers. In principle, this selective process appears to have paralleled the seating arrangements that He, as Joseph, had long before prepared when He met His brothers, years after they had sold him into slavery, and meticulously seated them according to the birth order:

> *And they sat before him, (Joseph) the firstborn according to his birthright and the youngest according to his youth; and the men marveled one at another. (Gen. 43:33)*

The Book of Genesis lists their birth order, from the eldest to the youngest, as: Reuben, Simeon, Levi, Judah, Dan, Napthalie, Gad, Asher, Issachar, Zebulun, Joseph and Benjamin. The birthing order of the sons was approximately the same order in which Jacob had subsequently blessed them.[496] Sig-

---
[496] Gen. Chh. 29-30.

nificantly, Jacob added two of his grandsons to the paternal blessing, Ephraim and Manasseh;[497] both destined to occupy vacant positions left by Joseph when he became empowered and moved up above the veil and by Dan who forfeited his position, as will be discussed.

Joseph's seating arrangements for his brothers also reflected the approximate order in which his father Jacob blessed his twelve sons. As far as can be ascertained, when Jesus selected the twelve Apostles, each represented a leader of one of the twelve tribes of Israel. Jesus would no longer be counted as one of the brethren because He was predestined to escalate above the heavenly hierarchy that composes the twelve earthly tribes. Each of the twelve remaining brethren, or perhaps in some cases a representative from that tribe, became an Apostle — a celestial being destined to rule over one of the twelve corresponding heavenly levels. By sifting through scriptures and correlating Old and New Testament verses, a pattern emerges which appears to provide a linkage between Jacob's sons and Jesus' Apostles. And though scriptures disclose the names of the twelve, it only partly records the order in which Jesus selected them. The New Testament discloses their names as follows:

> *Now the names of the twelve Apostles are these: The first, Simon, who is called Peter, and Andrew his brother; James the son of Zebedee, and John his brother; Phillip, and Bartholomew; Thomas, and Matthew the publican; James the son of Alphaeus and Lebbaeus, whose surname was Thaddaeus;*

---

[497] Gen. 48:20.

> *Simon the Canaanite, and Judas Iscariot, who also betrayed him. (Mt. 10:2-5)*

JACOB'S FIRST SON: REUBEN

In the prophetic sense, the Bible indicates that Jacob's firstborn, Reuben, who proved himself to be less favored because of his negative tendencies — or a successor of his tribe — may have been chosen as Jesus' first Apostle, Peter. When even souls of the highest heavenly order incarnate in the earth plane, the frequencies of their spirit necessarily decelerate causing them to lose much of their spiritual awareness as they take on the much slower vibrations of the 3rd dimension.[498] Except they are illuminated by the Christ Spirit, and receive the Spirit of Truth, they often become entangled in situations rendering them unable to recall and fulfill the missions they have set out to complete during an earth experience. The principle is patently revealed in the spirit that was Reuben on earth who, after the fall in the garden, had striven along with the Son who had been the First Adam, to reach for the Tree of Life in order to overcome lower states of consciousness. But the negative spirit force of the Archangel Satan is powerful and Reuben fell victim to the same wiles of Satanic desires and temptations that had felled Adam.

Reuben was distracted and drawn into temptation by his flesh desires, which ultimately led him to in-

---

[498] Cf. Heb. 2:9: Even Jesus *"...was made a little less than the angels for the suffering of death, crowned with glory and honour: that He by the Grace of GOD should taste death for every man."* And cf. Heb. 2:13-18.

[499] Gen. 35:22.

dulge in a sexual liaison with his father's concubine, Bilhah.[499] Jacob recognized this immoral activity as a sign of spiritual weakness in Reuben and accorded the birthright to Joseph's sons:

> *Now the sons of Reuben the firstborn of Israel, (for he was the firstborn; but forasmuch as he defiled his father's bed,* **his birthright was given unto the sons of Joseph the son of Israel:** *and the genealogy is not to be reckoned after the birthright. For Judah prevailed above his brethren, and of him came the chief ruler; but the birthright was Joseph's. (1 Chron. 5:1-2)*

At least partly because of his illicit affair with Bilhah, Reuben had lost his entitlement to full benefits and entitlements ordinarily reserved to a father's firstborn birthright son, but because of a biblically-inscribed spiritual rule specifically designed to protect the privileges of firstborn sons — a rule with which Jacob was doubtless aware — Reuben could not be fully deprived of his birthright:

> *If a man has two wives, one Beloved, and another hated, and they have born him children, both the Beloved and the hated; and if the firstborn son of her's that was hated: Then it shall be, when he makes his sons to inherit that which he has, that he may not make the son of the Beloved firstborn before the son of the hated, which is indeed the firstborn: But he shall acknowledge the son of the hated for the firstborn, by giving him a double portion of all that he has: for he is the beginning of his strength; the right of the firstborn is his. (Deut. 21:15-17)*

The highly spiritualized Jacob, unable to entirely remove Reuben from his birthright position nevertheless blessed him; albeit he had lost important features of the inheritance which would ordinarily have been accorded to him as firstborn. Jacob's second and third sons, Simeon and Levi, had also compromised their positions in the divine genealogy by using the rite of circumcision as a deceiving device to slay Shechem and his father Hamor along with others in their family.[500] This effectively removed both of these two sons from their prospects of inheriting the family birthright, and left Jacob with limited ways to remedy the situation confronting him. He needed to award the birthright to the next most spiritually qualified son in order to guarantee its being sustained through future generations at the highest possible spiritual level, to assure that he and his family could fulfill their destiny. Reuben retained only a portion of the family birthright he had gained as Jacob's firstborn son; it was all his father was able to convey to him under the circumstances.

The Bible reveals some excellent spiritual qualities of character in Reuben, some of which would carry through to manifest in his possible incarnation as Peter. When we consider the two separate earth experiences of the spirit that was the higher self of both Reuben and Peter, we find striking similarities. For example, when Joseph's brothers conspired to cast him into a pit and deceitfully tell Jacob that some evil beast had devoured him, it was Reuben who managed to deliver Joseph out of their hands, pleading with them not to kill him.[501] He implored them not to shed blood but

---

[500] Genesis Chapter 34.
[501] Gen. 37:18-21.
[502] Gen. 37:22.

rather to cast him into a pit close at hand and lay no hand on him, while all the while he was planning to return to deliver Joseph safely back to his father.[502] Reuben had then forthwith departed from the scene, perhaps thinking to draw his brothers away, but when he later returned after they had sold Joseph into slavery to a band of Midianite merchants, he found his brother gone. He rent his clothes in despair and returned to the company of his brothers to express his forlorn feelings:

> *The child is not; and I, whither shall I go? (Gen. 37:30)*

When the brothers later journeyed to Egypt to purchase grain to survive the great famine Joseph had foretold would come upon the land, they did not take Benjamin with them because Jacob, having already lost Joseph, feared to put at risk his only other son by Rachel by permitting him to accompany them. Joseph, having attained great power in Egypt, gave his brothers grain to take back to Canaan but he cautioned them not to return for more except they brought Benjamin with them.[503] They then counseled among themselves, conceding their guilt at what they had done to their little brother. It was Reuben who spoke up and explained his view of what had transpired; this leadership trait would remain with him as Peter, when he often spoke on behalf of the Apostles.

> *Spake I not to you, saying, Do not sin against the child; and ye would not hear? therefore, behold, also his blood is required. (Gen. 42:22)*

---

[503] Gen. 42:1-20.

Unknown to them, Joseph understood what they said, and after going apart from them to react in tears, he returned, took Simeon from them and had him bound before their eyes[504] as an assurance that they would return. When the brothers journeyed back home to Canaan, they sought to convince their father Jacob that they could only hope to have more grain from Egypt if they acceded to Joseph's demand that they bring Benjamin with them on their next trip. It was Reuben who first made an offer to Jacob:

> *Slay my two sons, if I bring him not to thee: deliver him into my hand, and I will bring him to thee again. (Gen. 42:37)*

But Jacob refused Reuben's request, even though he had offered his own two sons as markers. Jacob was disinclined to trust Reuben's offer, but rather was moved to accept a promise made by Judah.[505] He was aware of an instability in Reuben which he did not perceive in Judah.

The Bible divulges a number of similar character traits shared by Reuben — or a successor of his tribe — and Apostle Simon Peter. Often, these souls, perhaps the same soul, tended to leave off in his own

---

[504] Keeping in mind that Joseph was an earth experience of the Son of God, so that He knew the deeper spiritual mysteries, it is noteworthy that Simeon was the brother who had reacted with great anger and fury against Shechem and his father Hamor, and had slain them along with many others, *supra*, (Gen. Ch. 34); and it is also significant that Jacob later conferred a negative blessing upon Simeon (Gen. 49:5).

[505] Gen. 43:1-14.

direction; always with good intentions but at times missing the main point of what was taking place. In the matter of Reuben's attempt to save Joseph from being killed and cast into a pit, he failed to see that the end result would have been that if he had been successful in saving Joseph, the Lord's Will would have been thwarted. Joseph would have remained with his brothers, subject to their negative ill will toward him and spiritual history would conceivably have run a different course. Albeit it was all but impossible for Reuben to understand what the Lord had in mind, what was needed was for a way for Joseph to be guided into Egypt in order to fulfill Abraham's first dream.[506] It did subsequently take place when Judah later managed to persuade his brothers to sell Joseph to some Midianites who purchased him as a slave and carried him into Egypt, where he was sold.

That Jacob conceded to Judah's plea to allow Benjamin to go to Egypt with them instead of Reuben's plea, demonstrated that he recognized his son's spiritual frailty, causing him to be unreliable.[507]

JESUS' FIRST APOSTLE: PETER

Some of Reuben's characteristic traits later reflected in Apostle Peter, who often acted as leader of his brother Apostles in many undertakings. He is always mentioned as one of Jesus' *"Three"* most often assuming a leadership role over the other Apostles. For example, when Jesus revealed to His Apostles that he must go to Jerusalem to suffer, be killed and raised up the third day, Peter actually took the Master aside

---

[506] Gen. 15:13.
[507] Cf. Gen. 49:3-4.
[508] Mt. 16:20-22.

and began to rebuke Him, admonishing Him that no such fate should befall Him.[508] Though he had good intentions, his negative comment was clearly the result of Satan's negative intrusion into him, causing him to doubt Jesus' prophetic assertion; as was revealed by Jesus' reply to Peter:

> *But he turned and said unto Peter, Get thee behind me, Satan, thou are an offence unto me: for thou savorest not the things that be of God, but those that are of men. (Mt. 16:23)*

Another example of Peter's sufferance of powerful Satanic forces came to light during the Last Supper, when Jesus set about washing the feet of His Apostles. Satanic forces having rendered Peter insensitive to the spiritual import of this ritual, he advised Jesus that he would not take part in it. But the Master advised Peter that if he did not partake of this ritual He would have no part with him; after which Peter not only allowed the Master to wash his feet, but asked Him to also wash his hands and his head. Jesus explained the symbolic meaning of the washing of the feet.[509]

Possibly Peter's most serious misunderstanding took place just before Pentecost when he decided the Apostles should select another Apostle to replace Judas Iscariot, who had by that time taken his own life.[510] Peter, characteristic of the trait of a firstborn son, impulsively took the lead in setting out to fulfill what he truly believed was required for the selection of another Apostle, based on a prophecy in the Book of Psalms:

---

[509] Jn. 13:5-15.
[510] Acts. 1:15-16.

> *For it is written in the Book of Psalms, Let his habitation be desolate, and let no man dwell therein: and his bishoprick let another take. (Acts 1:20)*

The remaining eleven Apostles then appointed two from among their number — Joseph, surnamed Justus; and one named Matthias — and prayed, asking the Lord who knew the hearts of all men to show them which of the two should be chosen as the Apostle to replace Judas. Then they gave forth their lots and it fell upon Matthias, who was subsequently numbered among the eleven remaining Apostles.[511] On its face, this appears to have been a wise course of action. Judas had been removed in accordance with prophesies, and the scripture foretold that a replacement was to fill his position in order that there would be twelve special witnesses of Jesus who would continue to follow and teach His Gospel of love, truth and righteousness. But upon reflection, and in consideration of spiritual matters as they existed at that time, the decision was fraught with troublesome questions and considerations. For one, Jesus had Himself selected His Apostles from among all His other disciples, and had advised them **He knew whom He had chosen**. The remaining eleven Apostles had indeed conceived of a way the Lord could guide and direct them to select the candidate of His choice through prayers, but there was a fatal flaw in their reasoning; which, if Peter had in fact instigated the selection process, would have karmically redounded upon him.

The Apostles were closely acquainted with the disciples who had followed Jesus, and apparently presupposed He would choose His replacement Apostle from among them. Thus when they se-

---

[511] Acts 1:23-26.

lected two candidates, and asked the Lord to choose from between them the one they believed would be best qualified, they unintentionally limited Him to those two candidates. Peter and the remaining Apostles asked the Lord to guide and direct their decision, which seemed to them well and good. But instead of simply waiting patiently for Him to directly make known His choice, they impetuously set the parameters in which the decision was to be made by them, in the spirit of the flesh.

GOD having ordained man with free will, the Lord the Son does not restrict his use of it; albeit a proportionate karmic price may be required for its intentional or unintentional misuse. Individuals are free to act according to their desires and the thoughts that flow from them, without being blocked in their ways. But this decision by the remaining Apostles in the selection of Judas' replacement was of little or no effect. The Bible never again mentions the name of Matthias but, as will be discussed, the Lord had someone else in mind to replace Judas Iscariot. The risen Christ was fully capable of choosing His next Apostle from heaven, it was not necessary for anyone on earth to make that choice for Him, the best of intentions notwithstanding. As will be seen, Christ the Lord the Son had in mind a man on the earth who none of His eleven remaining Apostles would have even considered a prospective candidate. They weren't acquainted with him and knew nothing of his past earth experiences, much less the spiritual gains he had accumulated to that time. Even had they known his identity, they would have unquestionably shunned and disavowed him as one of Satan's followers, for reasons which will be explained. As it was, they acted on their own with the best of intentions.

Another example of Peter's characteristic ways was illustrated near the end of Jesus' Ministry, when He instructed His Apostles:

> *Little children, yet a little while I am with you. Ye shall seek me, and as I said unto the Jews, Whither I go, ye cannot come. (Jn. 13:33)*

Peter asked Jesus, *"Lord, whither goest thou?"* The Master responded, *Whither I go, thou canst not follow me now, but thou shalt follow me afterwards."* Peter then replied, *"Lord, why cannot I follow thee now? I will lay down my life for thy sake."* [512]

But Jesus foresaw the future, and He was well aware of the power Satan still exercised over Peter. He knew that Apostle had been struggling against the negative forces aligned against him, having on one occasion cautioned him:

> *Simon, Simon, behold, Satan hath desired to have you, that he may sift you as wheat: But I have prayed for thee, that thy faith fail not: and when thou art converted, strengthen thy brethren. (Lk. 22:31-32)*

Jesus knew the power of Satan, having contended against him through the many centuries that had ensued from the time He, the Son, had been Adam, and had been felled by the Devil's lies and deceits. Thus when Peter made his resolute promise to the Lord that

---

[512] Jn. 13:36-37.

he would willingly go into prison and to die with Jesus, the Master foresaw what would take place when Peter was under extreme pressure, and He replied:

> *I tell thee, Peter, the cock shall not crow this day, before that thou shalt thrice deny that thou knowest me. (Lk. 22:34)*

It came to pass precisely as Jesus had foretold. Shortly thereafter Jesus was taken before the high priest and condemned to death, and some of those present began to harass Him. Peter had hidden in the basement of the palace where a maid of the high priest observed him keeping warm and accused him of being one of Jesus' followers, which he three times denied.[513]

PETER'S SPIRITUAL AWAKENING

Apostle Peter's experience provides an illustration of what happens to soul-portions of the spirits of even powerful heavenly beings when they incarnate in the earth plane's slower vibrations, and become subjected to interfering Satanic influences, while at the same time being disadvantaged because of the diminishment of the spirit power they enjoy while in their angelic form in higher planes of existence.

It was after Pentecost that Peter and the remaining Apostles received the gift of the Holy Ghost sent by Jesus Christ as He had promised,[514] and underwent spiritual transformation. The Bible reveals that after

---

[513] Mk. 14:66-72.
[514] Acts 2:1-12; Jn. 14:15-17,26; 15:26; 16:7, 12-15.

Pentecost Peter was dramatically transformed, escalated in spiritual stature.

Biblical writings indicate that the angelic spirit that was the higher self of Peter, despite having sustained spiritual losses, gained so much from those earth experiences — and doubtless during other earth incarnations — that his position in heaven ranks high among the other eleven Apostles. Accordingly, as one of the twelve great Archangels, Peter, has been given the key to one of the twelve levels of the New Jerusalem.[515]

---

[515] Mt. 16:16-19.

—CHAPTER FOUR—

BENJAMIN
A SOUL INCARNATION OF
APOSTLE PAUL

When Jacob blessed his twelfth and youngest son, Benjamin, he did so in a way that foretold two of his son's future earth reincarnations: one as Saul son of Kish, first king of Israel; and the other as Saul of Tarsus, later renamed Paul. Subsequent events showed that in both of those future experiences the spirit of Benjamin did reappear in the tribe named for him. Benjamin's name means "*of the Light*," but Jacob's blessing foreshadowed some negative tendencies which would afflict him during his life as Saul son of Kish, and which would persist in his later experience as Saul of Tarsus. As was seen in the case of Peter, Benjamin, because he was one of the Lord's, was subjected to intense negative afflictions to the extent he also struggled in the wilderness of the earth plane. Eventually, the higher self angel who was the heavenly self of these respective souls, prevailed over the Satanic forces during his experience as Apostle Paul. He was counted as Jesus' twelfth Apostle, chosen by the risen Christ, the Son of GOD. It was written of Benjamin:

> *Benjamin shall ravin as a wolf: in the morning he shall devour the prey, and at night he shall divide the spoil. (Gen. 49:27)*

JACOB'S TWELFTH SON: BENJAMIN

Joseph and Benjamin were true blood brothers, sons of Jacob and Rachel. Jacob was deeply grieved when his beloved Rachel died while giving birth to their youngest son, Benjamin. Joseph was at that time presumed to be dead, his demise having been falsely reported to Jacob by his jealous sons, which caused Jacob to become closely protective of Benjamin. For that reason, when his older sons journeyed to Egypt to purchase grain during the famine, Jacob would not permit Benjamin to accompany them. And when they returned with grain, and with Joseph's promise to supply more if Benjamin would return with them, Jacob remained apprehensive. He rejected Reuben's offer to leave two of his sons for markers to assure Benjamin's safe return, but accepted Judah's verbal guarantee, and reluctantly allowed Benjamin to return to Egypt with the rest of his sons.

Joseph, who still had not divulged his identity to his brothers in Egypt at this point, was so delighted to see his younger brother that he ordered that bread be set on the table, and he sat the brothers before him, the firstborn according to his birthright: from Reuben the eldest to Benjamin the youngest. Significantly, he served Benjamin five times as much as any of his other brothers: a sign that disclosed their past and current close spiritual relationship, and forecasted that it was to continue in times to come.[516] The bread Joseph ordered set on the table was a sign that when Benjamin would long afterward incarnate as Apostle Paul, he would eat of the spiritual *"bread"* of life and light of the Lord — whose soul was at that time encased in Joseph's physical body.

---

[516] Gen. 43:31-34.

When the brothers embarked on their return trip to Canaan, laden with grain to stave off starvation of the family, Joseph commanded the steward of his house to fill the men's sacks with as much food as they could carry, and replace the money they had brought with them to buy grain. He also ordered that his silver divining cup be surreptitiously placed in the mouth of Benjamin's sack.[517] After they had departed from the city a little way, Joseph ordered his steward to overtake them and inquire why they had rewarded evil for good. The innocent brothers denied having stolen anything, and asked how they could have taken silver or gold without it having been noticed. They exclaimed that if any such items were to be found among them, the bearer should die. When the bags were searched, Joseph's silver cup was of course found in Benjamin's sack. Judah offered a heartfelt plea to Joseph, including his query as to how the brothers — including the one in whose sack the cup was found — could clear themselves. Joseph, although aware of his brothers' innocence, imposed a prophetic sentence upon Benjamin:

> *The man in whose hand the cup is found,* **he shall be my servant***; and as for you, get you up in peace to your father. (Gen. 44:17)*

That Benjamin was to be held accountable to Joseph as his servant carried future implications. He would much later — as Apostle Paul — become a servant of Joseph's when Joseph lived again as Jesus of Nazareth. Paul would through much tribulation carry the Lord's messages wherever He was sent.

---

[517] Gen. 44:1-2.

Judah, in the above-described scene in Egypt, briefly recapitulated all that had transpired from the time the brothers had come from Egypt to Canaan to purchase grain; including that their father Jacob would be disappointed and distressed to the extreme if Benjamin did not return safely with them.[518] Moved to tears by Judah's impassioned plea, Joseph then revealed his identity to his brothers, and prevailed upon them to bring Jacob and his whole family to Egypt where he could establish them safely; in that way fulfilling Abraham's prophecy as well as his own dreams.

Significantly, the silver cup placed in Benjamin's grain bag was Joseph's divining device.[519] Considered in the prophetic sense, it presaged that during a subsequent incarnation Benjamin would metaphorically drink of the same cup and obtain remarkable spiritual knowledge through the Spirit. It came to pass long afterward when Benjamin, reincarnated as Apostle Paul, testified that he had directly received through the Spirit of Christ the remarkable spiritual knowledge he taught: that it came from no man.[520] A subsequent earth manifestation in flesh of the spirit of Benjamin is understood to have been as Saul son of Kish, first king of Israel.

SAUL SON OF KISH: A SOUL INCARNATION OF BENJAMIN

Prophet Samuel described Saul as one who was so good that no one else in Israel could surpass him in his goodness:

---

[518] Gen. 44:18-34.
[519] Gen. 44:5.
[520] Gal. 1:11-12.

> *A choice young man, and a goodly: and there was not among the children of Israel a goodlier person than he: from his shoulders and upward he was higher than any of the people. (1 Sam. 9:1-2)*

According to the Book of Enoch, *"ruah"* is a Hebrew word describing and reflecting the inborn acquired level of knowledge, understanding and state of spirituality attained by every infant by the time of its birth in each new earth experience; representing the sum of its spiritual gains or losses through all its experiences to that time. Such a description would parallel Samuel's above-cited comment that from his *"shoulders and upward"* there was none that surpassed Saul in his knowledge and spiritual stature. Such a statement would be fitting of one who was an enlightened soul. But as Israel's first king he was tested by a host of negative spirit afflictions powerful enough to bring him down. His spirituality manifested when he underwent an unusual experience typical of that which marks the change from a *"natural"* man to a spiritual one.[521] One day, accompanied by a servant, Saul went off in search of some lost or strayed livestock. When they met with no success, the servant suggested inquiring of a man of God: which term in those days referred to a seer.[522] Moved by Divine Providence, Saul was guided to find Prophet Samuel; who had been already been advised by the Lord that the meeting was predestined to occur:

---

[521] 1 Cor. 2:14.

[522] I Sam. 9:6-8. As written in 1 Sam. 9:9: *"Beforetime in Israel, when a man went to inquire of God, thus he spake, Come let us go to the seer, for he that is now called a Prophet was beforetime called a Seer."*

> *Tomorrow about this time I will send thee a man out of the land of Benjamin, and thou shalt anoint him to be a captain over my people Israel, that he may save my people out of the hands of the Philistines: for I have looked upon my people, because their cry is come unto me. (1 Sam. 9:16)*

The prayers of the Lord's people are especially heard when their spirits are for some reason quickened, and the force and frequency of their vibrational levels intensified.[523] The Bible shows us that the Lord responds appropriately to those who are His. Thus when Prophet Samuel saw Saul, the Lord confirmed to him that Saul was the one of whom He had spoken the day before. When Saul asked Samuel where he might find *"the seer,"* he replied:

> *I am the seer: go up before me unto the high place, for ye shall eat with me today, and tomorrow I will let thee go, and will tell thee all that is in thine heart. (1 Sam. 9:19)*

The heightened level of spirituality of Prophet Samuel, combined with Saul's desire to find him to fulfill a noble spiritual purpose, activated the Lord's Guidance, and they were drawn to meet as if magnetically. The vibrations of Saul's spirit energy were at that time too slow to synchronize with the much faster vibrations of the Lord's Holy Spirit. This was not the case with Prophet Samuel, who by the process of spirit-attraction, had been drawn into his earth experience by his highly-spiritualized mother, Proph-

---

[523] Apostle James long afterward commented: *"The effectual fervent prayer of a righteous man availeth much."*

etess Hannah.[524] Later, however, Saul was quickened by the Lord's Spirit sufficiently to hear His voice, and to respond appropriately, which enabled him to become an effective king ruling over his people. This contrasts against the Christian Age in which, because of the Lord's New Covenant, each individual has the ability to directly reach GOD by the Intercession of the Christ Spirit [525] through the Holy Ghost, the Spirit of Truth and other Comforter.[526] After they had been guided to meet, Samuel proceeded to outline for Saul what would transpire when he would encounter certain prophets:[527] including that he was predestined to undergo a profound spiritual experience:

> *And the Spirit of the Lord will come upon thee, and thou shalt prophesy with them, and shall be turned into another man. (1 Sam. 10:6)*

This encounter led to Saul's spiritual rebirth, during which experience he was quickened by the Lord's Spirit, enabling him to become a spiritual man: as opposed to continuing that earth experience as a *"natural"* man, as he himself, as Apostle Paul, would later define the diminished spiritual state of being unable to comprehend GOD-inspired knowledge.[528]

---

[524] Chapters 1 Sam. 1 and 2 recount Hannah's exceeding great belief and faith in the Lord the Son — who she understood to be the Rock of Israel written of in Deut. 32:3-4. She knew He was able to kill and make alive, and would keep the feet of his saints: whose adversaries were to be broken in pieces when He would thunder out of heaven to judge the ends of the earth, and give strength to His king, and exalt the horn of His exalted.

[525] Heb. 7:25.

[526] Jn. 14:15-17,26; 15:26; 16:7,12-15 and note Jer. 31:31-34.

[527] 1 Sam. 10:2-5.

The Bible records that from that time Saul was much more spiritual, able to function at a much higher level of consciousness than before. In due time he was made king, and it was written of him that the Spirit of God had come upon him. He took hold of his kingship with surety because he knew beforehand that the Lord had ordained and positioned Him. The people, sensing the Lord's hand at work, accepted Saul's rule and followed him obediently.[529]

The soul incarnation of Saul first king of Israel is biblically illustrated as being a forerunner of the spiritual man he would long afterward turn out to be when he would be reborn as Saul of Tarsus, later renamed Paul, when he would be an example of how a negatively dis-spirited man could, under the New Covenant, repent, turn his life around, and set about following the Son of GOD whose Spirit had quickened and inspired him. Names are often subconsciously assigned through the Spirit by parents in ways which present subtle clues reflective of previous earth identities, and it was not by chance that king Saul would later be called by the same first name when He reincarnated as Saul of Tarsus. His spirit was still that of the king, reincarnated in a new flesh body, and still carrying vestiges of the character of his former self.

KING SAUL'S FALL

Despite king Saul's excellent start, problems arose when he succumbed to negative feelings of anger and jealousy. This caused the Lord to shut down his Spirit, and to bring in David, the seventh son of Jesse, to rule

---

[528] 1 Cor. 2:9-15.
[529] 1 Sam. 11:5-15.

in his place. As the Bible relates, Saul nevertheless continued his negative ways, even pursuing David with the intention of killing of him. The Lord in time found it expedient to banish Saul, cutting off all contact with him to the point that the frustrated king desperately sought to regain contact in an unacceptable way. During his rule, Saul had put away the wizards in the land, and those who relied upon familiar spirits,[530] in order that the people would not rely upon information given by low-level spirits but rather would seek the Lord's truth. When the frustrated Saul enquired of the Lord, He would not respond; neither by dreams, nor by Urim, nor by prophets.[531] By his negative ways Saul had exiled himself from His Lord in that earth experience.

At the end of his patience, Saul asked his servants to find some woman who had a familiar spirit that he might go to enquire of her. He was told that such a woman lived at Endor, so he disguised himself and visited her at night with two of his servants. He asked the witch to "*bring up*" a familiar spirit he would name, but the woman refused, asserting that king Saul (whom she did not recognize because of his disguise) had cut off all those who had familiar spirits. When Saul threatened to punish the woman for not doing as he commanded, she bent to his will and asked who she should *"bring up."* He named Prophet Samuel, who by then had passed beyond the veil.[532] Out of the eerie mists of the past appeared Samuel, covered with a mantle. He asked Saul why he had disquieted him to bring him into the earth again. Saul explained that he was sore distressed because the Philistines were making war against him, added

---

[530] 1 Sam. 28:3.

[531] 1 Sam. 28:6.

[532] 1 Sam. 28:3-11.

to which God had departed from him and would not answer him any more, and he felt compelled to call upon Samuel to advise him.[533] Samuel responded in a way that must have dumfounded Saul:

> *Wherefore then dost thou ask of me, seeing the Lord is departed from thee, and is become thine enemy? And the Lord hath done to him, as he spake by me: for the Lord hath rent the kingdom out of thine hand, and given it to thy neighbor, even to David: because thou obeyest not the voice of the Lord, nor executedst his fierce wrath upon Amalek,* [534] *therefore hath the Lord done this thing unto thee this*

---

[533] 1 Sam. 28:12-15.

[534] Cf. Ex. 17:13-16, which verses relate that when the Holy Spirit of the Lord the Son was incarnated as Joshua son of Nun, and Satan's spirit was incarnated as the warrior Amalek who strove early on in the Exodus to prevent Israel from returning to Canaan, its earthly promised land, the Lord GOD THE FATHER foresaw that the spirit higher-selves of Joshua and Amalek would continue to war against one another *"generation after generation."* In the prophetic sense it meant "life after life" on earth. The Lord admonished Saul that He remembered what Amalek had done to his people, laying a trap for them when they came up from Egypt, and He commanded Saul to go smite Amalek and his people: to utterly destroy them and their property (1 Sam. 15:1-2). Saul set out to fulfill that command, but he failed to fully execute the Lord's command, with the result that Samuel advised him: *"Behold, to obey is better than sacrifice, and to hearken than the fat of rams. For rebellion is as the sin of witchcraft, and stubbornness is as iniquity and idolatry. Because thou hast rejected the word of the Lord, he hath also rejected thee from being king." (1 Sam. 15:17-35)* Then Saul worshiped the Lord, repentantly seeking to turn back the negative effects of his errors.

> *day. Moreover, the Lord will also deliver Israel with thee into the hand of the Philistines:* ***and tomorrow shalt thou and thy sons be with me:*** *the Lord shall also deliver the host of Israel into the hand of the Philistines. (1 Sam. 28:16-19)*

This remarkable communication disclosed that Samuel — who had died and had passed on to the other side — remained fully aware of what the Lord had in mind at that time for Saul and for Israel. But as far as Saul was concerned, Samuel was a *"familiar spirit"* not to be sought by the king because the Lord had cut him off: at least during that earth experience. Samuel's prophetic words came to pass when Saul met his death:

> *So Saul died for his transgression which he committed against the Lord, even against the word of the Lord, which he kept not, and also for asking counsel of one that had a familiar spirit, to enquire of it: And he enquired not of the Lord: therefore he slew him, and turned the kingdom over to David, the son of Jesse. (1 Chr. 10:13-14)*

Fortunately for Saul, the cycles of reincarnation would provide him with future opportunities to be raised to a quickened state of spirituality in order to effectively fulfill his predestined earth mission. Those not yet familiar with the principles of reincarnation do well to ask themselves: if there were no further opportunities available to those who fall during an earth experience, what hope would the future hold for them? The process is graphically illustrated in the first Adam, who eventually returned as the *"last Adam"* to restore GOD's Holy Spirit to mankind.[535]

As Saul son of Kish, the reincarnated soul of Benjamin certainly did *"ravin as a wolf,"* as Jacob's blessing had foretold. His negative tendencies carried over with him into his earth experience as Saul of Tarsus: but fortunately for Saul, by the time of that subsequent experience the Son of GOD as Jesus of Nazareth had made His saving sacrifice on the Cross. Grace had been made available to those of Christ's, for which reason Paul — no longer under the Mosaic Law once he converted to Christianity — could repent, change his ways and erase all stains of sin he had to that time accumulated. In addition, he no longer needed to learn spiritual truths from a seer like Samuel, or any other human source or *"familiar spirit,"* He could receive it straight from the Lord. In his illustrious experience as Paul, the Lord spiritually revivified him, enabling him to fulfill the subtle sign given to him long before in Egypt when he had been Benjamin, and Jesus had been Joseph.

PAUL AS SAUL OF TARSUS

The angelic higher self of the soul of Benjamin son of Jacob, had passed through a particularly difficult testing as Saul son of Kish, first king of Israel. As has been noted, he had suffered serious spiritual losses; but given the Lord's forgiving nature, and his excellent experiences as Seth and Benjamin — and, as some have understood, as Prophet Jeremiah — Paul had not lost his spiritual equilibrium. He was undoubtedly one of those referred to by the Lord when He spoke through Prophet Malachi to those sons of Jacob who had fallen during their earth incarnations, but who were to be forgiven and afforded new and

---

[535] 1 Cor. 15:45; Heb. 5:8-9.

even more fruitful opportunities if they would return to Him.[536] As continually reiterated throughout the Bible, the Lord the Son, who had Himself fallen as Adam, personally understands the problems experienced by souls incarnated in flesh on earth. He is aware that everyone is tested — tempted by the negative spirit of Satan — and He is quick to forgive those who fall: provided they will overcome temptations at some point in their earth experiences, and no longer give in to them.

Moses' blessing of Benjamin reflected how Jacob's twelfth son would be continuously guided and protected by the Lord:

> *And of Benjamin he said, The Beloved of the Lord shall dwell in safety by him;* **and the Lord shall cover him all day long,** *and he shall dwell between his shoulders. (Deut.32:12)*

We are often, if not ordinarily, reborn within our own family lineages, and it appears that the chosen people of Israel generally reincarnated in the same tribe from one earth experience to the next. Saul of Tarsus was born an Israelite in his own tribe of Benjamin, even as he had before incarnated in that same tribe as Saul son of Kish, first king of Israel.[537] As might be expected, when he returned as Saul of Tarsus he picked up where he had left off as Israel's first king. His bitter attitude clearly unchanged, and still deeply entrenched in the Law of Moses, he set about persecuting Jesus' followers with a vengeance. It was spiritually reflective of the attitude he had before displayed as King Saul, when he pursued King David

---

[536] Mal. 3:16-18.
[537] Rom. 11:1; 1 Sam. 9:1.

and those who followed him. The same principle is seen when Elijah the Prophet reincarnated as John the Baptist, and in both experiences manifested similar characteristics.[538] Reborn as Saul of Tarsus, the soul which had resided in both Benjamin and King Saul was once again on earth, devoted to serving the Living God with undiminished fervency. When the spirit of the Lord came upon Paul on the Damascus Road, he doubtless had no idea it was the same Lord he had sought to serve as first king of Israel, who had cut him off because of his disobedience.

The Old Covenant had passed away, and it would take what some would describe as a miracle for Saul of Tarsus to be converted, given his venomous persecution of Christ's followers. But because his soul had been with the Lord the Son of GOD from the beginning, and had lived some excellent earth experiences, the Lord remembered him, and once again brought him under His wing in order that he might effectively fulfill his life's mission, and eventually dwell with Him in the higher levels of the New Jerusalem — as foretold in Moses' blessing of him, *supra*.

After Jesus Christ had been transformed and translated

---

[538] Mt. 11:9-15 and other biblical verses disclose that John the Baptist was the reborn Prophet Elijah. Some of the characteristics of Elijah (2 Ki. 1:7-8) are seen manifested again when that Prophet's spirit reincarnated as John the Baptist (Mt.). This illustrates that characteristics are carried by a soul from one life to another. In the matter of Saul son of Kish's transition to Saul of Tarsus — from Hebrew to Gentile — it is again seen illustrated that spiritual/mental characteristics are in some way imprinted and carried over from one earth experience to the next. Telltale signs of previous earth experiences frequently manifest in children at an early age.

into heaven, to the Right Hand of GOD and empowered there, a time came when He chose to select His last Apostle — the one to replace Judas Iscariot. Apostle Peter and his brother Apostles had sought to fulfill the place left vacant by Judas, as before explained. But Jesus knew who He wanted chosen,[539] and was well acquainted with Saul of Tarsus. He knew exactly where he was, and what he was doing. One reason He called Saul into His service was to notify all who would receive it that the same Lord of the hosts of Israel — who had spoken to them through His prophets — had manifested on earth as Jesus of Nazareth, and had brought in the New Covenant He had promised through Prophet Jeremiah. However, Saul could not effectively fulfill his mission in his comparatively negative state, and the Lord intervened, abruptly bringing to a halt his negative ways. Saul's spirit had been with the Lord from the beginning of earth incarnations, and he had undoubtedly accumulated outstanding spiritual gains in other life experiences, for which reason the Lord saw fit to choose Him as His faithful Apostle at a most opportune time. When the Lord the Son was raised above the veil that separates lower dimensions from higher dimensions,[540] He was empowered by His FATHER's Spirit to send the Holy Ghost, the Spirit of Truth.[541] In Paul's time, therefore, that Spirit was able to bring to Paul's remembrance knowledge deeply embedded in his soul memory. It served as a graphic example that Jesus, by His Crucifixion, had restored the gift of the Holy Spirit to mankind, thereby making the way into the Kingdom of GOD passable. Paul was called to demonstrate that development, and to teach it.

---

[539] Jn. 13:18.
[540] Heb. 6:19-20.
[541] Jn. 14:15-17,26; 15:26; 16:7,12-15.

BLINDED BY THE LIGHT

Saul's spiritual awakening, which would lead him to commence his ministry, began on a fateful day while he was on his way to persecute some Christians. He strode along the Damascus Road carrying a handful of arrest warrants by which to take into custody more of Jesus Christ's followers.[542] As the saying goes, he didn't have a clue as to what was really going forward, or what was about to transpire. But that was all destined to abruptly change when suddenly the Christ Spirit descended upon him as a light from heaven, and he fell to the earth hearing a voice saying to him, *"Saul, Saul, why persecutest thou me?"* Saul replied, *"Who are thou, Lord?"* And the Lord responded, *"I am Jesus whom thou persecutest."*[543]

At that point Saul's conversion began with an illuminating burst of the Lord's Holy Spirit: in a way perhaps similar to the change from his unspiritual state to his spiritual state when he had before been anointed as King Saul, as related *supra*. Saul underwent a painful chastening [544] of the kind which often accompanies spiritual rebirth, when the entire body is infused with the Spirit, causing dramatic spiritual, mental and physical changes to take place as the process of transformation begins. Because of his fall as Saul first king of Israel, Saul was destined to be especially severely tested, chastened long and tried hard during subsequent earth experiences as his acquired negativity was purged from him. It is the fate of all souls incarnated in flesh, who strive to at-

---

[542] Acts 9:1-2.

[543] Acts 9:4-5

[544] Deut. 8:5; Heb. 12:6-7.

tain to positions in the heavenly hierarchy GOD is rebuilding since Satan's defection, to undergo chastening, and Paul would afterward teach that we all must pass through much tribulation before being allowed to enter into the kingdom of God.[545] This was reflected in the Lord's words to Ananias when He instructed Him to lay healing hands on Paul in order to restore his eyesight after he had been blinded on the road to Damascus. To Ananias He said:

> *Go thy way: for **he (Paul) is a chosen vessel unto me**, to bear my name before the Gentiles, and kings and the children of Israel: For **I will show him how great things he must suffer for my name's sake**. (Acts 9:15-16)*

After the risen Christ converted Paul on the Damascus Road, having anointed and quickened him with His Holy Spirit, Paul became a new man. Despite his former negative ways, the Lord liberally accorded him Grace:

> *And I thank Christ Jesus our Lord who has enabled me, for that he counted me faithful, putting me into the ministry; who before was a blasphemer, and a persecutor, and injurious: but I obtained mercy, because I did it ignorantly in unbelief. And the grace of the Lord was exceeding abundant with faith and love which is in Christ Jesus. (1 Tim. 1:12-14)*

Jesus taught that once a man has undergone spiritual rebirth he depletes his spirit if he knowingly or intentionally returns to past negative ways:

---

[545] Acts 14:22; 2 Cor. 11:22-28; Heb. 12:5-11.

> *No man, having put his hand to the plow, and looking back, is fit for the kingdom of God. (Lk. 9:62)*[546]

Aware that to fall back after having been anointed by the Lord's quickening spirit would have been a grave mistake, Paul was careful from that time on to keep himself as free as possible of negativity. He disclosed to the Corinthians:

> *I keep under my body, and bring it into subjection: lest that by any means, when I have preached to others, I myself should be a castaway. (1 Cor. 9:27)*

Saul's name was apparently changed to Paul by the Lord in the same manner by which Abram's name had been changed to Abraham, Sarai to Sarah, etc. Paul, a Jew converted to Christian belief, became an exceptional example of how a man can be quickened by the

---

[546] The Bible emphasizes that this principal is to be considered extremely important by those who enter into spiritual rebirth. After the Lord's Spirit begins to work within an individual, that soul should use meticulous care to keep from falling back into former unspiritual ways, while struggling to develop spiritually. The Bible teaches this important requirement in several places; in particular Heb. 6:4-6; Heb. 10:26; and 2 Pet. 2:22-23. An especially compelling version of the rule is found in Heb. 12:14-17: *"Follow peace with all men, and holiness, without which no man shall see the Lord: Looking diligently lest any man fail of the grace of God; lest any root of bitterness springing up trouble you, and thereby many be defiled; Lest there be any fornicator, or profane person, as Esau, who for one morsel of meat sold his birthright. For you know how that afterward, when he would have inherited the blessing, he was rejected: for he found no place of repentance, though he sought it carefully with tears"*

Christ Spirit to enable him to receive GOD's Truth through the Holy Ghost in accordance with the terms of the governance of the New Covenant:

> *But I certify to you, brethren, that the gospel which was preached of me is not after man. For I neither received it of man, neither was I taught it, but by the revelation of Jesus Christ. (Gal. 1:11-12)*

But not all of Apostle Paul's teachings were received through the Spirit. Occasionally he would offer his personal opinion concerning certain matters; as reflected in his discourse about virgins. Though he conceded he had not received the Word of the Lord on that particular subject, he nonetheless believed his opinion to be worthy because the Lord had seen fit to grant him mercy, and had quickened his spirit:

> *Now concerning virgins I have no commandment of the Lord; yet I give my judgement as one that hath obtained mercy of the Lord to be faithful. (1 Cor. 6:25)*

BORN OUT OF TIME

Paul revealed that after Jesus' Ascension He was seen first by Cephas, then by the twelve, and afterward by more than five hundred brethren together, some of whom had passed away by the time Paul wrote.[547] After that he was seen by Apostle James, then all of the Apostles, and last of all by Paul, who conceded:

---

[547] 1 Cor. 15:5-6.

And last of all He was seen by me also, as one born out of due time. For I am the least of the Apostles, that I am not meet to be called an Apostle, because I persecuted the church of God. But by the Grace of God I am what I am: and his grace which was bestowed upon me was not in vain; but I labored more abundantly than they all: yet not I, but the Grace of God which was with me. (1 Cor 15:8-10)

Paul was *"born out of time"* for a number of reasons. For one, his negative experience as King Saul, which had carried over into his manifestation as Saul of Tarsus, was like a miscast anchor holding him back from making spiritual gains able to stimulate the Lord's quickening of his soul. The Bible reveals that there were only to be twelve Apostles, as there had been twelve sons of Jacob. After Judas Iscariot expired, there was an opening to be filled in their ranks, but Paul was not called when the eleven Apostles innocently but arbitrarily selected Matthias to replace Judas, as before discussed. He was called *"out of time"* because he had been selected as an Apostle after the other Apostles had already been chosen while Jesus was on earth. Unlike his brethren Apostles, he was chosen by the risen Christ. Because of the Son's empowerment by GOD the FATHER, Christ ordained His twelfth and last Apostle from beyond the heavenly veil.

Paul was predestined to bring the Lord's Word of the New Covenant to the Gentiles[548] in order that they might also become beneficiaries of it. That this was Paul's principle mission was outlined by the Lord when He first spoke to him on the Damascus Road:

---

[548] Gal. 1:1; 2 Tim. 1:7-11.

> But rise, and stand upon thy feet: for I have appeared unto thee for this purpose, to make thee a minister and a witness both of these things which thou hast seen, and of those things in the which I will appear unto thee; **delivering thee from the people, and from the Gentiles, unto whom I now send thee.** To open their eyes, and to turn them from darkness into light, and from the power of Satan unto God, that they may receive forgiveness of sins, and inheritance among them which are sanctified by faith that is in me. (Acts 26:15-18)

Paul described himself as "*the Apostle of the Gentiles*"[549] because he was to be a main connecting link between Jews and Gentiles, illustrating by his conversion and his teachings that the Old Covenant had been superceded by Jesus' New Covenant. In fulfillment of David's prophecy, many Jews had been blinded, unable to discern that Jesus was the flesh "*figure of Him who was to come.*"[550] Like many of Jesus' followers, Paul had been born a Jew, but he had been converted by Christ's Holy Spirit, which had been given to the Son by GOD without measure. As the above verses reveal, Paul was to be a witness of all he would see and experience: even as the Apostles of Jesus were to be witnesses of the events they had observed.[551] This witnessing takes place on the earth, although one of its principal functions may be reserved for the time of Judgment.[552]

---

[549] Rom. 11:13.

[550] Ps. 69:19-29; Rom. 5:14.

[551] Lk. 24:47-48; Acts 1:8,22; 1 Thess. 2:10; Rev. 11:3.

[552] Such prospects were raised by Apostle Paul at 1 Cor. 6:1-3, including: "*Know ye not that we shall judge angels? how much more things that pertain to this life?*"

The Bible reveals that after having undergone his spiritual awakening, Paul was able to bring himself into a trance state, during which time he was in contact with the Lord,[553] as had the Prophets of Israel before him. It was while in that state that Paul received the Word of God which guided, guarded, directed and moved him. On one occasion Paul, in a trance state, confessed certain sins to the Lord. Knowing his position to be precarious at that time because of his perilous situation, he prayed to the Lord, and heard Him say: *"Make haste, and get thee quickly out of Jerusalem: for they will not receive thy testimony concerning me."* Paul replied:

> *Lord, they know that I imprisoned and beat in every synagogue them that believed in you: And when the blood of your martyr Stephen was shed, I also was standing by, and consenting unto his death, and kept the raiment of them that slew him. (Acts 22:19-20)*

It was then that the Lord sent Paul upon his mission:

> *Depart, for I will send you far hence unto the Gentiles. (Acts. 22:21)*

That Paul was able to obtain instructions directly through the Spirit further attested to the terms of Jesus Christ's New Covenant, long before announced by Prophet Jeremiah.[554]

Despite the negative influences of dark spirits which the Devil had infused into Paul when he was King Saul, to break him down and cost him his position;

---

[553] Acts 22:17.
[554] Jer. 31:31-34.

the Lord the Son infused His Holy Spirit into Apostle Paul. It allowed him to overcome Satan's destructive influences, enabling him by his teachings and perfected lifestyle to serve as a remarkable example of how souls can potentially become beneficiaries of Jesus Christ's New Covenant. He was selected by the Lord to help bridge all souls across from the Age of the Hebrews into the Age of the Gentiles. It was part of the Son's Master Plan for mankind, which had been underway since the time of Adam's fall. His was a mission fitting of one whom the Lord had known from the beginning; one He chose to ordain as His twelfth and last known Apostle.

—CHAPTER FIVE—

DAN
A SOUL INCARNATION OF JUDAS ISCARIOT

CAIN

The Bible reveals that Satan's lower vibrational spirit manifested in Adam and Eve's first child, Cain, who having inherited a larger portion of Satan's spirit commenced the generations of a mixed seed in the earth plane. In the same way that the positive children of Adam had GOD's Spirit in them,[555] Satan's sons were composed of his own lowered vibrations because of their spiritual attunement with him. They accordingly became spirit children of the Devil, as taught by Jesus.[556]

The Apostle John reported that during a colloquy between Jesus and an enquiring group of Pharisees, the Master advised them:

> *I go my way, and ye shall seek me, and shall die in your sins: whither I go ye cannot come. Ye are from beneath, I am from above: ye are of this world; I am not of this world. I said therefore that ye shall die*

---

[555] The Son was eternally conceived in His FATHER's Spirit — He is the Progenitor of those souls who were formed after Him.

[556] Jn. 8:37-47.

> *in your sins: for if ye believe not that I am he, ye shall die in your sins. (Jn. 8:21-24)*

They then asked Him who He was, to which He replied He was the same who had spoken to them in the beginning, and that He had many things to say and judge of them — that if they would continue in His Word, then they were indeed His disciples and they would know the truth, and the truth would set them free.[557] The Lord taught that it is the Spirit that quickens — that the words He spoke were spirit and life [558] — but those who had not yet been sufficiently quickened by His Holy Spirit were unable to understand who He was. The Jews replied that they were Abraham's seed, never in bondage to any man, so how could He say they shall be made free?[559] Jesus replied that whosoever commits sin is the servant of sin, and the servant abides not in the house forever (i.e. because of sin) but the Son abides forever. Therefore, if the Son were to make them free, they would indeed be free. And He added:

> *I know that ye are Abraham's seed, but ye seek to kill me, because my word hath no place in you.* ***I speak that which I have seen with my Father: and ye do that which ye have seen with your father.*** *(Jn. 8:37-38)*

When His questioners responded, declaring that their father was Abraham, Jesus countered:

---

[557] Jn. 8:31-32 implied that they would receive the Holy Ghost, the Spirit of Truth and other Comforter (Jn. 14:15-17, 26; Jn. 15:26; Jn. 16:7,12-15).

[558] Jn. 6:63.

[559] Jn. 8:33.

> *If ye were Abraham's children, ye would do the works of Abraham. But now ye seek to kill me, a man that hath told you the truth, which I have heard of GOD: this did not Abraham.* **Ye do the deeds of your father.** *(Jn. 8:39-41)*

Abraham had himself heard the voice of the Lord and had followed it, doing as he had been commanded: even placing Isaac, his *"son of the promise,"* on an altar and preparing to sacrifice him after having been told by the Lord to do so at the time when He had tested Abraham's faith.[560] This same Lord, who later incarnated in flesh as Jesus of Nazareth, was now addressing this group of enquiring Pharisees, but they were unable to recognize Him. The spirit vibrations of their souls remained yet insufficiently quickened by GOD's Spirit for them to be in sync with Jesus' illuminated Holy Spirit of GOD. This explains what Jesus meant when He admonished certain Jews who did not believe in Him that if they were of GOD they would understand who He was, because those who had GOD's Spirit knew Him, and knew that He spoke the truth when He told them He had been sent by GOD.[561] Unaware of their spiritual plight, the Pharisees declared that they were not born of fornication; that they had one Father, even God; to which Jesus replied:

> *If God were your father, ye would love me: for I proceeded forth and came from GOD; neither came I of myself, but HE sent me. Why do ye not understand my speech? even because ye cannot hear my word.* **Ye are of your father the devil,** *and the lusts of your*

---

[560] Genesis Chapter 22.
[561] Jn. 8:39-47. Jesus explained this principle in several places as recorded in the Bible, exemplified in Jn. 10:25-31.

> *father ye will do.* **He was a murderer from the beginning**, *and abode not in the truth, because there is no truth in him. When he speaketh a lie, he speaketh of his own:* ***for he is a liar, and the father of it.*** *And because I tell you the truth, ye believe me not. Which of you convinces me of sin? And if I say the truth, why do ye not believe me? He that is of God heareth GOD's words: ye therefore hear them not, because ye are not of God. (Jn. 8:42-47)*

The Archangel *"who was the father of the lie,"* who *"abode not in the truth because there is no truth in him,"* was the Serpent in the garden, Satan, who deceived and lied to Adam and Eve. Cain was a son of the Devil, who had been *"a murderer from the beginning,"* having slain his brother Abel, *supra*.

DAN

Dan, Jacob's fifth son, had been born as the result of the negatively inspired union with Bilhah, Rachel's handmaid. It was negative because Bilhah was the maid who had defiled Jacob's bed with Reuben, Jacob's first son. That negative activity had caused Reuben the loss of the main portion of his birthright empowerment among the sons of Jacob.[562] By Dan's time it had already been made evident that the children of concubines would not be as spiritually quickened as those born of spiritualized parents; as had been seen when Sarah sent her Egyptian handmaid in with Abraham. She did so in spite of the Lord's promise to give her and Abraham a highly spiritualized son who would carry the Divine Lineage forward into future generations. The mating produced

---
[562] 1 Chr. 5:1.

Ishmael, who, according to the Bible, was removed from consideration for that exalted spiritual position: albeit the Lord did not abandon him.[563] According to the Bible, the Lord pointedly rejected Abraham's entreaty that Ishmael, the son born of his union with Hagar, be accepted as the son of the promise.[564]

In light of these considerations, when Dan was born from Jacob's union with Bilhah, he inherited from the time of his birth a difficult spiritual stumbling block under the 3 to 4 generation rule.[565] The liaison between Reuben and Bilhah caused a severe lowering of the spirituality in the child she would afterward birthe; which depletion was in turn inherited by Dan. This is a paramount reason why the Bible continually emphasizes that the generations of those who immorally defile GOD's Will inevitably suffer under the 3 to 4 generation rule for having done so. As Jesus taught, all things gained or lost on earth are gained or lost in heaven, and except for the Lord's mercy and grace, there is no antidote for the negative aspects of that rule.

From early in his life, Dan appears to have been negatively inclined. For example, when Joseph was seventeen, while he fed the flocks along with some of

---

[563] The Lord promised Abraham He would make Ishamael *"fruitful and multiply him exceedingly: twelve princes shall he beget and I shall make him a great nation. But my covenant I shall establish with Isaac..."* (Gen. 17:20-21). The entire Muslim nation afterward evolved through succeeding generations to become the powerful force it is today on the earth. It appears likely that Ishmael may have later reincarnated as the Prophet Muhammad.

[564] Gen. 17:18-21.

[565] Ex. 20:5; 34:7; Num. 14:18; Deut. 5:9

his brothers, including the sons of Bilhah, he brought back to his father a negative report of their activities. Dan was among the four sons he reported; and the other three were sons of Jacob by handmaids Bilhah and Zilpah,[566] thereby demonstrating the effects of depleted spirit upon those of a lower spiritual nature.

DAN'S BLESSING

Dan turned out to be a negative infiltrator into the twelve tribes of Israel.[567] Jacob, undoubtedly well aware of his fifth son's negative attributes, blessed him in a way that carried ominous overtones:

> *Dan shall judge his people as one of the tribes of Israel.* ***Dan shall be a Serpent in the way****, an adder in the path* ***that biteth the horse's heels, so that his rider shall fall backward****. I have waited for thy salvation, Lord. (Gen. 49:16-18)*

These three dramatic verses asserted what Jacob understood about his son Dan, and suggested the course he was predestined to follow. His blessing foretold a battle — one that had begun in the Garden of Eden, and would end with the empowerment of Jesus Christ of Nazareth. The Serpent in the garden that

---

[566] Gen. 37:2.

[567] During the Exodus when Moses took occasion to bless the fathers of the twelve tribes. He foretold of Dan: *"Dan is a lion's whelp: he shall leap from Bashan" (Deut. 33:22).* Bashan is in the kingdom of Og, an exceedingly fruitful place. When Moses prophesied that Dan at some future time was to leap from such a place, as a young lion might pounce on its prey, the implications were ominous

would bruise the heel of the woman's seed, Eve, was the same *"Serpent"* Jacob analogized in his blessing as his fifth son, Dan, who would later manifest as Judas Iscariot, as subtly disclosed in scriptures:

> *And I will put enmity between thee (Serpent) and the woman (Eve), and between thy seed and her seed; It (Eve's seed) shall bruise thy head and **thou (Serpent's seed) shalt bruise his heel.** (Gen. 3:15)*

The *"rider"* who fell backward because of the Serpent's venomous bite had been the *"First Adam,"* who would long afterward manifest in flesh as Jesus of Nazareth, *"the Last Adam."*[568] As recorded in the Book of the Revelation, the vengeful Serpent continued to successfully afflict all souls living in the earth realm until Jesus overcame him by the power of His blood shed on the Cross. Accordingly, it was the archangelic image of the empowered Christ (the First and Last Adam) John saw in a vision as sitting on a white horse, engaged in a battle with Satan during Armageddon:

> *And there was war in heaven: Michael and his angels fought against the dragon; and the dragon fought and his angels. . . . **And the great dragon was cast out, that old Serpent, called the Devil and Satan, which deceivth the whole world: he was cast out into the earth**, and his angels were cast out with him. . . . **And they (Christ and His army) overcame him by the blood of the Lamb**, and by the word of their testimony, and they loved not their lives unto the death. (Rev. 12:7, 9, 11)*

> *And I saw heaven opened, and **behold a white***

---

[568] 1 Cor. 15:45.

*horse; and he that sat upon him was called Faithful and True, and in righteousness he doth judge and make war. His eyes were as a flame of fire, and **on his head were many crowns**; and he had a name written that no man knew, but he himself. And he was clothed with a vesture dipped in blood; and his name is called The Word of God. **And the armies which were in heaven followed him upon white horses, clothed in fine linen, white and clean.** . . . And he hath on his vesture and on his thigh a name written, KING OF KINGS, AND LORD OF LORDS. (Rev. 19:11-16)*

SATAN AND HIS SONS

The Bible presents unequivocal evidence that the negative Archangel Satan, who in the beginning lied to and deceived Adam and Eve, not only infused a portion of his spirit as the soul in Cain, but also in innumerable other individuals who brought chaos into this earth plane. His goal was to disrupt all souls incarnated in flesh so they would not turn toward Christ the Son of GOD, who had entered into the world to remove the stains of sin from those trapped here so they could return to their first heavenly estates. The egoistic Satan was bent upon establishing a kingdom of his own by populating the earth with children dominated by his own spirit.

A KING OF TYRUS: PROBABLE SOUL INCARNATION OF DAN

That Satan would manifest a soul portion of his spirit on earth is reflected in one of the kings of Tyrus, upon whom the Lord commanded Prophet Ezekiel to "*take up a lamentation*":

> *Son of man, take up a lamentation upon **the king of Tyrus**, and say unto him, Thus saith the Lord God: Thou sealest up the sum full of wisdom and perfect beauty. Thou sealest up the sum, full of wisdom, and perfect in beauty. . . . **Thou hast been in Eden the garden of GOD**. . . . **Thou art the anointed cherub that covereth**; and I have set thee so: **thou was upon the holy mountain of God**; thou has walked up and down in the midst of the stones of fire. **Thou was made perfect in thy ways from the day that thou was created, till iniquity was found in thee**. (Ezek. 28:12-15)*

The King of Tyrus is referred to as the anointed cherub empowered to reign over the earth — the garden of Eden — before the transgression. He possessed great power, but was found to be iniquitous. The Lord's admonishment to the King of Tyrus through Prophet Ezekiel correlated with Isaiah's similar message to Lucifer, also known as the devil. In the following verses Isaiah describes Lucifer as the fallen son of the morning who, because of his iniquity, was cast down to lower dimensions of existence, the earth:

---

[569] This comment by the Lord given through Prophet Isaiah, refers to the "*cutting down to the ground*" of Satan as had been foretold in the beginning in Gen. 3:14. and as long afterward confirmed in Rev. 12:7-12.

> *How art thou fallen from heaven, O Lucifer, son of the morning! how are thou cut down to the ground,*[569] *which weakened the nations! For thou hast said in thine heart, I will ascend into heaven, **I will exalt my throne above the stars of God: I will sit also upon the mount** of the congregation, in the sides of the north: I will ascend above the heights of the clouds; **I will be like the most High. Yet thou shalt be brought down to hell, to the sides of the pit**. . . . But thou art cast out of thy grace like an abominable branch, and as the raiment of those that are slain thrust through with a sword that go down to the stones of the pit. (Isa. 14:12-15)*

Ezekiel and Isaiah both refer to the King of Tyrus and Lucifer, as having been cast into hell — the *"nether parts of the earth."* These biblical associations reflect back to Genesis, when the Serpent had first been sentenced to the earth plane because of his role in the Adamic transgression. As allegorically written, GOD declared at that time that the negative one was condemned to *"eat of the dust of the earth"* for the rest of his days. The Revelation confirms the Serpent's identity to be Satan, the devil, who, the Bible confirms, was indeed cast down to the earth plane. He has always attempted to establish his own kingdom on the earth, and to aggrandize himself above GOD by afflicting innocent souls who too easily fall prey to negative influences associated with the devil's lower states of consciousness:

> *And the Lord God said unto the Serpent. . . . **dust shall thou eat all the days of thy life**." (Gen. 3:14)*

Beloved John later confirmed the casting out of Satan and his followers from higher dimensions:

> *And there was war in heaven, Michael and his angels fought against the dragon, and the dragon fought and his angels. . . .* ***And the great dragon was cast out, that old Serpent called the Devil and Satan which deceivteh the whole world, he was cast out into the earth,*** *and his angels were cast with him. (Rev. 12:9)*

The Revelation leaves no doubt but that there were other angels cast out into the earth plane with the Serpent. These angels subsequently incarnated as sons of Satan, bent on helping him establish his kingdom in the earth plane. But Satan's modus operandi is far from fool proof. That even his own dissenting followers turned against one another is found in Ezekiel's revelation relating to two of Satan's leading angels, who incarnated as one of the Pharoahs, and as King Nebuchadnezzar.

A PHAROAH: A SON OF SATAN

Ezekiel's description of the King of Tyrus, and the Pharaoh correlates with Isaiah's description of Lucifer, *supra*. The Lord revealed through Prophet Ezekiel:

> *. . . .* ***his height was exalted above all the trees of*** *the field and his boughs were multiplied, and his*

> *branches became long because of the multitude of waters, when he shot forth. I have made him fair by the multitude of his branches so that **all the trees of Eden, that were in the garden of God, envied him**. Therefore thus saith the Lord God; Because **thou hast lifted up thyself in height;** I have therefore delivered him into the hand of the mighty one of the heathen;. . . . I have driven him out for his wickedness. I have made the nations to shake at the sound of his fall, when **I cast him down to hell with them that descend into the pit**; and all the trees of Eden, the choice and best of Lebanon, all that drink water, **shall be comforted in the nether parts of the earth. They also went down into hell with him unto them that be slain with the sword; and they that were his arm, that dwelt under his shadow in the midst of the heathen**. To whom art thou thus like in glory and in greatness among the trees of Eden? Yet shalt thou be brought down with the trees of Eden unto the nether parts of the earth. . . . **This is Pharoah and all his multitude**. (Eze. 31:5-18)*

KING NEBUCHADNEZZAR: A SON OF SATAN

Still another biblical writing asseverates that King Nebuchadnezzar was a son of Satan's, who, having received a dream of a tree, summoned Daniel, who interpreted its meaning for him:

> *The tree that thou sawest, which grew, and was strong, whose height reached unto the heaven, and the sight thereof to all the earth; Whose leaves*

> were fair, and the fruit thereof much, and in it was meat for all: under which the beasts of the field dwelt, and upon whose branches the fowls of the heaven had their habitation **It is thou, O king that art grown and become strong: for thy greatness is grown and reaches unto heaven and thy dominion to the end of the earth.** . . . And whereas they commanded to leave the stump of the tree roots; thy kingdom shall be sure unto thee, **after that thou shalt have known that the heavens do rule. (Dan. 4:20-26)**

The Bible appears to subtly suggest that the King of Tyrus had been a soul incarnation of Judas Iscariot and that the Pharoah and Nebuchadnezzar were two of Satan's leading sons. The multitude who formed these kingdoms are most likely those angels who were cast out of Eden with Satan at the beginning. (CF. Ezek. 31:1-18, synonymous with the "*multitude*" who had been with a Pharoah in the garden.) That being the case, the Adamic fall apparently impacted not only the Serpent and Adam and Eve but also a whole host of negative and positive angels. That the Pharaoh would battle against Nebuchadnezzar — one leading negative son aligned against another negative leading son — suggests that by his negative ways, Satan will eventually divide his kingdom into nothingness. This principle was taught by Jesus when He instructed:

> *Every kingdom divided against itself is brought to desolation.* . . . *And if Satan cast out Satan, he is divided against himself; how shall then his kingdom stand? (Mt. 12:25-26)*

Nebuchadnezzar forfeited his kingdom, but his spirit apparently remained tied to the earth until he would realize that the "*heavens do rule,*" as Daniel's prophetic comments implied, thereby suggesting that this king of Babylon would be required to subsequently reincarnate, because he had not in that particular life cycle lived in a way leading into a heavenly place. Otherwise, how can Daniel's prophesy be explained?

Satan's negatively inspired followers have appeared in a number of known prominent earth incarnations. It is related in Exodus[570] that the Lord, incarnated as Joshua Son of Nun, battled against Amalek, who early on in the Exodus sought to block Israel's journey under the command of Moses to the peoples' promised land of earth, Canaan. It was written at that time that the higher selves of these two incarnated souls (Joshua and Amalek) would war against each other "*from generation to generation,*" which, as biblically confirmed, came to pass through the centuries as each angelic figure repeatedly incarnated in flesh. Only by reincarnation could they have repeatedly manifested on earth to battle against each other life after life.

JUDAS ISCARIOT

It became apparent during the Last Supper that Jesus knew Judas Iscariot, one of his chosen Apostles, was a devil. The Master declared:

> *Have I not chosen you twelve, and one of you is a devil? He spoke of Judas Iscariot the son of Simon:*

---

[570] Ex. 17:13-16.

> *for he it was that should betray Him, being one of the twelve. (Jn. 6:70-71)*

That Judas would play a crucial role in fostering events destined to ultimately lead to Jesus' Crucifixion is biblically shown to be part of a plan foreordained at the time of the fall in the garden; which explains why Jesus chose him among His Apostles. During the course of the Last Supper, the Master explained:

> *I know whom I have chosen:* **but that the scripture may be fulfilled, he that eateth bread with me hath lifted up his heel against me.** *Now I tell you this before it come, that when it is come to pass, ye may believe that I am* **He.** *Verily, verily, I say unto you, He that receiveth whomsoever I send receiveth me; and he that receiveth me receiveth* **HIM** *that sent me. (Jn. 13:18-20)*

Jesus' reference to the fulfillment of scriptures co-

---

[571] Ps. 41:10-11 relates to Ps. 41:9: *"But thou, O Lord, be merciful unto me, and raise me up, that I may requite them. By this I know that thou favor me, because mine enemy doth not triumph over me."* This Psalm of David's suggests that David was aware that it was Satan — the Son of GOD's adversary — who was to manifest at some later time, and that the prayer quoted referred to the Son of GOD asking that GOD be merciful to Him, and raise Him up that He might requite (recompense or avenge) those of Israel. Heb. 2:13-18 discloses that Christ the Son's mission on earth was to overcome Satan, his angels and the iniquity they had brought into the earth plane; and verses from Ps. 41 indicate that it was known that the Lord the Son was bent upon avenging what Satan had done to Him when He was Adam in order that GOD might restore the Tree of Life's Holy Spirit to the earth plane.

incides with one of David's Psalms, in which he had centuries before foretold:

> *Yea, mine own familiar friend, whom I trusted,* ***which did eat of my bread, hath lifted up his heel against me.***[571] *(Ps. 41:9)*

It was brought to pass thousands of years later when Judas Iscariot *"lifted up his heel"* against Jesus of Nazareth. Yet, Judas' deceitful act appears to have been declared by GOD during the time of the Adamic fall.[572]

A SON FORFEITS HIS HEAVENLY CROWN

The spirit higher selves of the twelve sons of Jacob are, in higher dimensions, twelve leading angelic beings, who earned leadership roles while incarnated in the earth plane. After the fall they set out to serve the Son, and continued to do so through the centuries. They incarnated and reincarnated on the earth, continually battling against the negative forces of Satan and his angels. When the twelve divisions of the people of Israel were later established under Moses' leadership, the Lord separated them into their respective tribes. The souls of the twelve sons of Jacob in flesh were in heaven the angelic leaders of the tribes in that ethereal realm. These servants of GOD and Christ have always remained loyal and true, for which reason they have received his promise of exalted heavenly positions:

> *And I (Jesus) appoint unto you (Apostles) a kingdom as my Father hath appointed unto me; That ye may eat and drink at my table in my kingdom,*

---
[572] Cf. Gen. 3:15.

> *and sit on thrones judging the twelve tribes of Israel. (Lk. 22:29-30)*

Since the Lord's Crucifixion and subsequent empowerment, the heavenly hierarchy is being prepared to accommodate changes. No corruption will be allowed in the holy city of the New Jerusalem; otherwise the Son's victory over Satan and his angels would have been in vain. Accordingly, when the Lord returns in all His glory with His twelve heavenly princes to judge those worthy of dwelling in the New Jerusalem; the tribe of Dan/Judas will be removed, having been replaced by another leader.[573]

> *Let his days be few; and **let another take his office**. . . . Let them be before the Lord continually, that he may cut off the memory of them from the earth. . . . Let this be the reward of my adversaries from the Lord and of them that speak evil against my soul. (Ps. 109:8,15,20)*

That Judas's higher self was destined to be removed from Israel's Divine Genealogical Tree was noted by the Lord when he addressed him during his earth incarnation as a king of Tyrus. After noting the wickedness of this king who sought divinations by consulting with images and by "*looking in the liver,*"[574] the Lord directed His comments to the king's higher self spirit, Satan, in three prophetic verses:

---

[573] Refer to Chapter: "Manasseh: A Previous Soul Incarnation of Apostle James."

[574] Ezek. 21:21-24.

[575] At the time this was written, Satan still held sway over the earth as covering angel: the Son of GOD had not yet manifested as Jesus of Nazareth, when He would overcome Satan (Jn. 14:30; Jn. 16:33).

> *And thou, profane wicked prince of Israel, whose day is come, when iniquity shall have an end, thus saith the Lord God: remove the diadem, and take off the crown: this shall not be the same: exalt him that is low, and abase him that is high.*[575] *I will overturn, overturn, overturn it: and it shall be no more, until He come whose right it is; and I will give it Him. (Ezek. 21:25-27)*

The Lord's promise to "*overturn*" the king of Tyrus's kingdom was repeated three times, signifying its finality: the decision was thereafter inalterable. As the empowered Christ, the Son of GOD was predestined to inherit the whole of Israel's twelve-branched Divine Genealogical Tree. He would subsequently replace the heavenly higher self of Dan and Judas with another worthier prince. As biblically inscribed, "*that which is determined shall be,*" and Jesus Christ knew for a surety what Judas was to do. Because of his wickedness, Dan was deleted from among the hallowed names of Israel's divine genealogy as was shown to Beloved John in The Revelation[576] and his crown was given to an adopted son of Israel, as will be seen in the next chapter.

Precisely what took place in higher planes than the earth when this change was made remains yet unknown, but one important lesson learned is that negative desires, thoughts and actions are exceedingly costly to those seeking an eternal heavenly position in the Light of the new heavenly hierarchy: the place the Lord the Son has prepared for those who will be His.[577]

---

[576] Rev. 7:1-8.

[577] Jn. 14:1-4.

[578] Rom. 10:13.

The Bible leaves no doubt but that those who are spiritually "*of Israel*" share the Christ Spirit of the Son of GOD, the Spirit GOD gave the Son without measure. Those who are His belong to Israel, whether they have in past lives been Jew, Gentile or heathen. As Apostle Paul taught, whosoever shall call upon the name of the Lord shall be saved.[578] Every soul born in flesh, who has not overcome the world is composed of two spirit forces: a "mixed seed" to have inherited the spirit of both the Christ and Lucifer. Each is destined to be drawn to whichever place the Lord Wills at the time of Judgment. Jesus taught that there are "*many mansions*" where souls reside.[579] And as many negative near death experiences have illustrated, life in the dark pit where Satan is to be confined is truly a living nightmare. It appears that there are many kinds of gray places in between the heavenly levels and the Satanic pit. Accordingly, the place/level to which we will be directed at the end of our testing days on the earth will be determined by our particular beliefs, desires, thoughts and actions. Positions in the higher heavenly echelons are to be determined by Christ the Son of GOD at the great judgment.[580]

Only when a soul becomes one of GOD's by Christ can it be quickened into immortality, thereby raising up its vibrations to the level that it can be in sync with Christ the Son, and thus with GOD the FATHER. This principle explains GOD's having separated the sons of Adam in the beginning, when HE set the bounds of the people according to the number of the children of Israel in such way that the Lord the

---

[579] Jn. 14:2.

[580] 2 Cor. 5:10.

[581] Deut. 32:8-9.

Son's portion consisted of the people He inherited — Jacob's spiritual descendants thus *"became the lot"* of His inheritance.[581]

> *When the Most High divided to the nations their inheritance; when he separated the sons of Adam, he set the bounds of the people according to the number of the children of Israel. For the Lord's portion is his people; Jacob is the lot of his inheritance. (Deut. 32:8-9)*

—CHAPTER SIX—

EPHRAIM AND MANASSEH APOSTLES JOHN AND JAMES

> *Now the sons of Reuben the firstborn of Israel, (for he was the firstborn; but foreasmuch as he defiled his father's bed,* **his birthright was given unto the sons of Joseph** *the son of Israel; and the genealogy is not to be reckoned after the birthright. (1 Chr. 5:1)*[582]

The heavenly hierarchy has been under reconstruction since it was corrupted by Satanic rebellion. The inexorable changes by which the heavenly hierarchy was revamped were mirrored on earth by the activities of Jacob's twelve sons and their respective tribes. As the direct result of the opposing positive and negative actions of two of Jacob's sons, two earthly tribal and heavenly positions were vacated. One of these positions was held by Dan/Judas who forfeited his Apostleship. He was replaced with one of Jacob's two adopted grandsons, Manasseh, who was also Joseph's natural first born son. The second vacated position was that held by Joseph, the son of Jacob who was the

---

[582] The Bible teaches that because Reuben had defiled his father's bed, the spiritual birthright had been awarded to the two sons of Joseph, so the genealogy was not to be reckoned after the birthright, which was Joseph's (1 Chr. 5:1).

Star foretold by Prophet Balaam to come out of that Patriarch, *supra*. Joseph's angelic higher self later manifested on earth as Jesus Christ, the Son of GOD. When He was empowered by GOD after His subsequent incarnation as Jesus Christ of Nazareth, and was seated at his FATHER's right side, GOD vacated His position as leader of the tribe of Joseph, and escalated Him into the reigning position over all the twelve tribes of Israel: and over all the Gentiles and heathen as well. His position will presumably become occupied by Ephraim, Jacob's other grandson.

EPHRAIM

As previously recounted, when Jacob blessed his two sons Ephraim and Manasseh he adopted them as his own sons, declaring:

> *And now thy (Joseph's) two sons, Ephraim and Manasseh, which were born unto thee in the land of Egypt before I came unto thee into Egypt, are mine; as Reuben and Simeon,* **they shall be mine.** *(Gen. 48:5)*

By this adoption Jacob empowered Ephraim and Manasseh as his own two firstborn sons, while relegating Reuben and Simeon, his first two natural sons, to lesser spiritual positions in the family. As previously discussed, Jacob was unable to entirely eliminate Reuben from some aspects of his inheritance because of a spiritual rule in effect at that time,[583] but he foresaw an exalted future for Joseph's two sons. When he blessed them, he set Ephraim before Manasseh — the firstborn grandson — and foretold that al-

---

[583] Deut. 21:15-17.

though Manasseh would one day be great, and his descendants a great people, nevertheless his younger brother Ephraim would be greater than he, and in time would become a multitude of nations.[584]

Jacob's paternal benediction meant that Ephraim would inherit a lot in the land of Israel, and become a leader of his own people,[585] but even more importantly it foreshadowed his adopted grandson's phenomenal rise to spiritual power. Ephraim was destined to be ordained a prince: presiding over the tribe situated at the highest heavenly level and accordingly one of the twelve Archangels standing at one of the gates of the New Jerusalem. This is revealed by the history of his father Joseph, his identity and inheritance. Joseph was a soul portion of the Son of GOD, having dominion of one of the uppermost of Israel's twelve heavenly levels in the New Jerusalem. After His subsequent empowerment as Christ, He was escalated to sit at His FATHER's right side and given inheritance over all the twelve levels.[586] By that event a vacancy was thereby created in the leadership position of the tribe of Joseph.

Customarily, under the Mosaic Law, the firstborn son became the beneficiary of his father's inheritance, but in this case Ephraim, Joseph's second-born son, was predestined to occupy that position. These changes were set in motion when Jacob — the Spirit of the Lord profoundly influencing Him — wisely blessed Ephraim above Manasseh, Joseph's firstborn. The Lord — working through and by the spiritually

---

[584] Gen. 48:19-20.

[585] 1 Chr. 5:1

[586] Ps. 2:8-12

quickened Jacob, even as He worked through His prophets—conveyed His Word to Joseph. Some changes in the heavenly structure will not likely transpire until Christ returns to take dominion at the second coming. Ephraim's name is not yet listed in Israel's divine genealogy,[587] but it is understood by some that Joseph's position will be filled by Ephraim, a previous soul incarnation of Apostle John.

APOSTLE JOHN:
A SON OF ZEBEDEE

In accordance with Malachi's prophecy that the sons of Jacob were predestined to return, *supra*, the soul in Ephraim is understood to have reincarnated in Apostle John, and the soul in Manasseh as his brother James. Because Jacob had blessed Ephraim above his older brother, Manasseh, it is not surprising that he would later return as a highly spiritualized and learned Apostle, whose esoteric spiritual knowledge and understanding surpassed that of all his brethren Apostles; with the possible exception of Apostle Paul.[588] It was the Christ Spirit that opened the Apostles' understanding of the many parables and mysteries Jesus taught them as they followed Him during His ministry.[589] That John was able to under-

---

[587] Rev. 7:4-8

[588] Gal. 1:11-12 After Apostle Paul had been illuminated by the Christ Spirit, he succinctly described the heavenly role of Christ the Son of GOD. He noted that he, Paul, was a prisoner of Jesus Christ's on behalf of the Gentiles, who in the past had no knowledge of the mystery of Christ **because in other ages it had not been made known to the sons of men,** but was at last being revealed to Jesus' Apostles by the Spirit.

[589] Lk. 24:45.

stand what Jesus taught is indicative of his close spiritual attunement with Him. He is credited with having learned remarkable spiritual truths, as his writings bear witness. That noted, it is understood that the writings in the Book of John represent what others heard John teach, and afterward passed on to others, who spread the teachings. On the other hand, books 1 John, 2 John and 3 John are believed to more directly reflect that which had been written by John himself. John's Revelation, an unusually illuminating and often esoteric masterpiece, stands out as one of the most important of all scriptural writings.

Possibly the most illuminating of John's teachings is found in his explanation of the at-One-ment of GOD the FATHER, the Son and the Holy Ghost and his elucidation of how man can escape earth's third dimensional laws by becoming attuned to Christ the Son, to receive the Holy Ghost.[590] It was John who disclosed that Christ the Son of GOD was man's Maker and that in the beginning He was the Word of GOD, who, being made by GOD, was God in His own right — in Him was life and the life was the light of men.[591] It was not easily understood nor accepted that the heavenly higher self of Jesus of Nazareth had before been the Lord the Son of GOD who from heaven had shepherded the children of Israel from the beginning. It was John who reported Jesus' illuminating disclosure that no man has ascended from the earth into heaven, except he that had come down from heaven; and that at the very moment Jesus spoke those words His higher self Spirit *was in* heaven.[592]

---

[590] John Chapters 14, 15 and 16.
[591] Jn. 1:1-5; Eph. 3:8-11.
[592] Jn. 3:13.

In these verses, John subtly disclosed what we have come to understand to be the higher angelic self and lower self concept of man. Beloved John reported that Jesus conceded that He of Himself could do nothing — that it was GOD the FATHER working through Him who did the works — that He did what He saw His FATHER do.[593] Even as His Father raised the dead and quickened them, John taught, even so the Son *"quickens whom He will. For the Father judges no man, but has committed all judgment unto the Son."* [594] This disclosure was extremely important to those striving to acquire GOD's grace.[595] As John wrote, the only door open to GOD for mankind is by the Son's Intercession.[596] To attempt to go directly to GOD without Christ's Intercession, John taught, is futile, HE having turned all powers over to the Son Jesus Christ, because His Spirit Vibrations can be stepped down to the level of those who seek GOD by Him. GOD HIMSELF does not incarnate in flesh on the earth: but the Son is able to metamorphose His Spirit into lower dimensions of existence — in Spirit as the Beloved Archangel Michael, and in flesh as the soul in Jesus Christ of Nazareth.

Leaving aside an extended discussion of the multitude of John's reported teachings, several particular events and occurrences involving him require consideration. For example, at the scene of the Cross, when Jesus observed His precious mother Mary standing close by, with John His favored Apostle. Despite the excruciating pain He was suffering, Jesus de-

---

[593] Jn. 5:19-20.
[594] Jn. 5:21-23.
[595] Jn. 1:14-17. Cf. Rom. 1:1-6,17.
[596] Jn. 10:1-30.

clared: *"Woman, behold thy son !"* and to John, *"Behold, thy mother."* [597] The Bible reports that from that hour John took Mary into his home as his own mother — clearly representing an adoption — and she resided with him from that time. It was an adoption that carried much more significant implications than appeared on its face. In the spiritual sense, it signified that Jesus was at that time empowered to bring John into Jesus' heavenly family, no longer accountable to earth laws. It represented Jesus' acknowledgment of John's inheritance in the heavenly realms: which had been foretold of him long before when he was Ephraim, and his father Jacob had adopted him and placed him above his brother Manasseh.[598] Jesus' declaration also connoted that Beloved Mary had also sufficiently overcome as of that earth experience, and was no longer required to undergo cycles of life and death in the earth plane. It meant that after the Crucifixion, man's earth mother — Eve — had been restored, and she had again become the heavenly Mother of all who were the *remnant* of Israel. The so-called Marian apparitions emerged once Jesus Christ was empowered, indicating that when Jesus was taken up to GOD's Right Hand and empowered,[599] many radical changes took place in heaven and on earth. Jacob's adoption of Ephraim into his family and his placing him above Manasseh and all his other sons, precisely correlates with Jesus' subsequent adoption of His Beloved Apostle John — who had been Ephraim — into the heavenly family that He, Jesus Christ the Son, was already beginning to establish. These events also illustrate how earth families can help themselves ascend Jacob's ladder leading into

---

[597] Jn. 19:25-27.
[598] Gen. 48:5,20.
[599] Cf. Jn. 5:21-23; 2 Cor. 5:10.

the heavenly hierarchy by adopting one or more highly spiritual individuals.

After Jesus' Crucifixion, He met seven of His Disciples at the Sea of Tiberias: Peter, Thomas, Nathanael, John, James, and two unidentified followers.[600] The seven had gone fishing but the venture was unproductive. As they came ashore in the morning, the risen Christ was nearby, *"but the disciples knew not that it was Jesus."*[601] This lack of recognition illustrates that when a soul translates into higher realms of existence, its quickened state causes changes in the molecular structure of the physical body. Therefore, when it re-materializes on earth, as in the instant case, the regenerated body has a different appearance. The spiritual escalation of Apostle John was demonstrated by the fact that he was the only one able to recognize the transformed Jesus. What stands out predominantly here is that, as close to the Master as the other six were, they were unable to recognize Him in His resurrected form.[602] John's recollection of details of the meeting at the Sea of Tiberias,[603] reflects back to events that took place during the Last Supper. Peter, obviously interested in Jesus' close kinship with John, asked the Master which Apostle would betray Him; and, seeing John nearby, asked what John was to do. Jesus replied:

---

[600] Jn. 21:1-2.

[601] Jn. 21:3-4.

[602] This was also the case with Mary Magdalene from whom Jesus had cast out seven devils. When He appeared to her after the Crucifixion, she mistakenly thought him to be a gardener who tended the grounds of the sepulchers where Jesus had been laid to rest, and was unable to recognize Him in His resurrected form.

[603] Jn. Ch. 21.

> *If I will that he tarry till I come, what is that to thee? follow thou me. (Jn. 21:22)*

The Bible next discloses:

> *Then went this saying abroad among the brethren, that **that disciple should not die**: yet Jesus did not (say) unto him, He shall not die; but, If I will that he tarry till I come, what **is that** to thee? (Jn. 21:23)*

In the prophetic sense, this enigmatic disclosure by Jesus confirms the above-stated hypothesis that John was no longer required to undergo the earth cycles of life and death but that he would be able to manifest on earth in an incorruptible body after his physical death. That being the case, he has since that time been able to materialize in the earth plane without being subjected to earth's 3rd dimensional laws. This may explain why the Book of The Revelation is ascribed to John, albeit he had become known under the name *"St. John the Divine,"* and appears to have lived beyond the time of the other Apostles. After Jesus had by His Crucifixion payed the Adamic debt,[604] and had thereby restored the gift of the Holy Ghost to mankind, there was no longer any reason for him to manifest in flesh in the earth plane.[605] The thrust of the above verses is that He had selected John to *"tarry"* (i.e. remain, or bide one's time) to fulfill an important role until He, Christ, returned to take Dominion at Armageddon. The Master's words to Peter amounted to a precaution that he should not concern himself with John's destiny, but rather should focus his energies in following his Master. As disclosed in previous chapters, despite Peter's

---

[604] Rom. 5:12-21.
[605] Heb. 6:19-20.

remarkable works, his spiritual escalation does not appear, biblically speaking, to be nearly as exalted as John's.

Details of John's mission were revealed to him during his imprisonment on the Isle of Patmos. While he was in trance, an angel gave him a book, and commanded him to eat it. The book was an allegorical representation of the knowledge John had accrued to that time. Part of John's mission was to share it with all nations, and he was given an advisement which correlates with the biblical forecast that John would "*tarry*" in the earth plane in order to fulfill his mission:

> *And he said unto me,* ***Thou must prophesy again before many peoples, and nations, and tongues and kings****. (Rev. 10:11)*

Insofar as the Bible discloses, Beloved John did not in that earth experience fulfill the above prophesy; albeit there is much we do not as yet know about how he may have manifested. In the same way that we may reasonably expect to see Prophet Elijah (a previous soul incarnation of John the Baptist) on earth again in the Latter Days of man's decreasing spirituality,[606] it seems likely that the spirit of John the Apostle will also manifest again.

According to the Bible, Beloved John — actually his whole higher self spirit-being — stands to inherit an exalted heavenly position, as was subtly disclosed when, as Ephraim, he was blessed by Jacob above Manasseh, and above all his other sons. As aforementioned, Apostle John's adoption by Jesus Christ at the

---

[606] Mal. 4:5-6.

time of His Crucifixion signified his adoption into the heavenly family, and reflected Jesus' spiritual closeness to John. When we consider the past experience of John as Ephraim, we are able to better understand Jesus' spiritual relationship with this particular Apostle, of whom it was written:

> *Now there was leaning on Jesus' bosom one of his disciples whom Jesus loved. (Jn. 13:23)*

As Jesus remained in His FATHER's bosom, John in the same manner remained on Jesus's bosom during the Last Supper. And in relatively the same way GOD referred to Jesus Christ as His Firstborn, the Lord the Son when speaking through Prophet Jeremiah conceded that when He had been on earth as Joseph, Ephraim had indeed been His spiritually firstborn son, not Manasseh.

> *". . . . for I am a Father to Israel and **Ephraim is my firstborn.**" (Jer. 31:9)*

MANASSEH

When Jacob blessed Joseph's two sons, Ephraim and Manasseh, and placed them ahead of his own two firstborn sons, Reuben and Simeon,[607] he altered the sequential pattern established in the spiritual empowerment of the twelve tribes of Israel as it had stood until that time. And as previously noted, when Jacob then set second-born Ephraim ahead of his brother Manasseh, *supra*, still another change was made, which would echo through oncoming generations. The Bible confirms that when Ephraim and

---
[607] Gen. 48:5.

Manasseh were subsequently reborn as John and James, it was John who emerged as the most influential among Jesus' Apostles. James, on the other hand, is pictured as a stalwart dedicated teacher and preacher of Jesus Christ's New Covenant: so much so that king Herod considered him such a threat to his power that he ordered him executed.

When Jacob blessed and adopted his two grandsons and placed them above his own two firstborn sons, *supra*, it in effect forecasted that they would one day occupy exalted positions as two of twelve great Archangels to preside over their respective tribe/heavenly level. As previously noted, Ephraim — who manifested later as the Apostle John — is destined to take over the leading position of the tribe named for Joseph. Manasseh on the other hand, will by then have already assumed his position as titular head of Dan's tribe. That Dan's negative actions when he afterward incarnated as Judas Iscariot would cause him to lose his heavenly post to Manasseh — who later incarnated as Apostle James — raises the possibility that some of the souls composing Dan's tribe might be granted places in the tribe named for Manasseh. This possibility appears to be given life by Jesus' parable of the talents, in which Jesus teaches that everything an individual was given in the beginning may be taken away and turned over to another who is worthier, if he fails to make appropriate righteous use of that which he has been given:

> ***Take therefore the talent from him, and give it unto him which hath ten talents.*** *For unto everyone that hath shall be given, and he shall have abundance: but from him that hath not shall be*

> *taken away even that which he hath. . . . (Mt. 25:28-29)*

That Manasseh's tribe would not only replace Dan's tribe, but Manasseh might also become the leader of at least some of the souls in the fallen tribe of Dan, is an idea found in the Book of Joshua. Joshua prophesied that Ephraim and Manasseh were to be expanded:

> *And Joshua spake unto the house of Joseph, even to Ephraim and Manasseh, saying, Thou art a great people, and hast great power: thou shalt not have one tribe only. (Josh. 17:17)*

This supports the Lord's Word through Prophet Ezekiel that strangers brought into the Israeli fold could become potential beneficiaries of a heavenly inheritance:[608]

> *So shall ye divide this land unto you according to the tribes of Israel.* ***And it shall come to pass that ye shall divide it by lot for an inheritance unto you, and to the strangers that sojourn among you*** *which shall beget children among you and they shall be unto you as born in the country among the children of Israel:* ***they shall have inheritance with you among the tribes of Israel.*** *And it shall come to pass that* ***in what tribe the stranger sojourneth, there shall ye give him his inheritance****, saith the Lord God. (Ezek. 47: 21-23)*

These verses suggest the possibility that the prophesies of Joshua and Ezekiel may coincide with Jacob's blessing, in which he foretold that his grandsons would indeed become great nations.

---

[608] Gal. 3:6-29.

Although Ephraim was destined to attain to a higher position than his brother in the heavenly hierarchy, it appears that Manasseh was destined to assume the important task of guiding his own spiritually elevated tribe, while perhaps also re-orienting some of Dan's tribal members in accordance with GOD's divine laws.

APOSTLE JAMES: A SON OF ZEBEDEE

The Bible does not reveal much of significance about the works of Manasseh; nor do we read much about his revelation of spiritual mysteries when he later reincarnated as Apostle James. The biblical writings attributed to him record essential information important to the prescribed ideals and works of Jesus Christ's followers. By comparison, the works of his brother Apostle John indicate a more elevated level of spiritual knowledge and understanding. This again confirms the accuracy of Jacob's insightful blessing long before in which he had set second-born Ephraim ahead of his first-born brother Manasseh, and foretold that he would excel his brother, as discussed, *supra.*

James taught the value of exercising patience, while remaining stable and not double minded:

> *Let no man say when he is tempted, I am tempted of God: for God cannot be tempted with evil, neither tempteth he any man: but every man is tempted when he is drawn away of his own lust, and enticed. Then when lust hath conceived it bringeth*

> *forth sin: and sin, when it is finished, bringeth forth death. (Jas. 1:13-15)*

James' writings reflect a more gentle nature than the biblical characterization of him as one of the sons of Thunder[609] appears to imply. For example, he taught:

> *For the sun is no sooner risen with a burning heat, but it withereth the grass, and the flower thereof falleth, and the grace of the fashion of it perhisheth: so also shall the rich man fade away in his ways. Blessed is the man that endureth temptation: for when he is tried he shall receive the crown of life, which the Lord hath promised to them that love him. (Jas. 1:11-12)*

James' teachings are basic and fundamental, emphasizing the crucially important principle that faith without works is dead:

> *Was not Abraham our father justified by works, when he had offered Isaac upon the altar? Seest thou how faith wrought with his works, and by works was faith made perfect? And the Scripture was fulfilled which saith, ABRAHAM BELIEVED GOD, AND IT WAS IMPUTED UNTO HIM FOR RIGHTEOUSNESS: and he was called the friend of God. Ye see then how that by works a man is justified, and not by faith only. Likewise was not Rahab the harlot justified by works when*

---

[609] Mk. 3:17.

> *she had received the messengers, and had sent them out another way?* [610] *(Jas. 2:21-25)*

In his writings, James emphasizes the inestimably great value of helping to convert those who have not yet found The Way into heaven Made Passable by Jesus Christ, and he stresses that by such works one overcomes the stains of many sins:

> *Let him know, that he which converteth the sinner from the error of his way shall save a soul from death, and shall hide a multitude of sins. (Jas. 5:20)*

It is apparent that both Apostles John and James had, as Ephraim and Manasseh, been predestined to fulfill two preeminent positions as leaders of their respective tribes on earth; later to attain to exalted positions in the heavenly New Jerusalem. Jacob's other sons were also destined to fulfill important lead-

---

[610] Cf. Joshua Chapter Two, in which is described how Joshua sent spies into Jericho to view the land before he attacked that city, and Rahab a harlot — who in some way learned that the Lord had dried up the Red Sea in Moses' time, and that He was the Lord God in heaven above and in the earth below — assisted the spies so they were able to escape safely. The Bible notes that Joshua honored Rahab's request that she and her family be saved when Jericho was assaulted and overcome, making certain they were safely removed from the city when it fell (Josh. 6:25). Heb. 11:31 instructs that it was because of Rahab's faith, and what she had done, that she and her family did not perish when Jericho fell; albeit those around her who did not believe in the Lord, fell victim to the assault by Joshua's army. These verses carry a crucially important message in these Latter Days before the *"great and terrible day of the Lord,"* known as Armageddon.

ing positions at the head of each of their tribes, assisting the Lord in His efforts to escalate man's spiritual evolution toward eternal higher realms of existence. We can now only speculate that some of the sons may have, through the ages, been replaced by other representatives in particular tribes whose works have excelled their own.

CONCLUSION

Jesus of Nazareth, the Son of GOD clothed in flesh for the purpose of fulfilling the grand mission which providence had set before Him,[611] manifested in human form with the attributes of humanity, except that there was no sin in him, and His knowledge and understanding were phenomenal. He represented the biblically declared goal of a miraculous chain of interpositions dating back to the very foundations of the world. In the beginning He had been Adam, the first man in flesh, a living spirit; as Jesus of Nazareth He had become the Last Adam, a quickening spirit.[612] By His New Covenant He brought into the world a new order of things, a doctrine designed to help millions of souls trapped in the earth plane to assess their own character, shape their expectations, prune and purify their consciences, and cleanse themselves from the sinful thoughts, desires and actions that from the time of the Adamic fall had kept them bound to the material world and its Spirit-depleting ways.

At the time when GOD decreed having begotten HIS Son, He declared HIS intention to give Him the heathen for His inheritance, and the uttermost parts of the earth for His possession; and He commanded

---

[611] Heb. 2:13-18; and cf. Rom. 5:8-21.
[612] 1 Cor. 15:45.

that the Son was one day to break the heathen with a rod of iron, dashing them in pieces like a smashed potter's vessel.[613] This circumscribed in broad brushed terms all that was to take place after Archangel Satan's deceitful plan to establish his kingdom on earth until the Lord, with His angels, would long afterward return to take dominion at Armageddon. What has thus far transpired during that protracted period is the subject of the Holy Bible, which recounts details of what was gained and lost during the struggle of the Lord the Son and certain of His Angels, who strove to make a way passable through the perilous earthly minefield by which good souls could safely return to their original spiritual estate. They eventually were able, as Jesus of Nazareth and His Apostles on earth, to bring down Satan, and confine him and his angels to the earth plane,[614] rendering them unable to return to heavenly dimensions where they had, by their disobedience to GOD, brought about their own downfall.[615]

The Holy Bible traces the pathway embarked upon by the Son of GOD when He voluntarily undertook his sublime earth mission of restoring GOD's Holy Spirit to all of mankind who remained stranded in the earth plane. As related in the text of this work, it was when the Son returned as Enoch after His experience as Adam that He was able to regain for himself the Holy Spirit, the life-giving essence of the Tree of Life.

Certain of those who had entered into the earth plane with Him when He was Adam continued to reincarnate with Him through the centuries, always

---

[613] Ps. 2:6-9.

[614] Rev. 12:7-12.

[615] Jude 6. Cf. Heb. 5:8-9.

striving to help Him overcome the earth and the devilish forces that had taken control over it. As has been seen, there were certain special souls who strove with Him to overcome Satan and his angels. In Jacob's time — as a providence of the 3 to 4 generation rule governing spiritual escalation or depletion — the Lord's divinely guided lineage was established within the boundaries of Jacob's spiritual descendants.[616]

From that time on, those who were to ultimately compose the elect of the Lord the Son — those who were to be among the remnant of the chosen children of Israel, having through many incarnations and centuries been preserved by Him — were numbered among the 144,000 elite souls written of in the Bible. These souls, having started in the beginning with the Lord to make a way passable into heaven for those spirit-sheep who had lost their way, were to be granted exalted positions in the new heavenly hierarchy He had set about rebuilding after the fall, as the Bible reveals.

The Age of Egypt had seen man's institution of many gods. Melchizedek ended the idolatrous Egyptian Age by introducing and establishing the concept of One GOD. The Law of Moses became the vehicle which man was to understand had been designed as a *"schoolmaster"* to bring him to Christ the Son, in order that he might be justified by faith, thereby to be one of Abraham's seed according to the promise.[617] But when the children of Israel began to stray and failed to adhere to the terms of the First Covenant, the Lord promised through Prophet Jeremiah to replace it with a New Covenant, which would pro-

---

[616] Deut. 32:8-9.
[617] Gal. 3:18-29.

vide man with a more direct way to be in touch with GOD through the Intercession of one eternal heavenly Priest after the order of Melchizedek.[618]

That Priest was Jesus Christ. It was He who brought in the New Covenant He had Himself promised through Prophet Jeremiah. It applied to all on earth — Jews, Gentiles and the heathen alike — and was so radically advanced beyond the Old Covenant that it could not be suddenly absorbed into man's impaired spiritual knowledge and understanding as it existed at that time. It relied upon man's overcoming of the negative earthly mentality he had acquired as the result of his fall into materiality.[619] To partake of the fruits of the New Covenant, man was required to curtail evil, remain righteous, loving and accomplish good works, in order to be transformed by the Spirit of the Son, whom GOD has empowered to conduct all things for HIM — including judgment.[620] It was written of the Son: *the Law was given by Moses, but Grace and Truth came by Jesus Christ."*[621] Because of His fullness of knowledge and spiritual power, Jesus was exalted above all the prophets who had preceded Him. In fact He was the Prophet foretold by Moses[622] — the Messiah at His First Coming.

The New Covenant He brought in was divine in its nature, but the spiritual ignorance and blindness of mankind at that comparatively early stage of his spiritual development, made it improbable it would be readily accepted. The Mosaic Law was by that time so deeply

---

[618] Jer. 31:31-34. Cf. Ps. 110:1,4-6; Heb. 7:25.
[619] 1 Jn. 2:14-17.
[620] Jn. 3:34; 5:21-23; 2 Cor. 5:10.
[621] Jn. 1:17.
[622] Deut. 18:18-19.

imbedded in the hearts and minds of the people of Israel it could only be at best partly overcome by the remarkable miracles Jesus was able to perform to authenticate His replacement of it. Religious and spiritual beliefs belong to the invisible world, for which reason man has in all ages demanded teachings not only understandable to him, but presented in an authoritative way to stamp them in his mind as truth.

The problem was that Jesus was the only man on earth who knew what His New Covenant was to embrace. It was perfect in itself, but existed nowhere but in His own mind; and the minds of those to whom it was to be taught were not blank pages on which could be easily inscribed the radically innovative principles of His entirely new spiritual concept. On one hand, the heathen were still without a clue as to what was taking place; and on the other, the Jews were not about to accept annihilation or effacement of the beliefs they had treasured for some 1,500 years of striving to fulfill the Mosaic Law. Jesus selected the sound planks from the Old Covent edifice, set aside the rest, added His new spiritual timbers and incorporated the whole of it into His New Covenant. But the basic principle that underlaid His new doctrine was simply too radical for many to accept. Jews were wont to ask how a man who had sinned during his life could <u>erase the stains of the sins built up by his iniquity, by simply repenting it and embarking on a new and better course.</u>

There was no tenable way for Jesus to have simply taught a new religion without attaching it to the fundamental Law which had before been given to the chosen people through and by Moses; and it would have made no sense to do so. <u>He had Himself, as Enoch, illustrated</u>

that obedience to GOD was mandatory: that it was by "walking with GOD" for 300 years that He was able to overcome the negative karma He had built up as Adam.[623] Then He had returned in a series of remarkable earth appearances — including Melchizedek, Joseph son of Jacob, Joshua son of Nun, Asaph in David's time, and Jeshua son of Josedech — before returning as Jesus of Nazareth to fulfill His mission of making The Way passable into heaven for all who would ever afterward follow Him there. It would have been impossible for Him to have effaced all He had before accomplished by simply ignoring it, and starting off on a totally new and different course than the one He had Himself instituted. When it was time for the New Covenant to be introduced, the foundations were already in place, because He had through the centuries been unceasingly constructing it; even predictively painting a picture of what it was to be through His prophets.

Through Prophet Joel the Lord had spoken of a time to come when He would pour out His Spirit upon many, enabling them to prophesy and experience prophetic dreams and visions; which would be a sign of the nearness of the *"great and terrible day of the Lord"* — Armageddon. The Lord foretold that at that time those who would call upon His name would be delivered into the Holy Mount, the heavenly New Jerusalem.[624] We are today seeing palpable evidence that this time is beginning to draw near, heralding the return of the Lord from heaven *"with a shout, with the voice of the Archangel,"* to take dominion and start the Millennium of the First Resurrection.[625]

---

[623] Gen. 5:21-23.

[624] Joel 2:28-32.

[625] 1 Thess. 4:15-17; Rev. 20:1-6.

It is a time for all souls incarnated on earth to repent, forgive everyone their trespasses and turn away from all negative flesh desires, thoughts, intentions and actions which corrupt men's souls, making it impossible for them to partake of the glorious redemption and resurrection which the Lord has promised to those who are His.